Eugene C Schrottky

The Principles of rational Agriculture

Applied to India and its staple Products

Eugene C Schrottky

The Principles of rational Agriculture
Applied to India and its staple Products

ISBN/EAN: 9783337061289

Printed in Europe, USA, Canada, Australia, Japan

Cover: Foto ©ninafisch / pixelio.de

More available books at **www.hansebooks.com**

THE PRINCIPLES

OF

RATIONAL AGRICULTURE

APPLIED TO

INDIA

AND ITS STAPLE PRODUCTS.

BY

EUGENE C. SCHROTTKY, G.C.U.G.

Bombay:
TIMES OF INDIA OFFICE.
1876.

Dedicated

TO THE MEMORY

OF THE LATE

BARON JUSTUS von LIEBIG

BY HIS DEVOTED PUPIL

THE AUTHOR.

PREFACE.

ANY book having for its object the furtherance and improvement of Indian Agriculture, will, no doubt, be welcomed not only by those who are interested, directly or indirectly, in the subject, but also by all those who have the interests of this country, and the interests of its commonwealth, at heart; and I therefore with great confidence bring this work on "The Principles of Rational Agriculture applied to India and its Staple Products" before the critical eye of the public. Though I am conscious it will be found defective in many points, I have no doubt but that its shortcomings will be leniently dealt with in consideration of its general object.

When entering upon this work, I was stimulated by the belief, which is growing stronger and stronger with my prolonged sojourn in Bombay, that India, far from being that country about whose wealth and resources I delighted to read in my youthful days, is, on the contrary, a poor, impoverished land, the majority of whose millions of inhabitants are living in abject and squalid poverty, trying to gain from Mother Earth the little remnant of its former wealth and fruitfulness which the recklessness and ignorance of preceding generations have left it, and that the reason of this poverty is the neglect of agricultural improvements which past and present rulers have been guilty of, and the utter disregard which past generations have paid to the interests of their children's children by exhausting the resources of a soil which once was remarkable for its fertility.

This, therefore, is an attempt to bring the subject in all its bearings more fully to the notice of the public, and to remove that indifference and want of interest with which everything connected with Indian Agriculture is usually received.

I have dedicated this book to the memory of the late Baron Von Liebig, in whose death we mourn the loss of one of the greatest chemists of the age. I have to thank him that I feel confidence enough to diffuse his great ideas more generally in India, and to contribute my mite to the benefit of my fellow-creatures. The merit of my venture in writing this book in a (to me) foreign language is entirely his; it is due to the influence of his ideas, which he never failed to impress deeply upon all who came in contact with him. If I am able to further his principles by means of this book, and can succeed in the task by following the way he pointed out, the honor will be due to him alone; it will be the fruit of the seed he has sown.

The second part of this book, which treats exclusively on the " Rational Culture of the Staple Products of India," is a digest of most that is known about them. Reports to Government, and scraps of information found scattered throughout the volumes of the *Agricultural Gazette of India,* have been very useful to me in compiling this portion.

EUGENE C. SCHROTTKY.

BOMBAY, *July* 1876.

CONTENTS.

PART I.

The Principles of Rational Agriculture.

INTRODUCTION.

Agriculture advanced to the rank of a science in Europe, but neglected in India, the style of cultivation being the same now as it was thousands of years ago.—The disregard of the principle of restoration to the soil.—The impossibility of success in agricultural operations whilst disregarding this principle.—The soil deprived of its fertilizing constituents by the crops removed.—The exhaustion of the soil a natural consequence.—The ryot of India makes a certain return to the soil.—The inadequate nature of this return.—Lord Mayo acknowledging the primitive and backward state of agriculture in India, and the just claims which the ryot has upon the Government, upon which rests the duty of improving agriculture.—Her Majesty's Secretary of State admitting that the Government of India has a direct and immediate interest in the improvement of agriculture, such as is possessed by no other Government.—The Indian ryot does badly because of his never having been taught better. —He lives on the capital instead of the interest, and naturally becomes poorer and poorer.—The father lives at the expense of the son.—The conservative ideas of agricultural classes in general, and that of the Indian ryot in particular; his keen appreciation of improvements notwithstanding.—The Government of India, in its peculiar position as landlord, suffers by the present mode of cultivation, which takes away from the soil and gives nothing back.—Increasing impoverishment the consequence.—The necessity of teaching the ryot how to do better and improve agriculture.—The futile attempts of Government to effect this.

Evidence of the gradual diminishing outturn of the Indian soil.—The *Ayeen Akbary*, and its statistics of the average produce of India.—Comparison with the present outturn.—Alarming declension in full concord with the laws of husbandry.—Special mention of the gradual decline of the outturn of cotton in the Broach zillah, the figures being given by the *Ayeen Akbary*, Colonel Monier Williams, Dr. Burn, Mr. Rivett-Carnac, and others.—The necessity of acting in accordance with the Principles of Rational Agriculture if the example is to be avoided of the foolish husbandman who expected to reap where he had not sown.—Comparison between the results of European and Indian agriculture.—Comparison between the condition of the European farmer and the Indian ryot.—Their respective conditions with reference to the relative outturn of the soil.—The poverty of the Indian ryot and the deficiency of food.—India's necessity, the development of all her agricultural resources.—The means to accomplish this.—Irrigation and manure will increase the outturn fourfold.—The advisability of beginning at the root of the evil: the ignorance of the husbandman.—Advice and instruction to be given to the most intelligent farmer of each village.—Also guarantee to make good all losses resulting from his adopting the style of cultivation recommended, and from using manures whose effects are unknown to him.—Annual prizes for the largest outturn and for superior produce.—Circulation of pamphlets in the vernaculars.—Experimental farms to improve the staple products of the district, to select and distribute superior seed, and to obtain statistics.—The results of the experimental farms to be made widely known among the agricultural classes.—Criticism upon the model-farms in the Bombay

Presidency, the talent and energy of superintendents being exclusively devoted to making them self-supporting.—The fallacy of this system.—Experimental farms to be considered remunerative only by the improvement they effect in the agriculture of their districts.—The inability of Government to effect all these improvements single-handed, and the necessity for the co-operation of an AGRICULTURAL SOCIETY 1

CHAPTER I.

THE PLANT.

A knowledge of the **nature of plants** and their component parts necessary to understand the Principles of Rational Agriculture.—The organic and inorganic parts of the plant.—Their origin.—The conditions of plant life.—The seed in its relation to the plant.—The cosmic conditions of germination.—The process of germination.—Seeds will germinate and produce miniature plants in water from the store of nourishment they contain.—The condition of the young plant depends upon the quality of the seed.—The advantages of seed selection.—Superior plants from superior seed.—The condition of the soil in relation to the germinated seed.—The delicate root-fibres prefer a loose, porous soil.—Cato's teachings on tillage are still the foundation of agriculture.—The roots are the medium through which human skill can reach the plant.—The properties of the root.—Its absorbing power.—The rootlets absorb from the soil the inorganic food of plants.—The stem the conveyor of the sap to the different parts of the plant.—Silica one of the chief inorganic constituents of the stems of **cereals and grasses.**—It forms the bones of vegetable life.—Leaves and their functions.—The exposure of the crude sap in the leaves to the influence of light and atmospheric air, and the changes it undergoes.—The seed, and its connection with the plant.—Selection and change of seed.—Seed and seed-sowing. 22

CHAPTER II.

THE ORGANIC PARTS OF PLANTS.

Four elements (carbon, nitrogen, oxygen, and hydrogen) form the organic parts of plants.—Their origin, the atmospheric air.—Plants cannot assimilate these elements in their pure state.—The three great suppliers of organic plant-food, water, ammonia, and carbonic acid.

Carbon.—The erroneous belief of the early philosophers that carbon, and the other elements of organic plant-food, were derived directly from the decaying vegetable matter in the soil.—The fallacy of the "Humus Theory." —Soils can most raise luxuriant vegetation after every trace of vegetable matter has been expelled from them.— The certainty that the organic parts have been derived from the atmospheric air.—The presence of humus in the soil tends to increase its fertility only by affording a surplus of organic plant-food.—Vegetable respiration.— The absorption of carbonic acid and the expulsion of oxygen.—The connection between animal and vegetable respiration.—The replenishment of carbonic acid withdrawn from the atmospheric air.—The necessity of carbonic acid being also present in the soil, it being a solvent of the alkaline earths and insoluble phosphates.— Baussingault's experiments on the absorption of carbonic acid.—The decomposition of carbonic acid under the influence of light and atmospheric air, and its assimilation by the plant.

Hydrogen and oxygen.—The source whence they are derived. —The several functions of water.—Its absolute indispensability for vegetable life, being the first stimulator and supporter of it.—The property of leaves to inhale moisture from the atmosphere when absent in the soil.

Nitrogen.—Its inert nature in the pure state.—Ammonia and nitric acid the two sources of nitrogen.—Their presence in the atmospheric air.—Its balance, how preserved.— The relation between nitrogen and our edible crops 40

CHAPTER III.

The Inorganic Parts of Plants.

The small percentage of the inorganic parts of the plant when compared with the organic parts.—The functions of the former with regard to the latter.—The importance of inorganic parts in the vegetable kingdom.—Vegetable life cannot exist in the absence of any one of their number.—The ashes of different plants vary in their composition.—The importance of analyses.—Potash and soda.—Their functions in vegetable life.—Potash a solvent for silica.—The same amount of potash serves to dissolve many times its maximum of silica by repeated circulation through the system of the plant.—Mr. Lawes' experiments on the circulation of the sap and the quantity of inorganic matter deposited.—Silica and sand.—Lime a prominent constituent of root-crops and leguminous plants.—Magnesia.—The property of lime and magnesia to take each other's places.—Lime and silica form the bones of vegetable life.—Sulphuric acid.—Phosphoric acid.—Phosphoric acid forms the principal mineral constituent of the seed.—No grain can be formed in its absence.—The gradual reduction of its percentage in the soil affects chiefly the outturn of the seed.—The Indian method of cultivation has deprived the soil of this important substance in far greater proportion than of any of the other inorganic parts.—No restoration has been made for the loss occasioned by the annual withdrawal of the grain crops.—Where is all the phosphoric acid gone to?—The export trade of bones deprives India of the means to repair the waste of past generations.—The value of bones as manure.—The percentage of phosphoric acid in rice.—The estimated quantity withdrawn from an acre by a cultivation extending over two thousand years.—The deficiency of phosphoric acid in the soil of India proved by analysis.—The small average outturn due to this deficiency.—The quantity of phosphoric acid required by the rice-plant, and the quantity available.

The yield of the soil is regulated by that inorganic plant constituent which is present in smallest proportion.—The Minimum Theory applied to **phosphoric** acid.—The stores of phosphoric acid available.—Guano.—Animal refuse.—Bones.—Coprolites.—A conservancy **department** for the animal kingdom necessary.—The **assimilation by** the plant of its inorganic parts.—Endosmose.—The transformation of the sap in the leaves.—Prince Salm **Horstmar's** experiments proving the relative necessity of each **of the** mineral plant constituents.—The absence of a single **one** in the soil affects the whole organism of the plant.—The division **of** plants into groups according to their principal inorganic constituents.—The different kinds **of** soils best suited **for the** different kinds of plants............ 51

CHAPTER IV.

The Soil and its Functions.

The soil is the supplier of the inorganic constituents **of** plants.—The condition in which these inorganic substances must be present.—Their mere presence does not prove the fertility of a soil.—The fallacy of judging by **a chemical** analysis **of the** capabilities of a soil.—Tables to "measure" the fertility of a soil.—The injury done to scientific agriculture **by** hasty conclusions drawn from imperfect experiments.—The constituent parts of the soil are in their original form insoluble in water.—The action of moisture, heat, and atmospheric air renders them soluble.—The peculiar absorptive power of the soil **to** abstract the elements **of** inorganic plant-food from their solutions.—The capillary absorbing power of the soil.—Its bearing upon vegetable life.—The physical force of attraction of the soil **is** stronger than the solvent power of **water**; but yields **when** "Endosmose" comes into play.—To judge of the capabilities of a soil, it is necessary to distinguish between the assimilable and unassimilable portion of inorganic plant constituents present in it.

Inorganic plant-food in physical and chemical combination.—Inorganic plant-food necessary in physical combination for the immediate requirements of the soil, in chemical combination for its lasting fertility.—A sufficient quantity of plant-food in the first state indispensable for the purposes of husbandry.—Fallowing.—Its meaning, purport, and action upon the component parts of the soil.—An analysis of a soil should exhibit the physical condition as well as the chemical composition of its ingredients.—Necessary details of a soil analysis to render it useful and interpretable for the purposes of agriculture.—Surface and subsoils of the Concan.—Their relative bearing power.—Subsoils, at first sterile, become fertile.—The subsoil of India contains sufficient inorganic plant-food to make it, if judiciously treated, once more "the Garden of the East."—Surface and subsoils of Salsette.—Difference of chemical composition.—The improvement of the soil by heat, moisture, and atmospheric air.—A knowledge of the condition of his soil necessary to the farmer.—The means to change the inorganic plant-food from the unassimilable to the assimilable state.—The mechanical operations of agriculture.—Their meaning and purport.—The results depend upon the amount of inorganic plant-food present.—The help of science to ascertain what is wanted.—Drainage.—The use of manures to aid the mechanical operations of agriculture.—Lime.—Common salt, saltpetre, ammonia.—Colonel Corbett adding to the evidence of the exhausted nature of India's soil.—Irrigation, with constant cropping, hastens the impoverishment of the soil: wheat-lands degenerate into rice-lands, rice-lands are abandoned to reeds and rushes.—Irrigation will impoverish the soil unless a different system of cultivation is adopted, and the balance of inorganic plant-food more carefully preserved.—The *Oriental* on irrigation-works in India, and manures.—The natural state of the plant compared with its artificial or cultivated state.—The difference between soils bearing a natural growth of plants and those under cultivation by mankind.—The enrichment of the one and the impoverishment of the other. 106

CHAPTER V.

MANURES.

History of using manures.—First manure, animal and vegetable refuse.—A farm in ancient times returned to the field what was taken away from it.—A decrease in the outturn first perceptible when the farmer exported his produce.—Rotation of crops forced upon the farmer by the declining fertility of the soil.—Fallowing the next step.—The soil ceases to be remunerative and requires rest.—The rational solution of the difficulty.—The importation of manure as an equivalent for the exportation of produce.—Artificial manures; their use and abuse.—Different manures for different crops and soils.—Special manures; their nature, **and relation** to the soil.—The disappointment which must follow their **indiscriminate** use.—Monetary waste in supplying phosphoric acid to **a soil already** containing it in abundance.—An intimate knowledge of a soil necessary **in order** to obtain the highest results by the smallest outlay.—Liebig on manures in their relation **to crops** and soils.—**The** Minimum Theory.—An analysis necessary to point out the Minimum 116

CHAPTER VI.

MANURES AVAILABLE IN INDIA.

Mr. R. H. Elliot on the future prospects of agriculture in India, the want of manure, and the degeneration of man **and** animal.—The fertility of a soil depends upon the quantity of inorganic plant-food which it contains in physical combination.—The chief object of agriculture should **be** to maintain this fertility.—The progressive exhaustion of the soil, **under the present** system of agriculture **in** India, **expressed in figures.**—Man and animal part of the soil.

The total consumption of food-stuffs by **the** Indian subjects of Great Britain.—The ashes, or inorganic parts of these food-stuffs, are to be found in human refuse.—The welfare **and**

ultimate existence of nations depend upon the proper utilization of this fertilizing matter.—The calculations of Liebig—730 crores of rupees the value of food-stuffs consumed annually in British India.—The loss to the commonwealth by the waste of the inorganic constituents contained in the refuse of food, which, if carefully restored, would have enabled the soil to yield another crop worth 730 crores.—Public opinion awakening to a knowledge of the enormous waste going on.—The *Times* on the River Pollution Commission.—The conservation of human and animal refuse in India offers no difficulties.—The project of a system adapted for all small towns and villages.—Mr. Buck on the utilization of town-refuse at Furrukhabad.—Experiments made in the Deccan with human refuse as manure give remarkable results, more than doubling the outturn.—Town-refuse adopted as manure for all food-stuffs.—Its approximate composition.—Its mode of application... 117

CHAPTER VII.

Earthy Phosphates and Lime.

The importance of phosphoric acid as the predominating mineral constituent of the seed.—Bones are the principal source of phosphoric acid.—Their composition.—Bones the chief necessity of high agriculture.—Their behaviour to pure water, and to water containing carbonic acid.—Their comparative solubility depends upon their state of division.—The solvent action of carbonic acid upon bone phosphates in solutions of common salts, saltpetre, and ammonia.—Superphosphate] of lime.—Coprolites.—Phosphoric acid, the chief loss sustained by the soil of India.—Its application to the soil will double the outturn.—The use of phosphoric acid in Cheshire.—The action of superphosphate is immediate, and chiefly confined to the upper layers.—Bone-dust, on the contrary, penetrates deeper, and requires some years before the maximum result is obtained.—Mr. Robertson's experiments with bone-dust.—Soils most profited by bone-manure.—The action of phosphates on soil and plant.—Quantity used per acre.

Lime.—Its extensive use as a **manure.—Its** composition.—*Kunkur.*—Quicklime.—Action of lime on clay and soils in general.—The liberation of alkaline silicates from their unassimilable compounds.—Lime a powerful **aid** to the mechanical operations of agriculture.—Shell-sand.—Its extensive use in Ireland and France.—Quantity used **per** acre.—Lime increases the assimilable store of inorganic plant-food, resulting in a corresponding increase of the outturn.—Its use must go hand in hand with a careful restoration to the soil of what is withdrawn.—If not, lime **will enrich** the father and impoverish the son.—Experiments **of lime-manuring at** Oberbobritzsch.—Mr. Robertson's **experiments on the Madras** Model Farm.—Quicklime has the greatest effect **on stiff, clayey,** or marshy soils.—The permanent improvement of the soil **effected by** lime, and its effects upon different crops.—The action **of** lime on soil and plant 134

CHAPTER VIII.

GYPSUM, NITRATE OF POTASH, AND AMMONIA.

Gypsum allied to lime in its composition and general effects.—**Preferable** for green crops and grass-lands.—Dr. Pinkers' experiments.—How Gypsum is applied.—Its effects upon leaves and stems.—Highly appreciated in Europe.—Aden pumice.—Mr. Smith's experiments on clover and wheat.—Mr. Robertson's experiments.—Refuse of soda-water manufactories.

Nitrate of potash.—*Sora Khar.*—Mr. Robertson's **experiments.**—Consumption **of nitrates** steadily increasing.—Quantity per acre, and mode of application.—Effect on the plant.—Common salt checks the tendency **of** saltpetre to make **the crop** run into grass.—Ammoniacal liquor of gas-works.—Its usefulness for kitchen plants, and mode of application.. 151

CHAPTER IX.

JAPANESE HUSBANDRY A MODEL FOR INDIAN FARMING.

Extracts from the Report to the Minister of **Agriculture** *at Berlin on Japanese Husbandry ; by Dr. Moran,* **Member of the** *Prussian East Asiatic Expedition.*

The climate of Japan.—Cotton and rice, buck-wheat and barley.—The soil of Japan ; its fruitfulness the artificial product of proper cultivation.—Advantages of soil and climate turned to good account by an industrious people.—Agricultural questions yet unsolved in Europe have long been settled in Japan.

The Japanese axiom of agriculture: "Without continuous manuring, no continuous harvest."—Kind of manure, and mode of collecting and storing it.—Way of using it.—Japanese compost-manure.—Manuring with every crop.—"Fallow" not known in Japan.—Export of farm produce and import of manure.—The Japanese lives truly on the interest of the capital of the soil.—Tillage.—Deep cultivation.—Drill-cultivation brought to perfection in Japan...... 157

PART II.

The Staple Products of India.

CHAPTER I.

RICE.

Rice, the principal food of one-third of the human race, **chiefly cultivated in Asia.**—The varieties of rice.—Mode of cultivation in Salsette and the Concan.—Ploughing, sowing, and transplanting.—An improved culture resulting in an improved staple.—The superior quality of Carolina rice **attributable** to superior cultivation.—The endeavours of **the Court of** Directors to introduce this variety into India. —Mr. Kittredge's instructions.—History of Carolina rice. —Mode of cultivating it in South Carolina.—The importance of Carolina rice as a subsoil-feeder.—Experiments made **by** the Indian Government to acclimatize this variety.—The general advantages of its cultivation.—The improvement of indigenous rice equally important.—Careful **cultivation** the means of accomplishing it.—Rice soils, **and the means of improving** them.—Limeing.—Cultivation **in** furrows.—Deep-ploughing.—Selection of seeds.—Manuring, 187

CHAPTER II.

WHEAT.

Indian wheat in the European markets.—The exports **from** Bombay.—The high quality of **wheat** and the increasing demand.—The successful cultivation of wheat demanding a thorough knowledge of the Principles of Rational Agriculture.—Exhaustion **of** the soil rendering wheat-plants liable to be attacked by disease and parasites.—Deficiencies in soils on which wheat has been grown for any length of time.—Available silica in its relation to wheat.—How to increase available silica in wheat-soils.—Rotation **of** crops.—The agricultural advantages of India in connection with irrigation.—The defects of wheat-soils determinable by studying the mineral elements contained in wheat.—Nitrogen and wheat.—Mineral constituents necessary for the development of a long, well-filled ear.—The composition of wheat-ash.—Salt a fertilizer for wheat.—Composition of wheat-straw.—The relation between seed and straw, and the mineral constituents relatively required.—The manuring of wheat-soils to be adapted to the wants of the plant.—The first step of profitable farming in India is the accumulation of the raw material, *i.e.*, manure, for good harvests.—The deepening of the soil.—An acre twelve inches deep is worth more than four acres six inches deep.—General instructions for sowing, ploughing, and manuring.—The Cultivation of Wheat in the Central Provinces by A. C. Elliot 203

CHAPTER III.

SUGARCANE.

The antiquity of the cultivation of sugarcane in India.—Annual production.—Average outturn per acre.—Composition of sugarcane.—The varieties cultivated in India.—Their relative qualities.—China sugarcane.—Puttaputti producing the best Jaggery.—Otaheite and Bourbon sugarcane.—History of introduction into India.—Soils best suited for sugarcane.—Calcareous matter essential for the production of superior sugarcane.—Analysis of soils famed for the production of sugarcane.

Manures.—Rotten straw.—Mud from tank-bottoms.—Crushed bones.—Salt.—Preparation of the soil.—Ploughing and planting in the Rajahmundry district.—Watering, manuring, and ploughing in the Mysore and other districts.—Preparation of the fields in general.—The cutting of "sets."—Quantity of tops required per beegah, and average yield.—The planting of sugarcane.—Mr. Vaupell on the most successful mode of cultivating the Mauritius cane in Bombay.—After-culture.—Watering, weeding, and digging.—Draining.—Propping and wrapping the cane.—

Harvesting.—Injuries to which the plant is liable.—Effects of different manures upon sugarcane.—Experiments made by the Superintendent of the **Poona** Botanical Gardens ... 230

CHAPTER IV.

Cotton.

Cotton, the staple clothing of India.—Cotton in the **East, and** cotton in the West.—The superiority of American **cotton,** due to what causes.—Difference between "New Orleans" and "Fair Dhollera."—Causes of the inferiority of **Indian** cotton.—The ryot and the middleman.—The cotton industry of England in its relation to America and India. —**The** attempts of the Indian Government to introduce the **American** variety.—The deterioration of acclimatized exotic **cotton in** India.—Deterioration **of** cotton **in** America.— **Extract from** the Report **of** the Agricultural Department, Washington.—Improvement of the indigenous staple *versus* the acclimatization of an exotic staple.—Cotton cultivation in the Berars, and the influence of railways **and roads.**

The rational culture of the cotton plant in India.—Soils adaptable for cotton.—Preparation of the soil.—The tap-roots of the species "Gossypium."—Deep-ploughing.—Mr. Rivett-Carnac on deep-ploughing of cotton-fields, **and** results obtained on the Berar model-farms.—Levelling and ridging. —**Mr.** Login on "Ridging" in India.—Selection of seed.— The time for sowing.—Soaking the seed and sowing.— Thinning the plants and weeding.—Topping.—The time and mode of gathering.—The drying of cotton.—Noxious influence of sun and dew.—Mr. Login's experiments.—Cost and results of the Egyptian method of cotton cultivation. —The object of cotton-culture.—Improvement of the **soil** should affect the **parts** of fructification.—Analysis of cotton-wool and cotton-seed.—The proportion **of** phosphoric acid in "Orleans" and "Surats."—Cotton manures. —Return of plant and seed to the soil.—Professor Hilyard on the withdrawal of soil-ingredients by cotton-wool and cotton-seed.—Experiment of manuring cotton with superphosphate of lime, and results 262

PART I.

THE PRINCIPLES OF RATIONAL AGRICULTURE.

INTRODUCTION.

Agriculture advanced to the **rank of a science in Europe, but** neglected in India, the style of cultivation being the same now **as it was thousands of** years ago.—The disregard of the principle of restoration to the soil.—The impossibility of success in agricultural operations whilst disregarding this principle.—The soil deprived of its fertilizing constituents by the crops removed.—The exhaustion of the **soil** a natural consequence.—The ryot of India makes a certain return to the soil.—The inadequate nature of this return.—Lord Mayo acknowledging the primitive and backward state of agriculture in India, and the just claims **which the ryot** has upon the Government, upon which rests the duty of improving agriculture.—Her Majesty's Secretary of State admitting that the Government of India has a direct and immediate interest in the improvement of agriculture, such as is possessed by no other Government.—The Indian ryot does badly because of his never having been taught better. —He lives on the capital instead of the **interest, and** naturally becomes poorer and poorer.—The father lives at the expense of the **son.—The conservative** ideas of agricultural classes in **general, and** that of the Indian ryot **in** particular; his keen appreciation of improvements notwithstanding.—The Government of India, in its peculiar position as landlord, **suffers by the** present mode of cultivation, which takes **away from the** soil and gives nothing back.—Increasing impoverishment the consequence.—The necessity **of teaching the ryot** how to do better and improve agriculture.—The futile attempts of Government to effect this.

Evidence of the gradual diminishing outturn of the Indian soil.—The *Ayeen Akbary*, and its statistics of the average produce of India.—Comparison with the present outturn.—Alarming declension in full concord with the laws of husbandry.—Special mention of the gradual decline of the outturn of cotton in the Broach zillah, the figures being given by the *Ayeen Akbary*, Colonel Monier Williams, Dr. Burn, Mr. Rivett-Carnac, and others.—The necessity of acting in accordance with the Principles of Rational Agriculture if the example is to be avoided of the foolish husbandman who expected to reap where he had not sown.—Comparison between the results of European and Indian agriculture.—Comparison between the condition of the European farmer and the Indian ryot.—Their respective conditions with reference to the relative outturn of the soil.—The poverty of the Indian ryot and the deficiency of food.—India's necessity, the development of all her agricultural resources.—The means to accomplish this.—Irrigation and manure will increase the outturn fourfold.—The advisability of beginning at the root of the evil: the ignorance of the husbandman.—Advice and instruction to be given to the most intelligent farmer of each village.—Also guarantee to make good all losses resulting from his adopting the style of cultivation recommended, and from using manures whose effects are unknown to him.—Annual prizes for the largest outturn and for superior produce.—Circulation of pamphlets in the vernaculars.—Experimental farms to improve the staple products of the district, to select and distribute superior seed, and to obtain statistics.—The results of the experimental farms to be made widely known among the agricultural classes.—Criticism upon the model-farms in the Bombay Presidency, the talent and energy of superintendents being exclusively devoted to making them self-supporting.—The fallacy of this system.—Experimental farms to be considered remunerative only by the improvement they effect in the agriculture of their districts.—The **inability of Government to effect all these improvements single-handed, and the necessity for the co-operation of an AGRICULTURAL SOCIETY.**

AGRICULTURE, as practised in Europe, has always been considered a noble art, and Kings and Cæsars have mounted the throne from the plough, and have laid aside the cares of State for an agricultural life. The ancient Romans, especially, held Agriculture in very high estimation, their greatest men having practised it before and after filling the highest State appointments and earning the most distinguished honours. Consequently, the improvements effected in Europe in the mode of cultivation, as well as in the implements used, have been great, and in keeping with the general advance of education and civilization.

In Eastern countries, on the contrary, we find that Agriculture, as an art, has been entirely neglected, it being carried on very much in the same way now as it was two to three thousand years ago; and the backward state of this most important of all arts is prominently apparent in India. No advancement, no improvement, has been effected during several ages; the implements of husbandry are the same as before, and so is the mode of cultivation; thus reducing a land of once boundless wealth to comparative poverty. For there can be no doubt that the wealth of India lies in her soil, and in the products she can raise therefrom ; that in her soil lies a capital, the judicious employment of which should make her the richest country in the world ; it should raise her ryots to the position of **well-to-do farmers,** instead of being, as at present, the poorest and most ignorant of the population. Attention will be drawn **further** on to the small outturn of the fields of **India as** compared with that of well-nursed and properly tended soils of other countries, which, though **not** enjoying the advantages of a tropical climate, yield **more** than double the average of India. It will be shown that the **outturn** of the rice-fields of India must originally have been **much larger,** and that we have to seek the causes which have reduced it to its present **low level in the reckless style** of Indian cultivation.

The riches and resources of India **lie** buried in **her soil, and it is** only by developing these resources, these riches, that we can permanently improve the country. Government has laid down hundreds of miles of railway ; it is sowing an education broadcast among the masses, which only tends to fill its offices with underpaid officials ; but the true development of the **natural** wealth of this vast country with an essentially agricultural population has hitherto hardly been attempted. Indeed, the efforts which Government has made to improve Indian Agriculture have been few and far between, and it must also be said that, while few, they have been conducted in a most negligent and unsystematic manner.

The Indian ryot ploughs, **sows, and reaps in the** same manner now as his forefathers **did before him,** at a time when our ancestors were **picking acorns** in Germany, or painting their bodies blue in Britain; but with this difference, that the soil has **become** exhausted, and the **products raised therefrom, so** far from showing such improvements as we **notice** in other countries, **have** become reduced in quantity and deteriorated in quality, and consequently both man and beast have degenerated. We are not surprised to find that the ryots of India plough with the same primitive instrument, and still adhere to the barbarous custom of twisting the tails **of their** cattle, as their forefathers did centuries ago ; but we have reason to be surprised that an enlightened Government has not yet succeeded in inducing them to improve their antiquated method of cultivation, that nothing has been done to rouse them long before this to energetic self-action and **to adopt** modern improvements. No ordinary measure, however, will remove the inherent stubbornness and constitutional apathy of the Indian ryot, who **cultivates** the soil in the manner described, not **because the** method is good or best adapted to the country, but because it has been sanctioned by immemorial usage. He says, when any improvements are suggested to him—" Why should I alter my system ? I must do as my father has done before me." To improve Indian Agriculture, therefore, while being one of the most important, is yet one of the most difficult, things which Government has to accomplish ; it is a task which requires no ordinary energy, patience, and indefatigable perseverance.

From time immemorial the soil has not only been cultivated in the rudest possible manner, but the very first principle of Agriculture, *i.e.*, " To give back to the soil what is taken from it," has been utterly disregarded. Harvest after harvest has been reaped, crop after crop has been removed, and when we consider that with every bushel of rice, with every bundle of straw, we take away from the soil a certain amount of inorganic substances which formed originally a most important part of it, we may justly feel surprised that it yields still as much as it does. On the presence of these substances in sufficient quantities depends all vegetable life ; it is therefore evident that, without adequate restoration of what is withdrawn, it would be impossible to carry on agriculture for any length of time without gradually but surely impoverishing the soil. This fact is now being realized in India, a country which has been almost entirely ruined by the ignorance and recklessness with which past generations have squandered its resources, and dissipated the treasures Nature so lavishly had stored up in its soil.

Every year enormous quantities of grain and other food-stuffs are consumed; large quantities are annually exported to foreign countries, which means that we yearly deprive the soil of a certain amount of its component parts, a quantity of mineral substances which form the most important portion of it, and which are essential to the growth of the crops. Just as the world rotates in endless circles, so these substances ought to circulate, and return whence they came, after fulfilling their purpose of sustaining life—and only thus can the laws of nature be satisfied and the balance of fertility preserved. But in no land more than in India has this great law of restoration been so utterly ignored, and consequently her soil, from being once the most fertile, has become sterile, and the once renowned Garden of the East has become a comparatively barren country.

It is true that the ryot, the native cultivator, does make a certain return to the soil; he burns the remaining stubble of the previous crop, as also leaves, grass, &c., which are gathered for the purpose, and the ashes of which, spread over the fields, are supposed to compensate for the loss sustained. But the ashes of leaves and stalks will only supply the mineral food for the creation of similar parts; and as the value of a crop consists in the quantity of the grain, and not in the quantity of straw, it is apparent that such an inadequate restoration will have very little beneficial effect on the outturn of the more valuable portion of the crop.

The fact that most of our fields are deficient in the mineral food necessary for the proper development of the grain, and that this deficiency has been caused by the exhaustive processes of past and present cultivation, cannot be disputed in the face of statistics showing the relative outturn of the past and present. Considering the rapid advances Agriculture has made in Europe during the last century—advances which have raised this pursuit to the rank of a science—it is astonishing that not one of the principles on which alone it can be carried on profitably, and without injury to future generations, has found its way into India.

Lord Mayo, in one of his despatches in 1870, says:—"It cannot be denied that Indian Agriculture is in a primitive and backward condition, and the Government has not done for its improvement all it might have done. When the light of science has been properly brought to bear upon Indian Agriculture, the results will be as great as they have been in Europe. The duties which in England are performed by a good landlord, fall in India, in a great measure, upon the Government. The only Indian landlord who can command the requisite knowledge and capital for the improvement of the land, is the State. There is perhaps no country in the world in which the State has so immediate and direct an interest in such questions. The land-revenue yields twenty millions of our annual income. The means of obtaining agricultural instruction in India are no better now than they were fifteen years ago." (Lord Mayo might have said, with equal truth, fifteen *hundred* years ago.) " The work that is performed by the great agricultural societies of Europe must be performed in India by the Government, or not at all." Her Majesty's Secretary of State for India says :—" It is certain that, with the exception of the permanently-settled provinces of Bengal, the Government has a direct and immediate interest in the improvement of Agriculture which is possessed by no Government in Europe."

The Government, therefore, it would appear from the above extracts, is fully aware of the neglected state of Indian Agriculture ; but no reason is assigned to explain the absence of the necessary measures to effect the desired improvements. From the most remote ages it has always been the chief object of wise and provident rulers to encourage Agriculture in all its branches, knowing, as they did, that the products of the land, and the men who raise them, are the principal foundation and pillars of Empires. Does it not, then, seem strange that our rulers should neglect the first duties of governors, and, while concentrating their attention on the intricate complications of State machinery, should yet overlook the primary moving-power, the indispensable requisite that sustains the vitality and maintains the well-being of nations, but by their passive behaviour suffer its efficiency and organism to become seriously impaired ?

The Indian cultivator *has* some idea, vague and undefined though it is, of that great law of restoration which governs Agriculture ; he is aware that he should give the land something in return for the crop he takes away from it ; but that is all. He does not know what essential element he is taking away, nor how to compensate for it adequately. The great question of modern Agriculture —how to improve the land, and obtain the highest permanent return with a minimum outlay—does not trouble his mind for a moment. He draws year after year a certain percentage from the capital contained in the soil, instead of living on the interest ; and consequently, year after year, the capital, *i.e.*, the fertility of the soil, dwindles down, and the percentage which can now be extracted from it is barely sufficient for his maintenance. He is poor, but in the natural course of things his children will be poorer still. It is well known that, of all liege-subjects, the tillers of the soil are the most conservative, not only in their allegiance to the reigning power, but also in their ideas generally, being greatly adverse to innovation. Although the Indian ryot is no exception to this rule, but, on the contrary, is an exceptionally conservative man, who prefers walking in the footsteps of, and following the example set by his ancestors, yet he is not the less fully alive to his own interests, and will be only too eager to adopt any mode of cultivation which would ensure him a larger crop than is obtained by his own method, provided he is personally convinced that such advantages can be secured.

The Government of India, in its peculiar relative position to the cultivator, has very responsible obligations to discharge. It must be considered as representing an extensive land-owner, holding the acres of the State in trust for future generations. But does not Government betray that trust to the detriment of the resources of the country, and therefore to the prejudice of succeeding generations, by permitting its tenants, the ryots, to carry on Agriculture in the present ruinous method, in suffering them to draw continuously from the resources of the land, without a reasonable return, a percentage which must ultimately, although gradually, dwindle down to a degree which will be inadequate for their existence ? Besides these cogent reasons for immediate and strenuous action, the present pernicious system will, manifestly, be detrimental to the interests of Government itself in a fiscal point of view, inasmuch as, consequent upon the meagre outturn, the cultivator will ultimately find himself unable to pay his quota of the revenue, while large tracts of country will be abandoned as barren, thus considerably reducing the chief source of contribution to the public finances.

Government is lending the ryot the capital of the State, *i.e.*, the soil of the country, in order that, by his labour, he should make it yield an interest from which to maintain himself and his family, and to pay his share towards the requirements of Government. But it will be proved in the following pages that, as has been asserted before, the ryot maintains himself and pays his dues, not from the interest, but from the capital itself. Is it not, then, incumbent upon us to endeavour to prevent what will be the inevitable result of this system— increased pauperism of the cultivator, and sterility of the soil? Should we not try to inculcate in the ryot some of the principles of an improved method of cultivation, convince him of the indispensability of observing the great principle of giving a return to the soil for the annual defection, and show him how to attain maximum results with the minimum of expenditure without detriment to the soil, or impairing its prolific capabilities in any way?

Quoting the words of Dr. Mouat, the Hon'ble the Court of Directors stated, in their well-known despatch of the 19th July 1854, on the subject of education in India, that there was " no single advantage that could be afforded to the vast rural population of India that would equal the introduction of an improved system of Agriculture." But though twenty-three years have elapsed since the penning of that despatch, nothing, or next to nothing, has been done in the matter. Though I may be guilty of repetition, I cannot avoid asking again whether it can for a moment be supposed that we could raise year after year the same kind of crops on the same soil, without rotation, without any manure worth mentioning, and not bring about a gradual but certain falling-off in the yield? Or that we could withdraw year after year from the soil a certain quantity of fertilizing substances, without ultimately rendering it utterly sterile?

I am in possession of ample evidence to prove that the yield of India's soil has gradually diminished since the last century. I will mention here only a few facts in support of the charge I advance of reckless cultivation—a recklessness which has resulted in our crops being now grown on an exhausted surface-soil, yielding a return which would be utter ruin to any farm in Europe.

The *Ayeen Akbary* contains a set of tables showing the average produce of food-stuffs and other agricultural products throughout India, which, dating from the middle of the seventeenth century, were prepared in the reign of Akbar by order of his great minister, Tudar Muhl, and were based upon the records of nineteen years' careful observation of the seasons. (The natural philosophers of that age regarded nineteen years as a lunar cycle, in which the seasons were supposed to run through all their variations.) These statistical tables appear to have been prepared with extreme care, and their reliability is incontestable—an assurance which cannot unfortunately be always made in connection with the agricultural statistics collected in these days. According to these tables, the average produce of rice in India amounted in the middle of the seventeenth century to 1,338 lbs. per acre, of wheat 1,155 lbs., of cotton (unpicked) 670 lbs., equal to about 223 lbs. picked. On reference to the statistics of the nineteenth century, and especially of this decade, we find the average yield of rice to be 800 to 900 lbs. per acre, of wheat 660 lbs., of cotton (picked) 52 lbs. Have we not reason to stand aghast at the fact thus revealed, that the soil of India is rapidly approaching exhaustion? For thousands of years the soil of India has nourished millions of souls; but during all that time it has, with every recurring year, been deprived of a large portion of its plant-food of organic and inorganic elements which are indispensable to the growth and development of crops, while the restoration of these essential elements has either been *nil*, or of an extremely inadequate character. Can we, then, be surprised at the alarming declension the above figures indicate?

A very striking instance of the gradual deterioration and inevitable exhaustion of the soil under the existing method of agriculture, is shown in the results of the cultivation of cotton at different periods. The yield of picked cotton in the middle of the seventeenth century was 223 lbs. per acre. No information of a reliable character regarding the staple seems to be available from that time until the present century, but I would ask my readers to refer to Colonel Monier Williams' memoir, in which, speaking of the Broach zillah and its black soil, he states that it produced in his time (1828) 128 lbs. of cotton per acre. Much later (1844), we learn from Dr. Burn, who had charge of the Broach experimental farm, that, under the most careful treatment, only 83 lbs. of cotton were obtained from one acre. In the last decade the average produce was 67 lbs. per acre, and now it has declined to an average of 52 lbs. !

Mr. Rivett-Carnac, until lately Cotton Commissioner, when reporting upon the cotton cultivation of Ahmedabad, said he was "at a loss to account for the continuous yearly decrease" of this staple. But this decrease can easily be accounted for, if we consider the natural laws, the Principles of Rational Agriculture, which demand a conscientious restoration to the soil of the elements of plant-food which are taken away from it. If we do not desire a diminution in the yearly outturn, we should act in consonance with those laws ; otherwise we shall only be following the example of the foolish husbandman, and expect to reap where we have not sown. If due consideration is accorded to the facts and figures I have adduced, there will hardly be any further proof needed to support the charge of reckless cultivation.

If we now compare the results of European Agriculture with the yield of the once fertile soil of India, we can hardly be surprised at the wretched condition of the Indian ryot. In Bavaria, in Italy near Piedmont, in the Lombardy plains of the Po Valley, where rice is cultivated, the yield is on the average 2,500 lbs. per acre, while in this Presidency it is only 700 to 800 lbs. ! The average yield of wheat in Europe is 1,500 lbs. per acre, while the average in India is 660 lbs. ; 200 lbs. of cleaned cotton are picked from an acre in America, 300 to 400 lbs. in Egypt, while in India we get an average of 52 lbs. ! We can understand, then, by what means the farmer of Europe and America is enabled to live in comparative opulence, while the ryot of India is compelled to vegetate in squalid poverty, his implements of the rudest possible description, and his cattle pitiful specimens of a gradual degeneration. Starved is the soil, starved is the tiller of the land, starved are his cattle. The soil craves for food, and man and beast likewise crave for food.

Mr. C. A. Elliot, Settlement Officer, N. W. P., expresses himself very strongly on the miserable condition of the Indian ryot. I quote his own words :—" I do not hesitate to say that half our agricultural population never know from year's end to year's end what it is to have their hunger fully satisfied. The ordinary phrase in these parts when a man asks for employment is, that he wants half-a-seer of flour ; and a phrase so general must have some foundation. I believe that it has this much truth in it, that 1 lb. of flour is sufficient, though meagre, sustenance for a non-labouring man. That a labouring adult can eat 2 lbs. I do not doubt ; but he rarely, if ever, gets it. But take the ordinary population in a family of five, consisting of a father, mother, and three children. The father will, I would say, eat a little less than 2 lbs., the mother a little more than 1 ℔., the children about 3 lbs. between them. Altogether 7 lbs. to five people is the average, which, after much enquiry, I am inclined to adhere to. I am confident that with our minutely divided properties, our immense and cramped population, and our grinding poverty, any attempt at heavier taxation would result in financial failure to the Government, in widespread distress and ruin to the people."

To quote a Bengal journal, " What India wants is the development of all its agricultural resources, of rice and wheat and millet, as well as of cotton; of jute and silk, as well as of china grass ; of tea and coffee, as well as of cinchona and ipecacuanha."

The means by which we can develop these resources are well known, but we must strike at the root of the evil, namely, the ignorance of the cultivator; and we must commence with agricultural education at the home of the farmer, and spread among the masses an elementary knowledge of the rational Principles on which alone Agriculture can be pursued successfully, and a strict observance of which can alone prevent the alarming decrease in the fertility of the soil. With the possession of such a knowledge, added to the advantages of a tropical climate, where everything favours the luxuriant growth of vegetable life, we could, here in India, achieve far greater results than are obtained in more temperate climes; and if, in addition to the natural advantages, we had a system of canals and irrigation-works, we would be enabled to grow *four* blades where formerly but one grew, and India would become once more the Garden of the East.

I am, however, not an advocate for agricultural schools and colleges, which I think would be decidedly premature at this period of total ignorance, but am of opinion that education should commence at the home of the cultivator. I would select the most intelligent farmer in each village, and advise him, not to alter, but how to improve, his present mode of cultivation. I would explain to him the uses of the different manipulations of husbandry, and their effects upon the crop; I would instruct him how to obtain suitable manure for his land and his crop, and, to induce confidence in the proposed measures, would stipulate that half the increase over the usual yield should be assigned to me, while I bound myself to compensate him for any loss he may sustain by the adoption of the method I recommend. I would have prizes, of sufficient value to attract competitors of all classes, distributed annually, for the largest outturn per acre and for superior descriptions of grain. I would have circulated pamphlets in the vernaculars, stating the principles of modern Agriculture in the most simple and comprehensive language, and adapted generally to the native style of thinking. I would have model-farms where the products of the district could be reared under an improved system, where selection and distribution of seed could be undertaken, and whence we could obtain reliable statistics as to the results of adopting a certain treatment and certain manures. The facts and figures obtained at these model-farms should then be annually printed in English and the different vernaculars, and distributed throughout the land.

There are some model-farms in this Presidency with trained agriculturists and superintendents, but we fail to see the benefits they are effecting. Do they show the ryots how to improve their crops, how to enhance the yield, how to manure this peculiar soil and effect the permanent improvement of others ? Is it not their obvious duty, before all other considerations, to apply the recognised Principles of Modern Agriculture to the staple products of the country, and adapting them, after close observation, to the peculiarities of the climate ? Should they not, first of all, exercise their practical and scientific knowledge in effecting an improvement in the soil of the surrounding country, as well as of the different crops grown, and try to diffuse agricultural knowledge among the native cultivators ? Instead of doing all this, however, they only keep experimenting upon the introduction of all sorts of exotic plants—experiments which occupy much valuable time, and are very seldom attended with satisfactory results or any benefit to the country. It should be observed, however, that I fully recognise the usefulness of such experiments ; but they should be treated as of secondary importance, the improvement of indigenous products being of primary consequence. That is to say, we should first endeavour to improve the indigenous staple products, and only turn our attention to experimentalizing on exotic plants when everything necessary is accomplished for the former, and no further improvement is possible.

It may not be out of place here to draw attention to the fallacy of the system of 'self-support' which has been adopted in connection with these model-farms. When a superintendent is appointed over a farm, he is carefully impressed with an idea of the paramount importance of making it support itself. That is considered the chief object, and the only indication of the indubitable success of a farm. What possible good, may I ask, can be expected under such a system? The chief duty of superintendents ought, manifestly, rather to consist in raising native agriculture in their districts to the highest standard possible, the expenditure incurred in doing so being willingly borne by the State. The Agricultural Department of the small State of Prussia spends yearly the equivalent of nearly six lakhs of rupees, exclusive of salaries and the cost of administration, solely for agricultural purposes; and never surely was the public money employed in a better object. It is my opinion, however, that Government, single-handed, will be unable to accomplish much for the advancement of Indian Agriculture, but that our first step must be the establishment of an *Agricultural Society*, composed of members sincere and zealous in their aims, and who recognise fully the importance of the work to be undertaken.

CHAPTER I.

THE PLANT.

A knowledge of the nature of plants and their component parts necessary to understand the Principles of Rational Agriculture.—The organic and inorganic parts of the plant.—Their origin.—The conditions of plant life.—The seed in its relation to the plant.—The cosmic conditions of germination.—The process of germination.—Seeds will germinate and produce miniature plants in water from the store of nourishment they contain.—The condition of the young plant depends upon the quality of the seed.—The advantages of seed selection.—Superior plants from superior seed.—The condition of the soil in relation to the germinated seed.—The delicate root-fibres prefer a loose, porous soil.—Cato's teachings on tillage are still the foundations of agriculture.—The roots are the medium through which human skill can reach the plant.—The properties of the root.—Its absorbing power.—The rootlets absorb from the soil the inorganic food of plants.—The stem the conveyor of the sap to the different parts of the plant.—Silica one of the chief inorganic constituents of the stems of cereals and grasses.—It forms the bones of vegetable life.—Leaves and their functions.—The exposure of the crude sap in the leaves to the influence of light and atmospheric air, and the changes it undergoes. —The seed, and its connection with the plant.—Selection and change of seed.—Seed and seed-sowing.

To fully understand the natural laws on which the Principles of Rational Agriculture are based, it is essentially necessary to possess an intimate knowledge of the nature of plants and their component parts ; of the relation which these latter bear to, and the influence they exercise upon, the whole organism. We have to acquaint ourselves with the different elements of which plants consist, and to enquire whence they are derived and how they are assimilated.

If we subject a plant, or a portion of it, to the process of combustion, we reduce its component parts to their elementary form; we call those which are combustible the *organic*, and those which are incombustible the *inorganic parts* of the plant.

The organic parts are chiefly derived from the atmosphere ; they consist of four elements—

    Carbon,   Hydrogen,
    Nitrogen,   Oxygen,

and are assimilated through the leaves and the roots in the form of *Carbonic Acid*, *Water*, and *Ammonia*.

The inorganic parts—the ashes of the plant—are all derived from the soil, and the most important elements we find in them are—

    Potash,   Phosphoric Acid,
    Soda,   Silicic Acid,
    Lime,   Sulphuric Acid,
    Magnesia,   Chlorine.

The inorganic parts are assimilated by the underground part of the plant—the root.

All these organic and inorganic elements constitute what we call the food of plants : every plant requires them in an available form for its development. Heat, light, and moisture are the other conditions under which vegetable life exists, as they rouse to action the slumbering vital power in the seed, and develop the plant from it, if the situation is such that the young plant can obtain its inorganic food from the soil and its organic food from the atmosphere.

The seed contains within itself all the organic constituents of plants in the form of starch, albumen, and fat, as well as the inorganic elements; and is thus enabled to supply from its own resources any element which nature may find necessary for the further development of the plant.

When the seed is brought under the influence of heat, air, and moisture, some curious changes take place in its component parts; it absorbs moisture, begins to swell, and from that time absorbs oxygen rapidly, which, affecting first the nitrogenous compounds, changes completely the nature of the compounds present in the seed, converts the starch into cellulose, and, by depositing it in the shape of cells, produces a root downwards into the soil, and a shoot—developing subsequently into one or two leaves—upwards into the air, which parts have thenceforth to absorb from without the nourishment necessary for the further development of the plant.

If seed is allowed to germinate in water instead of in the soil, the plant will continue growing, although it receives no portion of its inorganic food from the soil. It will continue for a few weeks to develop new leaves, the old ones becoming yellow and dying off; thus showing that its constituents have been withdrawn for the formation of new parts. A miniature plant may thus be produced, and vitality kept up for some time, until the inorganic elements become insufficient for its increased growth, and it then dies. Under natural conditions however, *i.e.*, when the seed is placed in contact with the soil, the plant will, as soon as the first leaves are formed, begin the process of assimilating food from without—the inorganic portion through the rootlets, the organic portion chiefly through the leaves; the elements absorbed increase the mass, the plant gradually expands, and the process of development goes on now more or less vigorously, according to the amount of nourishment the plant can obtain within reach.

Until the first leaves are produced, the plant depends entirely on the nourishment contained in the seed for the formation of the organs which subsequently absorb food from without. The number and strength of these organs will be in exact proportion to the amount of nourishment contained in the seed: a large, well-developed seed will produce during the course of germination large and vigorous organs, while a poor, imperfectly-developed seed will not only take much longer to germinate, but the rootlets and leaves produced will be weak and fewer in number. That is to say, by the time the assimilating organs of the small seed become sufficiently strong and numerous to push on the growth of the plant, the large seed will have raised a strong, vigorous plant several inches above the ground. This difference of growth will be perceptible in all the further stages of development, and the grain produced will also be of the same nature as the seed.

The advantages, therefore, which the farmer derives from a judicious selection of seed, will be evident. A crop of rice reaped from one and the same field, exhibits considerable difference in the size of grains, some being larger, some smaller, according to the maturity and the development of the ears.

If, then, only the larger and well-developed grains were selected for seed, we could not only secure a harvest showing a pretty uniform size of grain, but by careful cultivation we could obtain grain even of a superior description to the seed sown; and by further judicious selection from these again, the improvement could be continued. In the general selection of seed for sowing, some regard must be had to the soil and climate. Seed from a poor soil will be found best adapted for a rich soil; the seed of mountainous districts should be preferred to that of the plains.

Not less important than the selection of the seed

is the nature of the soil, which exercises an immediate and most powerful influence upon the first development of the plant. The soil should be prepared in accordance with the construction of the root, whatever sort of crop it may be intended to grow. The radiation and extension of the part of plants underground depend greatly upon the porosity or stiffness of the soil. The roots, which are extended and lengthened by the addition of new cells, have to encounter a certain degree of obstruction, and will therefore always extend in the direction offering the least resistance. Consequently, while a stiff, clayey soil may be well adapted for plants with strong and thick root-fibres, it will be found uncongenial to those with delicate fibres, and will materially retard their extension. Small seeds, moreover, will require a finer division of the soil than large ones.

It may, then, be accepted as a rule that the soil can never be too much operated upon. The teachings of Cato in his *De Re Rustica*, with regard to the tillage of the soil, are still the fundamental principles of Agriculture. In answer to " *Quid est agrum bene colere ?*" he says, " *Bene arare. Quid secundum ?—Arare. Tertio ?—Stercorare.*"

The farmer cannot devote too much attention to the peculiarities and nature of the roots of the particular description of crop he desires to cultivate; for it is through the roots alone that he can exert any influence upon the plants. The more care, therefore, he bestows upon the proper development of the root, the more satisfactory and remunerative will be the result of his labour.

The fibres of the root are the medium through which the plant assimilates that kind of food which is derived from the soil, and through which it expels the excessive moisture, as well as all those substances which have incidentally entered into the system of the plant, but which it refuses to assimilate. The rapidity with which the root absorbs water is very great, and it is easy to make one's own observations to demonstrate the fact.

Let a small plant drawn out of the soil be placed in a tumbler of water, another glass containing a like quantity of water being placed alongside. The water will disappear far more rapidly from the glass containing the plant than from the other ; and if the plant is able to exist at all in water, it will absorb many times its weight. I had a plant of spearmint growing for sixty days in water, and although at the end of that time it weighed only ninety-five grains, it had absorbed not less than fourteen thousand grains of water, or nearly one pint and three-quarters. The plant had therefore retained only a minute portion of this large quantity of water ; the remainder must have been got rid of, mostly by exhalation through the leaves. The reason for this enormous absorption is, that the inorganic constituents of plant-food require very large quantities of water for their solution. Mr. Lawes calculated that two thousand grains of water have to pass through the vegetable system before one grain of solid matter can be deposited within the cells of the plant.

From the root, the liquid, containing the inorganic elements obtained from the soil, travels up the *stem*, and is distributed among the different parts of the plant, to assist vitality and impart nourishment to the leaves, buds, flowers, and fruits. On examining a stalk of Indian corn or sugarcane cut for the purpose, there can be seen, even with the naked eye, a number of very minute cells, enclosed by a thin cuticle, called epidermis, which contains (this is the case in all grasses, canes, cereals, &c.) a large percentage of silicious earth, which seems necessary to protect it from injury, and to impart to the stalk the strength required to bear the weight of the ear. This fact explains why silica in an assimilable state is indispensable to the growth of cereals. The minute cells which this epidermis encloses are the conveyors of the sap, as the fluid which rises from the root is termed; they are also the storers and assimilators of the vegetable food. The sap travels, through all those minute sexagonal cells, to the leaves, where it is exposed, in numerous little tubes and cells, to the chemical influence of heat, light, and atmospheric air, whereby the crude fluid is converted into a nutritious sap to assist the development of new formations. Here in these leaves, under the influence of the atmospheric air, an incessant chemical change is going on, presenting very interesting phenomena which will be discussed later on. But many observations have yet to be made before we can fully understand the mystical chemical processes by which the water of the sap is decomposed, receives new elements, assimilates them for the different functions of vegetable life, and returns them eventually to the cellular system of the stem, to be utilized in the further development of the plant, or, if superfluous, to be expelled through the medium of the roots.

A superficial observation of a leaf will show that the two sides are different in colour : the upper side, which is generally glossy, seems to be a continuation of the epidermis of the stem, and serves for the transmission of the light ; while the under side, which presents a dull appearance, contains all those little cells and tubes by which moisture is evaporated or absorbed, and gases inhaled or exhaled, and which are called the stomata of the leaves.

The processes of vegetation and the purposes of the plant culminate in the production of the seed ; and its importance as the propagator of new plants is of course apparent.

It has been mentioned before that the seed stands in closer connection to the plant which is raised therefrom, and exerts a greater influence upon it—apparent in all the different stages of plant-life—than is generally known. This will be further apparent from the remarks of the *Canada Farmer* on "The Selection and Change of Seed":—

"This [selection of seed] is a matter of primary importance to the farmer, for, however well he may manure and cultivate his land, his labour will be but thrown away if he neglects to obtain clean and sound seed of the most approved varieties of whatever crop he intends to grow. It is the opinion of many practical men that the crops of most kinds of grain will deteriorate when confined to selection of seed grown on the same farm, or even the same region of country, for many years in succession. Others maintain that, by always selecting the best seed from the crops grown on the farm, and taking particular care to have only such as is plump and well-matured, the quality will improve from year to year. We think there is truth on both sides. We have known a farmer to sell off the best of his grain and reserve that of inferior quality for seed, remarking that, small as it was, it would grow, and that, he thought, was all that was necessary. Such an idea is a common but erroneous one, as, although plant will be produced from inferior seed, it will be wanting in the healthful vigour that is the characteristic of one grown from a plump and well-developed seed, which contains not only a large and strong germ, but also a full amount of the plant-food requisite to support that germ until the young rootlets can eliminate food from the soil for the support of the plant.

"It is the want of a proper appreciation of this fact that leads many to imagine that a change of seed, even between near neighbours, is of great value. Thus, a farmer who does not take the trouble to select his seed-wheat from the best portion of his crop when growing, and to separate and reserve it for future use, or who never frees his seed from the presence of chess, cockles, or other noxious weeds before sowing, finds a great advantage in obtaining seed of the same variety from a neighbour who has the reputation of growing good crops, and who has a nice, plump, clean sample of seed grain for sale. In such a case, the advantage gained is ascribed to change, when in reality it is due to selection. But, on the other hand, varieties of grain, grasses, &c., have originated or become common in one part of the country, and their introduction to another portion of the same or an adjoining country, proves of signal advantage to the cultivator of the soil, for a time at least. A farmer who takes an agricultural journal, often reads in it an account of some new variety of grain as yet unknown, except in some distant locality. He sends for a small sample (perhaps a few bushels), sows it, and soon discovers that it possesses some quality that gives it superior advantages over the varieties that have usually been grown in his neighbourhood. His neighbours find out this fact, and then comes a rush to him with ' Please, let me have some seed of that new kind of wheat you grew last year.' It is just here that we find the benefit of change, which is the discarding of one variety for the purpose of giving place to another and better variety of the same article; and it would only be fair that the person who introduces and tests the qualities of any new variety of cereal, should have a sort of patent right to make something out of his enterprize and outlay, by charging a higher price for the seed he grows than the ordinary price of the commonly grown sorts of the same article."

The *Agricultural Gazette of India* contains a most valuable article on "Seed and Seed-sowing," which is quoted here entire :—

"When will our cultivators learn that bad seed never produces good crops? The cost of seed, even of a really good quality, is one of the least expensive items in the charges incurred for raising a crop, and yet, small as the cost is, there are few cultivators that do not grudge the expense. They will sow any seed possessing the ordinary characteristics of the seed of the variety of crop they wish to produce, provided that they have it already of their own producing, or can buy it at a low rate. Thus, to save half a rupee, or a rupee at the most, per acre, they will risk the value of their labour on cultivation, the loss of the crop, &c. The difference in the return, obtained from a crop produced by good seed and from a crop produced by bad seed, may be 25 per cent. in favor of the former, say Rs. 5 per acre—certainly a large return for the extra rupee spent in procuring the good seed. But this is not all; for the sickly crop produced by inferior seed, or by old seed, is always more liable to be injured by blight, by weather, and by insects, than a healthy crop, the produce of well-grown, well-developed seed. By good seed we mean not only that the seed must be large and well-formed, true to its kind, regular in colour, fresh, and free from all mustiness, &c., but that it must have been produced under favorable conditions, that is, must not have been grown year after year on the same land, or on land of the description and quality of that on which it is intended to be sown, and must, when tested, yield at least 75 per cent. of vital grains. Our cultivators do not fully appreciate the benefits that arise from a change of seed. Instead of, year after year, sowing the produce of their own soil, they should endeavour to obtain seed by exchange, or by purchase, from some neighbour who farms soil of a different kind to that farmed by them; or, what is even better, obtain it from some distant part of the district, in which the soils are of a different character, but in which the climate is somewhat similar to their own. Under a very good system of agriculture, it is possible to get fair results by sowing on the same land, year after year, the produce of each preceding harvest; but the practice is not to be commended when it is possible to get a fair sample of seed from a soil differing from that on which it is to be sown. The heaviest and plumpest seed should always be selected, provided it also possesses the other qualities that characterize good seed. The fact is, we should deal with our seed as with our breeding stock—select the parent which possesses the qualities we wish to find in that to be produced. European agricultural seeds have greatly improved in quality during the last ten or fifteen years, and this, to a considerable extent, is due to the greater care and skill now employed in their cultivation. The result is chiefly to be attributed to selection, that is, to the best grains in the best ears or heads only having been for years used for seed. In this way, superior qualities can be stamped with some degree of permanency or any variety of seed. But when we have secured the seed with these higher qualities, it becomes all the more necessary that the circumstances to which it must be exposed should be those of a favorable character. A seed elevated in this way will yield worse results when opposed by unfavorable circumstances, than seed of the same kind in the unimproved state. It is a well-ascertained fact that plants, like animals, can in time adapt themselves to circumstances which at first they may dislike, and which at that time may be actually injurious to them.

"The seeds of plants that have gradually become habituated to unfavorable agricultural conditions, will grow and give fair results under circumstances that might prove quite fatal to the prospects of a crop from seed which had not been so trained. But we may have obtained seed which meets the conditions we have laid down, and yet find that we have not secured all the conditions necessary to ensure, even to a moderate degree of certainty, a good result for all our care. We allude here to the danger of obtaining seed tainted by disease. It is a well-ascertained fact that many of the diseases from which our crops suffer are to be traced to the seed, either from the germs of disease having been actually present in the seed, or from the seed having been the produce of plants which had been attacked by disease, and whose vigour and constitution had thereby been injured. It is to meet evils of this kind that the European farmer employes washes and steeps, in which he prepares his seed for sowing. We think it would be a wise act on the part of the Indian farmer were he to adopt the same practice. These washes are solutions of sulphate of copper, of chloride of lime, of chloride of sodium (common salt), of sulphate of iron, of sulphate of soda, of arsenic, &c. The arsenic solution is objectionable as a steep for grain, from the danger of putting large quantities of so poisonous a substance in the hands of ordinary agricultural labourers, and from the danger of the prepared grain finding its way amongst the food of the live-stock. Sulphate of soda (Glauber salt) possesses some merit, but as the grain which has been dressed by it must be dried by lime-powder, a great deal of trouble is produced. Sulphate of iron (green vitriol) is useful, but is not effective in all cases, while it is very little cheaper than the more effective blue vitriol. Chloride of sodium has little effect on seed infected by the spores of parasitical fungi; chloride of lime is destructive to the spores of some fungi that attack farm crops, but not to all.

"Sulphate of copper is, without doubt, the most effective and most useful of all the chemical salts used in the preparation of seed pickles. It destroys the spores of all the fungi that attack farm crops, while the vitality of the seed is in no way injured by its action, and not only as regards efficacy is it the most valuable of all the saline substances used, but it is the easiest to apply. It is used in the following way :—Take three-quarters of a pound of the salt and dissolve it in a gallon of hot-water; after allowing it to cool, it is fit for use. The solution thus prepared is sufficient for about 200 lbs. of ordinary field seed. Before applying the solution, spread the grain equally over a hard earthen floor, to a depth of about six inches, then sprinkle it with the solution, at the same time mixing the whole thoroughly with a shovel until all is uniformly damped; it will dry in two or three hours, when it will be fit for sowing. We have used a much stronger solution of blue vitriol than this, not only without injury to the seed, but with benefit. As a general rule, old seed requires less of the solution than new seed. It is the safest plan to subject all seed to the action of this pickle, even though the crop which produced it was quite healthy, as it may have met with the spores of the fungi in the granary or store-room, and may thus be in no better state than if produced by unhealthy plants. When we say that all seeds should be subjected to the action of a solution of sulphate of copper before being sown, we refer only to the ordinary agricultural seeds; some seeds may be too delicate to resist, uninjured, even its moderate action, **but the** farmer should experiment and decide this for himself. In many European countries—in Scotland especially, the use of the blue vitriol solution as pickle for seed has effected an immense amount of good in that country. Less than thirty years ago it was usual to lose, by blackball and other fungoid diseases, from one to eight bushels of grain per acre, while at the present day, in the best-farmed districts, it is difficult to find a single diseased head of grain; to some extent this is due to other causes, but the result is chiefly to be attributed to the general use of blue vitriol in pickling the seed.

" But all the foregoing goes for little or nothing if the seed is not placed in the soil in a proper manner, and to this we would invite particular attention ; for of all the evils that result from the wretched agricultural practice followed in this country, not the least is the loss produced by bad sowing, especially by sowing too thickly. Indeed, from thick-sowing alone we have no hesitation in asserting our belief that, on at least two-thirds of the arable land of India, an annual loss is experienced equal in amount to the full rent demanded by Government on dry land, and equal to one-quarter of the rent demanded **for** wet land. We have known instances of native cultivators sowing as much as 300 lbs. of **paddy-seed on each acre of** land to be cropped. The quantity of paddy-seed generally broadcasted for a crop **is not so much as this ; it varies** between 100 and 200 lbs. per acre—a quantity still far in excess of the amount needed ; for some of the best crops of **country** paddy that were ever produced under broadcast sowing, were raised from less than 50 lbs. of seed per acre. The waste of seed thus caused by the low agricultural practice of the country, represents in the total a heavy national loss. But this is far from being the only bad result that arises from inefficient sowing ; for, after the ill-effects produced by bad seed, there are no influences more active for evil, during the growth of a crop, than those which result from thick-sowing. In the crowd of plants produced, each struggling for mastery over the other, we have a most productive source of injury. Each plant is wasting its energies in the attempt to secure the means of existence, and in the endeavour to resist the ill-effect produced by the close proximity of its neighbour—energies which ought to be directed to meet its wants during a healthy progressive development. At first sight it would appear that the right practice in sowing is to place each seed in the position to produce the maximum result, equi-distant from each other, so that each may get its full share of soil, air, and light ; but there are other considerations to be taken into account, *viz.*, the weeding and tillage of the crop during its growth—operations which can only be performed at an economical rate when the crop is cultivated in lines, but the distance can readily be adjusted, and the seed so sown in the lines as to secure each plant in the position to produce the largest result with the least expenditure of field labour in its cultivation. Broadcasting seed is only justifiable under very peculiar circumstances ; as, a hasty season, scarcity of labour, damp soil, an uneven surface, or a surface covered by rock, trees, and other impediments. In broadcast sowing, the seed is placed irregularly in the soil, and there is always a considerable waste from seed being left uncovered, or by being covered too deeply ; hence, to provide against a deficiency of plant from this cause, it is necessary to sow a little more seed than would otherwise be needed.

Thick-sowings on rich or highly-manured soil **produce a close luxuriant** growth of prematurely-developed plants, which generally become matted **and laid long** before harvest. Crops in this state are invariably attacked **by** mildew, under the influences of which **their yield is greatly** lessened. In rich and poor soils alike, thin sowing is beneficial—not **too thin on poor soil, though** on very highly-manured soils seed can scarcely be **too thinly sown**. The desideratum is to produce a good standing regular crop, through which air and light may get. As a rule, thick-sown crops require an abundant **supply** of manure to enable them to perfect their development. The competition for support must be specially provided for, if the soil is not in a high manural condition. But rules cannot be laid down for all conditions of soil, of crop, of climate, &c.; each farmer should experiment and ascertain **for** himself what quality of seed of each variety best suits **his** soil and climate."

CHAPTER II.

THE ORGANIC PARTS OF PLANTS.

Four elements (carbon, nitrogen, oxygen, and hydrogen) form the organic parts of plants.—Their **origin, the atmospheric air.**—Plants cannot assimilate these **elements** in their pure state.—The three great suppliers of **organic plant-food, water, ammonia, and carbonic acid.**

Carbon.—The erroneous belief of the early philosophers that carbon, and the other elements of organic plant-food, **were derived directly from the** decaying vegetable **matter in** the soil.—The fallacy of the "Humus Theory."—Soils can most raise luxuriant vegetation after every trace of vegetable **matter has** been expelled from them.—The certainty that **the** organic parts **have** been derived from the atmospheric air.—The **presence of** humus in the soil tends to increase its fertility only by affording a surplus of organic plant-food.—Vegetable respiration.—**The absorption of carbonic acid and the expulsion of oxygen.**—The connection between animal and vegetable respiration.—The replenishment of carbonic acid withdrawn from the atmospheric air.—The necessity of carbonic acid being also present in the soil, it being a **solvent** of the alkaline earths and insoluble phosphates.—Baussingault's experiments on the absorption of carbonic acid.—The decomposition of carbonic acid under the influence of light and atmospheric air, and its assimilation by the plant.

Hydrogen and **oxygen.**—The source whence they are derived.—The several functions of water.—Its absolute indispensability for vegetable life, being the first stimulator and supporter of it.—The property of leaves to inhale moisture from the atmosphere when absent in the soil.

Nitrogen.—Its inert nature in the pure state.—Ammonia and nitric acid the two sources of nitrogen.—Their presence in the atmospheric air.—Its balance, how preserved.—The relation between nitrogen and our edible crops.

It was mentioned before that the organic parts of plants consist of four elements—one of which is Carbon, which we find in its purest state in the diamond; and three are gases, namely, Hydrogen, Oxygen, and Nitrogen. The combustible nature of these organic parts, and their easy conversion into gaseous compounds which escape into the atmosphere, give us the clue whence these substances have been obtained, and where we have to seek for them, on the basis of that great law governing animal and vegetable life, that whenever vital power has ceased to exist, all the elements will, under ordinary circumstances, return whence they came—earth to earth, air to air.

Most exhaustive experiments have proved that plants are incapable of absorbing in a pure state these four elements which constitute their organic parts: a plant may be set in pure carbon, supplied with pure oxygen, hydrogen, and nitrogen, and will yet die for want of nourishment. Therefore, as already observed, no plant can absorb and assimilate these substances in their elementary form; it is only from certain, now well-known, compounds that it is able to abstract them; and these great suppliers of all organic plant-food are *Carbonic Acid*, *Water*, and *Ammonia*.

Carbonic Acid—a gaseous body consisting of one part of carbon and two of oxygen—is the source from which all plants derive their carbon, and it claims our attention first. The natural philosophers of a former generation, even the celebrated Sir Humphrey Davy, believed that the organic food of plants—carbon of course included—was directly derived from the decaying vegetable matter contained in the soil, and they considered the relative presence or absence of such as the sole reason for the fertility or sterility of the soil. When leaves, branches, trees, or any other vegetable matter in short, are heaped together and left exposed to the action of moisture and atmospheric air, a gradual decay or slow combustion takes place, on account of the affinity which the oxygen of the atmospheric air possesses to the carbon and hydrogen of vegetable matter. In course of time the whole becomes a black mouldy mass, which some chemists have called *humus*. The so-called "Humus Theory" rested on the erroneous belief that, as stated above, plants derived their organic food directly from this substance. The fallacy of this theory was, however, soon demonstrated, and Liebig showed by extensive experiments the mistake that was made.

From an acre of good meadow or grass land there is obtained year after year, on the average, 2,500 lbs. of hay, which contain 984 lbs. of carbon and 32 lbs. of nitrogen ; and, with proper irrigation and a fair soil, even greater results may be obtained. Whence, then, do the plants derive all this carbon and nitrogen ? Not from the soil—for meadow soils have been analyzed and found not to contain a single year's supply of carbon in humus ; no vegetable or animal manure is ever used ; and yet year after year undiminishing quantities of carbon and nitrogen are taken away, and the humus, or decaying vegetable matter in the soil, is increasing instead of decreasing. It is therefore evident that these substances must have been derived from some other source than the soil—a conclusion which of course is diametrically opposed to the Humus Theory.

Soils have been subjected to a red heat in order to expel every trace of decaying organic matter, and, when cooled down, were sown with various seeds, which germinated and grew plants as luxuriantly as possible, arriving at complete perfection in all their organs. There is thus not a shadow of a doubt left that the atmospheric air is the principal and primary source of carbon and nitrogen.

Our early philosophers apparently noticed the more than ordinary fertility of a soil rich in humus, rich in decaying vegetable matter ; but were led to form wrong conclusions on the cause of this fertility. The fact that the presence of humus in a soil tends to a most luxuriant growth of plants is of course indisputable, but it is solely because it affords the plant a surplus of organic food by the products of its decomposition, which are principally carbonic acid, ammonia, and water, and which are either returned to their original element, the atmospheric air, to be absorbed by the leaves, or dissolved by the moisture in the soil and assimilated through the roots. We can therefore easily understand the importance of decaying vegetable matter in a loose, porous soil, where all particles are accessible to the influence of the atmospheric air and its oxygen, out of contact with which vegetable matter is inert, and instead of increasing the fertility of the soil, has, on the contrary, a sterilizing effect—a striking example of which we have in the extensive bogs of northern climates. A great amount of carbonic acid is undoubtedly derived from decaying vegetable matter in the soil; but by far the greater portion is absorbed directly from the atmospheric air, which must therefore be regarded as the principal source of this important element.

The absorption of carbonic acid from the atmosphere is that phenomenon which is termed vegetable respiration, and is conducted through the small pores or openings in the cuticle of the leaves, called stomata. Atmospheric air, the bulk of which is oxygen and nitrogen, contains, besides ammonia, invariably a quantity of carbonic acid, which, although relatively very small, being only two volumes in five thousand volumes of air, is quite sufficient to supply carbon for the growth of a most luxuriant vegetation all over the globe. For the prodigious extent of the atmosphere raises the total amount of carbonic acid contained therein to about 8,440 billions of pounds.

The plant absorbing this gaseous compound retains the carbon and returns the oxygen to the air. This continuous absorption would, in course of time, naturally diminish the percentage of carbonic acid in the atmospheric air, if an all-wise Nature had not provided for such an exigency. For, while plants inhale carbonic acid and exhale oxygen, animal respiration does just the reverse; animals absorb oxygen and expel carbonic acid—a wonderful connection between these two kingdoms, by which the one supplies the necessary means of existence for the other. Then the decay of the plants themselves, which sets in immediately on their vital power becoming extinct, contributes towards the supply for succeeding generations. Further, any loss incurred by nature in storing up carbon in coal, peat, turf, &c., is made good by the periodical eruptions of volcanoes, which supply from time to time enormous quantities of carbonic acid, and also ammonia, to our atmosphere; so that the constitution of the atmosphere is rarely changed to a perceptible degree.

But although the larger quantity of carbonic acid

is thus assimilated by the leaves, and would be sufficient for the requirements of the plant, yet it is absolutely necessary for the well-being of our cultivated plants that it should likewise be present in the soil, where it serves to bring the alkaline earths and insoluble phosphates into a state of solubility and available for assimilation.

We see, therefore, the value of decaying vegetable matter in the soil ; for the products of its decomposition, being principally carbonic acid, are eagerly absorbed by the moisture present in the soil. Should this source of carbonic acid be not available to the soil, the necessary quantity is supplied by every rainfall, which dissolves it to a perceptible extent while descending through the atmospheric air, and brings it down to the soil to suit the requirements of vegetable life. As carbon forms the basis of all organic compounds, it is necessarily of great importance ; and carbonic acid being the only source from which plants derive it, special attention to the subject is particularly requisite when discussing the natural laws of husbandry.

Baussingault, a very eminent agricultural chemist, proved the absorption of carbonic acid by the leaves of plants in the following ingenious manner. Through one of the apertures of a large three-necked receiver he introduced a vine branch bearing about twenty leaves, and then closed air-tight the little space between the stem and the glass. The second aperture he connected with an aspirator, which drew air gradually through the third opening of the receiver. This aspirator was connected with an apparatus for the accurate determination of the amount of carbonic acid. By these means he proved that the air passing through the receiver lost three-quarters of its carbonic acid; for whereas, before the air entered the receiver, it contained four volumes of carbonic acid in every ten thousand volumes of air, after having been in contact with the leaves, only one volume of it remained.

The decomposition and assimilation of carbonic acid seems to be only possible under the influence of light and heat: when the sun shines upon a plant, then the leaves absorb the largest quantity of carbonic acid. This vital process is continued only during the day, while at night and in darkness no such assimilation can take place, but the plant, on the contrary, instead of expelling oxygen then, expels carbonic acid. A wrong conclusion may be drawn from this observation; for it would be incorrect to believe that this exhalation of carbonic acid is the product of any chemical process taking place in the plant, or the result of a slow combustion of the carbon, such as occurs in the animal system.

The carbonic acid exhaled by plants during the night is derived from the soil through the medium of the roots; for the circulation of the sap does not even cease during the night, but goes on unintermittently ; and as there is always a considerable quantity of carbonic acid taken up along with the moisture by the roots, but which, in the absence of sun-light, cannot be assimilated, we consequently find it expelled by the stomata of the leaves. Vital power is, however, not altogether extinct during the night, for an absorption of oxygen undeniably takes place, which element is retained in the system, to take part in some chemical process not quite understood as yet.

Hydrogen and oxygen, which next claim our attention, we find in most of the vegetable compounds in the relative proportion of 1 to 8—the same proportion in which they form water ; so that it has been correctly inferred that water is the source from which the different organs of plants derive and assimilate these two elements. But water has several functions to fulfil in vegetable life ; for it not only furnishes hydrogen and oxygen to assist in the direct formation of the different parts of the plant, but also serves as the sole medium by which all the mineral substances derived from the soil pass into the vegetable system. It serves as a solvent for all the inorganic food which plants require, and which it thus renders assimilable.

On account of these various functions which water has to fulfil, it is absolutely indispensable for all vegetation, and therefore without it no plant can exist; from the first indications of the germination of the seed, till the ripening of the grain, water is always the first stimulator and supporter of life. A great deal of the water which serves to convey to the plant the necessary food from the soil, is, as I have mentioned before, evaporated through the stomata of the leaf; but the quantity exhaled depends entirely on the amount of moisture already present in the atmosphere. This process of absorption and evaporation has been compared by some one to the burning of a wick fed by oil: the greater the evaporation of water through the leaves, the larger the flame of the wick—the greater the consumption of oil, the more rapid the circulation of the sap.

Leaves not only exhale, but also inhale, watery vapour, and that with great rapidity whenever the soil becomes dry and the roots cannot find sufficient moisture for the purposes of the plant. The beneficial effect of dew is entirely owing to this peculiar property of the leaves. Thus it can be explained how trees in India preserve their beautiful green foliage throughout the dry season, when not a drop of rain moistens the ground for months. These plants seem to store up during the monsoon sufficient inorganic food within their cells to meet their requirements throughout the remainder of the year; and a wise Nature has given to the leaves the power to absorb sufficient moisture from the atmospheric air to maintain the circulation of the sap.

Nitrogen, the organic element which now remains to be considered, is present in its pure state in our atmosphere, and constitutes two-thirds of it; but it is such an inert substance in this pure state that it will not combine with any other substance. Most exhaustive experiments have conclusively proved that plants are incapable of assimilating it in its pure state, and the only known sources from which plants derive it are—*Ammonia*, a compound of nitrogen and hydrogen; and *Nitric Acid*, a combination of the same element with oxygen.

Ammonia is principally absorbed by the roots, it being highly soluble in water; and though it is present in the atmospheric air in such small quantities that we can barely detect it with our finest reagents, yet we can trace it distinctly in all rain-water. The balance of its percentage in our atmosphere is preserved in the same way as carbonic acid—by the decay of vegetable and animal matter, and by the eruptions of volcanoes. Ammonia and nitric acid are compounds very important to the farmer, being the only sources which supply to our edible crops nitrogen, the relative proportion of which stands in close connection with their nutritive qualities; and therefore they cannot be too highly valued.

Nitrate of Potash and Soda, when in contact with decaying vegetable matter, will also yield ammonia; hence their importance as chemical manures.

CHAPTER III.

THE INORGANIC PARTS OF PLANTS.

The small percentage of the inorganic parts of the plant when compared with the organic parts.—The functions of the former with regard to the latter.—The importance of inorganic parts in the vegetable kingdom.—Vegetable life cannot exist in the absence of any one of their number.—The ashes of different plants vary in their composition.—The importance of analyses.—Potash and soda.—Their functions in vegetable life.—Potash a solvent for silica.—The same amount of potash serves to dissolve many times its maximum of silica by repeated circulation through the system of the plant.—Mr. Lawes' experiments on the circulation of the sap and the quantity of inorganic matter deposited.—Silica and sand.—Lime a prominent constituent of root-crops and leguminous plants.—Magnesia.—The property of lime and magnesia to take each other's places.—Lime and silica form the bones of vegetable life.—Sulphuric acid.—Phosphoric acid.—Phosphoric acid forms the principal mineral constituent of the seed.—No grain can be formed in its absence.—The gradual reduction of its percentage in the soil affects chiefly the outturn of the seed.—The Indian method of cultivation has deprived the soil of this important substance in far greater proportion than of any of the other inorganic parts.—No restoration has been made for the loss occasioned by the annual withdrawal of the grain crops.—Where is all the phosphoric acid gone to?—The export trade of bones deprives India of the means to repair the waste of past generations.—The value of bones as a manure.—The percentage of phosphoric acid in rice.—The estimated quantity withdrawn from an acre by a cultivation extending over two thousand years.—The deficiency of phosphoric acid in the soil of India proved by analysis.—The small average outturn due to this deficiency.—The quantity of phosphoric acid required by the rice-plant, and the quantity available.

The yield of the soil is regulated by that inorganic plant

constituent which is present in smallest proportion.—The Minimum Theory applied to phosphoric acid.—The stores of phosphoric acid available.—Guano.—Animal refuse.—Bones.—Coprolites.—A conservancy department for the animal kingdom necessary.—The assimilation by the plant of its inorganic parts.—Endosmose.—The transformation of the sap in the leaves.—Prince Salm Horstmar's experiments proving the relative necessity of each of the mineral plant constituents.—The absence of a single one in the soil affects the whole organism of the plant.—The division of plants into groups according to their principal inorganic constituents.—The different kinds of soils best suited for the different kinds of plants.

THOUGH, when compared with the large bulk of the organic parts of a vegetable compound, the inorganic parts constitute a very small percentage —amounting, on the average, to only 5 per cent. of the whole—yet the influence they exert upon vegetable life is most important. The functions they have to fulfil in assisting in the transformation and transmission of the various elements of organic life, are unhappily but imperfectly known, and we must fain be content with such ideas and theories as experiments and observations lead us to deduce; but even then it is sometimes extremely difficult to express our ideas of certain processes in suitable and comprehensive language.

By the influence of acids, woody fibre can be converted into starch, and starch into sugar; but as to the nature and causes of the chemical transformation of their elements, chemists have not as yet agreed—in fact, it must be confessed that we know very little about them up to the present time. All that *is* actually known is, that these inorganic substances, the constituents of the ashes of plants, are of vital importance to the vegetable kingdom, and indispensable to the existence of the plant ; and it has been proved by actual experiments that vegetable life cannot be supported in the absence of *any one* of them—and our knowledge ends here. What functions these mineral substances have to perform in vegetable life, can only be conjectured. It will require indefatigable experiments and vast powers of discernment to reveal to us the more subtle operations of nature.

The ashes of the different plants vary naturally in the composition and proportion of their various ingredients, but we find generally present—first, the soluble alkalis *Potash* and *Soda*, sometimes combined with *Chlorine;* secondly, the alkaline earths *Lime* and *Magnesia*, more or less in combination with *Phosphoric* and *Sulphuric Acid;* and lastly, *Silica*, with a small portion of *Iron*, and sometimes *Alumina*. As different plants contain these substances in various proportions, and all are exclusively derived from the soil, it will be admitted that an analysis of the ashes of the different plants is of great importance, as it will guide us in the selection of the soil on which it is intended to grow a certain crop.

The knowledge of the proportion in which a

certain plant requires certain minerals, is one of the principal means by which we can explain satisfactorily why a certain plant will not grow upon a particular soil where another species may flourish; and such knowledge will enable us, at the same time, to improve that soil by supplying the absent mineral, or counteracting the injurious influence of others.

The analysis of the ashes of the different plants enables the educated farmer to select his land for a particular crop or devise some particular mode of improving it; but the more mechanical requirements and necessary properties of the soil, to which I shall refer further on, must not be neglected. These analyses will guide the farmer in the selection of certain manures for certain crops, having due regard for the requirements of different soils. Those analyses have now all been made by the most reliable authorities, and as a complete list of them may be useful, I think I may appropriately give them here *in toto* :—

Table showing the quantity of inorganic matters in 100 *parts of different plants dried at* 212 *degrees.*

SEEDS.	
Wheat .... 1·97	Maize .... 1·20
Barley .... 2·48	Pease .... 2·88
Oats (with Husk) .... 3·80	Beans .... 3·22
,, (without Husk) .... 2·06	Kidney Beans .... 4·09
Rye .... 2·00	Lentils .... 2·51
Millet .... 3·60	Tares .... 2·60
Rice .... 0·37	Buckwheat .... 2·13
	Linseed .... 4·40

Hemp Seed	5·60
Rape Seed	4·35
Sunflower	2·95
Guinea Corn	1·99
Gold of Pleasure	4·10
White Mustard	4·15
Black Mustard	4·31
Poppy	6·56
Horse-chesnut	2·81
Grapes	2·76
Clover	6·19
Turnip	3·98
Carrot	10·03
Sainfoin	5·27
Italian Rye Grass	6·91
Mangold Wurzel	6·58

STRAW AND STEMS.

Wheat	4·54
Barley	4·99
Oats	7·24
Winter Rye	5·15
Summer Rye	5·78
Millet	8·32
Maize	3·60
Pease	4·81
Beans	6·59
Tares	6·00
Lentils	5·38
Buckwheat	4·50
Hops	4·42
Flax Straw	4·25
Hemp	4·14
Gold of Pleasure	6·05
Rape	4·41
Potato	14·90
Jerusalem Artichoke	4·40

ENTIRE PLANT.

Potato	17·70
Spurry	10·06
Red Clover	3·79
White Clover	8·72
Yellow Clover	8·56
Crimson Clover (T. carnatum)	10·81
Cow-grass (T. medium)	11·31
Sainfoin	6·51
Rye Grass	6·42
Meadow Foxtail (Alopecurus pratensis)	7·81
Sweet-scented Vernal Grass (Anthoxanthum odoratum)	6·32
Downy Oat Grass (Avena pubescens)	5·22
Bromus Erectus	5·21
,, Mollis	5·82
Cynosurus Cristatus	6·38
Dactylis Glomeratis	5·31
Festuca Duriuscula	5·42
Holcus Lanatus	6·37
Hordeum Pratense	5·67
Lolium Perenne	7·54
Poa Annua	2·83
,, Pratensis	5·94
,, Trivialis	8·33
Phleum Pratense	5·29
Plantago Lanceolata	8·68
Poterium Sanguisorba	7·97
Yarrow	13·45
Rape Kale	8·00
Cow Cabbage	10·00
Asparagus	6·40
Parsley	1·10
Furze	3·11
Chamomile (Anthemis arvensis)	9·66
Wild Chamomile (Matricaria chamomilla)	9·10
Corn Cockle (Agrostemma githago)	13·20
Corn Bluebottle (Centaurea cyanus)	7·32
Foxglove	10·89
Hemlock (Conium scraculatum)	12·80

Sweet Rush (Acorus calamus) ...... 6·90
Common Reed (Arundo phragmitis) ...... 1·44
Celandine (Chelidoneum majus) ...... 6·85
Equisetum Fluviatile ...... 23·60
" Hyemale ...... 11·80
" Arvense ...... 13·80
" Linosum ...... 15·50

LEAVES.

Turnip ...... 9·37
Beet ...... 20·30
Kohl Rabi ...... 18·54
Carrot ...... 10·95
Jerusalem Artichoke ...... 28·30
Hemp ...... 22·00
Hop ...... 17·25
Tobacco ...... 22·62
Spinach ...... 19·76
Poplar ...... 23·00
Red Beech ...... 6·00
White Beech ...... 10·51
Oak ...... 9·80
Elm ...... 16·33
Horse-chesnut ...... 9·08
Maple ...... 28·05
Ash ...... 14·76
Acacea ...... 18·20
Olive ...... 6·45
Orange ...... 13·73
Potato ...... 15·10
Tussac Grass ...... 7·15

ROOTS AND TUBERS.

Potato ...... 4·16
Jerusalem Artichoke ...... 5·38
Turnip ...... 13·64
Beet ...... 8·27
Kohl Rabi ...... 6·08
Rutabaga ...... 7·34
Carrot ...... 5·80

Belgian White Carrot ...... 6·22
Mangold Wurzel ...... 8·78
Parsnip ...... 5·52
Radish ...... 7·35
Chicory ......
Madder ...... 8·33

WOODS.

Beech ...... 0·38
Apple ...... 1·29
Cherry ...... 0·28
Birch ...... 1·00
Oak ...... 2·50
Walnut ...... 1·57
Lime ...... 5·00
Horse-chesnut ...... 1·05
Olive ...... 0·58
Vine ...... 2·57
Larch ...... 0·32
Fir ...... 0·14
Filbert ...... 0·50
Chesnut ...... 3·50
Poplar ...... 0·80
Hazel ...... 0·50
Orange ...... 2·74
Vine ...... 2·57

BARKS.

Beech ...... 6·62
Cherry ...... 10·37
Oak ...... 6·00
Horse-chesnut ...... 7·85
Filbert ...... 6·20

FRUITS.

Plum ...... 0·40
Cherry ...... 0·43
Strawberry ...... 0·41
Pear ...... 0·41
Apple ...... 0·27
Chesnut ...... 0·99
Cucumber ...... 0·63
Vegetable Marrow ...... 5·10

TABLE of the Composition of the ASH of different PLANTS in 100 parts.

	Potash.	Soda.	Chloride of Potassium.	Chloride of Sodium.	Lime.	Magnesia.	Oxide of Iron.	Phosphoric Acid.	Sulphuric Acid.	Carbonic Acid.	Silica.
Wheat, Grain	30·02	3·82	......	......	1·15	13·39	0·91	46·79	......	......	3·89
Straw	17·98	2·47	......	......	7·42	1·94	0·45	2·75	3·09	......	63·89
Chaff	9·14	1·72	......	......	1·88	1·27	0·37	4·31	......	......	81·22
Barley, Grain	21·14	......	5·65	1·01	1·65	7·26	2·13	28·53	1·91	......	30·68
Straw	11·22	......	......	2·14	5·79	2·70	1·36	7·20	1·09	......	68·50
Oats, Grain	20·63	1·93	1·03	4·27	10·28	7·82	3·85	50·44	3·35	......	4·40
Straw	19·46	3·93	2·71	0·24	7·01	3·79	1·49	5·07	9·61	1·36	49·56
Chaff	6·33	0·39	......	......	1·95	0·38	1·58	1·04	0·17	......	72·85
Rye, Grain	33·83	1·74	0·30	0·60	2·61	12·81	1·04	39·92	0·80	......	9·22
Straw	17·20	1·74	......	trace.	9·10	2·40	1·40	3·80	......	......	64·50
Maize, Grain	28·37	1·14	......	2·29	0·57	13·60	0·47	53·69	......	......	1·55
Stalks and Leaves	35·26	2·49	......	......	10·53	5·52	2·28	8·09	5·16	2·87	27·98
Rice, Grain	20·21	2·11	......	......	7·18	4·26	2·12	62·23	4·47	0·82	1·37
Pease (gray), Seed	41·70	4·22	3·82	1·24	4·78	5·78	0·18	36·50	8·68	12·48	0·68
Straw	21·30	0·54	......	......	37·17	7·17	1·07	4·65	3·05	3·42	3·23
Beans (common field), Grain	51·72	2·77	......	11·54	5·20	6·90	0·61	28·72	1·40	25·32	0·42
Straw	32·85	......	3·27	4·03	19·86	2·53	0·65	0·49	2·52	18·73	2·61
Tare, Seed	32·82	1·69	7·41	4·55	20·78	5·31	0·50	10·59	4·67	20·37	1·28
Straw	31·72	......	......	0·36	15·71	1·66	5·58	10·34	1·56	0·22	3·57
Flax, Seed	34·17	3·68	......	9·21	8·40	13·11	1·79	38·54	8·39	15·75	1·45
Straw	21·53	0·34	......	0·96	21·20	4·20	1·30	7·53	5·38	5·44	7·92
Rape, Seed	16·33	10·57	......	2·53	8·30	8·80		31·90	3·90	23·04	19·98
Straw	16·63				21·51	2·92		4·68			11·80

TABLE of the Composition of the ASH of different PLANTS in 100 parts.

	Potash.	Soda.	Chloride of Potassium.	Chloride of Sodium.	Lime.	Magnesia.	Oxide of Iron.	Phosphoric Acid.	Sulphuric Acid.	Carbonic Acid.	Silica.
Spurry	26·12	1·14	......	8·90	14·46	8·88	......	10·20	1·79	27·38	1·14
Red Clover	25·60	......	9·08	6·02	21·57	8·47	1·26	4·09	2·96	18·05	1·95
Cow-grass (Trifolium medium)	22·78	......	12·39	1·86	24·42	8·86	1·09	4·94	2·66	20·16	1·12
Yellow Clover	27·48	......	11·72	8·16	17·26	8·39	1·40	......	4·82	4·31	1·76
Alsike Clover	29·72	......	6·29	1·05	26·83	4·01	0·71	5·64	3·25	20·74	1·73
Lucerne	27·56	......	11·64	1·91	20·60	5·22	2·23	6·47	4·80	15·94	2·63
Anthoxanthum Odoratum	32·03	......	7·03	4·90	9·21	2·53	1·18	10·09	8·39	1·26	28·35
Alopecurus Pratensis	37·03	......	9·50	......	3·90	1·28	0·47	6·25	2·16	0·65	38·75
Avena Pubescens	31·21	......	4·05	5·66	4·72	3·17	0·72	10·82	3·37	......	36·28
Bromus Erectus	20·33	......	10·63	1·38	10·38	4·99	0·26	7·53	5·46	0·55	38·48
,, Mollis	30·09	......	......	3·11	6·64	2·60	0·28	9·62	4·91	9·07	33·34
Cyriosurus Cristatus	24·99	......	11·60	......	10·16	2·43	0·18	7·24	3·20	......	40·11
Dactylis Glomerata	29·52	......	17·86	3·09	5·82	2·22	0·59	8·60	3·52	2·09	26·65
Festuca Duriuscula	31·84	......	8·17	0·62	10·31	2·83	0·78	12·07	3·45	1·38	28·53
Holcus Lanatus	34·83	......	3·91	6·66	8·31	3·41	0·31	8·02	4·41	1·82	28·31
Lolium Perenne	24·67	......	13·80	7·25	9·64	2·85	0·21	8·73	5·20	0·49	27·13
Annual Rye-grass	28·99	0·87	......	5·11	6·82	2·59	0·28	10·07	3·45	......	41·79
Poa Annua	41·86	......	0·47	3·35	11·69	2·44	1·57	9·11	10·18	3·29	16·03
,, Pratensis	31·17	......	11·25	1·31	5·63	2·71	0·28	10·02	4·26	0·40	32·93
,, Trivialis	29·40	......	6·90	......	8·80	3·22	0·29	9·13	4·47	0·29	37·50
Phleum Pratense	31·09	......	0·70	3·24	14·94	5·30	0·27	11·29	4·86	4·02	31·09
Plantago Lanceolata	33·26	......	4·53	8·80	19·01	3·51	0·90	7·08	6·11	14·40	2·37
Poterium Sanguisorba	30·26	......	3·27	1·35	24·82	4·21	0·86	7·81	4·84	21·72	0·83

TABLE of the Composition of the ASH of Different PLANTS in 100 parts.

	Potash.	Soda.	Chloride of Potassium.	Chloride of Sodium.	Lime.	Magnesia.	Oxide of Iron.	Phosphoric Acid.	Sulphuric Acid.	Carbonic Acid.	Silica.
Achillea Millefolia	30·37	......	20·49	3·63	13·40	3·01	0·21	7·13	2·44	9·36	9·92
Potato, Tuber	43·18	0·09	......	7·92	1·80	3·17	0·44	8·61	15·24	18·29	1·94
Stem	39·53	3·95	......	20·43	14·85	4·10	1·34	6·68	6·56	......	2·56
Leaves	17·27	......	4·95	11·37	27·69	7·78	4·50	13·60	6·37	......	6·47
Jerusalem Artichoke	55·89	......	4·88	......	3·34	1·30	0·45	16·99	3·77	11·80	1·52
Stem	38·40	0·69	......	4·68	20·31	1·91	0·88	2·97	3·23	25·40	1·51
Leaves	6·81	3·72	......	1·82	40·15	1·95	1·14	6·61	2·21	24·31	17·25
Turnip, Seed	21·91	1·23	......	......	17·40	8·74	1·95	40·17	7·10	0·82	0·67
Bulb	23·70	14·75	......	7·05	11·82	3·28	0·47	9·31	16·13	10·74	2·69
Leaves	11·56	12·43	......	12·41	28·49	2·62	3·02	4·85	10·36	6·18	8·04
Mangold Wurzel, Root	21·68	3·13	......	49·51	1·90	1·79	0·52	1·65	3·14	15·23	1·40
Leaves	8·34	12·21	......	37·66	8·72	9·84	1·46	5·89	6·54	6·92	2·35
Carrot, Root	49·73	12·11	......	......	5·64	2·29	0·51	12·31	4·26	18·00	1·11
Leaves	17·10	4·85	......	3·62	24·05	0·89	3·43	6·21	5·08	23·15	11·61
Kohl Rabi, Bulb	36·27	2·84	......	11·90	10·20	2·36	0·38	13·45	11·43	10·24	0·83
Leaves	9·31	......	5·99	6·66	30·31	3·62	5·50	9·43	10·63	8·97	9·57
Cow Cabbage, Head	40·86	2·43	......	......	15·01	2·39	0·77	12·53	7·27	16·68	1·66
Stalk	40·93	4·05	......	2·08	10·61	3·85	0·41	19·57	11·11	6·33	1·04
Poppy, Seed	9·10	......	7·15	1·94	35·36	9·49	0·41	31·38	1·92	......	3·24
Leaves	36·37	......	2·50	2·51	30·24	6·47	2·14	3·28	5·09	......	11·40
Mustard Seed, white	25·78	0·33	......	......	19·10	5·90	0·39	44·97	2·19	......	1·31
Radish Root	21·16	......	1·29	7·07	8·78	3·53	1·19	41·09	7·71	......	8·17

Potash and *Soda* have long been known to form a considerable portion of the mineral constituents of plants. Potash is the more important of the two, Soda preponderating only in plants which exist on sea-shores, from the ashes of which we formerly derived all our Carbonate of Soda. Potash is the alkali essential to most of our crops, and constitutes a large percentage of the ashes of every plant—on the average fully 30 per cent. It is always found present in greater proportion in the ashes of leaves and stalks than in those of grains ; and while forming nearly 40 per cent. of the ashes of leaves, it constitutes only 20 per cent. of the ashes of the grains of cereals.

The functions which potash performs in vegetable life are not sufficiently studied as yet ; but as, by chemical experiments, it is known that potassa will change woody fibre into different organic acids, as acetic, oxalic acid, &c., we may fairly suppose that it has similar duties to perform within the cells of the plant ; while it is absolutely indispensable for bringing the silica, so essential to the growth of cereals, into a state of solution, to be carried through the cells of vegetable life for assimilation. It must be remembered that not a grain of an inorganic substance can enter the system of a plant unless dissolved by the medium of water ; otherwise, not the thousandth part of a grain of solid substance could enter into the absorbing cells of the root ; and we can therefore understand why a plant dies in the absence of water.

I have no hesitation in advancing the theory that the same portion of Potash does its work over and over again; that is to say, the same quantity of Potash, after dissolving a minute portion of Silica, conveys it through all the sap cells, from the root to the utmost extremity of the leaves, and, after depositing the required quantity, returns for a fresh supply to be deposited as before. There is no doubt that a portion of the alkali itself is retained within the cells in the course of these journies, but the greater portion is returned to the soil.

This theory is based upon many facts and observations. From an analysis of wheat-straw, I find that, in every 100 parts of ashes, there are present 22 parts of Potash to every 61 parts of Silica; and as we know that it requires at least two parts of Potash to dissolve one part of Silica in combination, we have to account for 100 parts of Potash which are wanting. Where is this balance gone to? It cannot have evaporated. It must be concluded, then, that the same quantity has been employed repeatedly in carrying through the system of the plant the different minerals otherwise insoluble in water. Another phenomenon has been observed which tends to strengthen this conclusion, namely, that we find the largest percentage of ashes in a plant when life and growth are most vigorous, and that this percentage diminishes as the plant approaches perfection; the balance, therefore, must have been returned to the soil, after fulfilling its function of acting as a solvent medium for such minerals as are insoluble by themselves.

I will mention two instances in which this difference has been remarked. An analysis of an entire plant of sunflower showed before flowering 14·7 per cent. of ashes, while when bearing seed it contained only 9·3 per cent. of inorganic substances. And a wheat plant gave 7·9 per cent. of ashes before flowering, and 3·3 per cent. when bearing the ear. What other conclusion, then, can be drawn, but that the balance was only employed as a solvent, and was returned to the soil when no longer required?

Some idea may be formed of the rapid circulation of sap in plants by a reference to the careful experiment made by Mr. J. B. Lawes of Rothamstead, the celebrated patent manure-maker, who, as mentioned in a previous chapter, has shown that, for every grain of mineral matter fixed in the plant, two thousand grains of water have to pass through its system. This explains the presence of some minerals which are found in plants, such as iron and manganese, for which potash and other alkalis do not act as solvents.

It is now known that all substances, even gold,

when in an impalpable state of division, are soluble in water; but the extent of it is infinitesimal, so that often with the most delicate reagents their presence can barely be detected. The fact, however, of their solubility being established, and knowing that two thousand grains of water have to pass through the cells of plants to every grain of mineral matter contained therein, we cannot, then, be surprised to find in a plant one or two grains of a substance which is considered, generally speaking, insoluble.

Silica, as mentioned before, is dissolved by potash, and thus brought into the system of plants; but the Silica here referred to must be distinguished from sand, which is Silica also, but which, as such, is incapable of being used as food by plants; for sand cannot be dissolved and carried into the vegetable system by any common means at the command of nature. (But sand has functions to fulfil in the soil, as will be shown when the subject of soils will be treated; but they are merely mechanical.) So, when speaking of Silica in connection with the nourishment of plants and their chemical constituents, I mean the Silica existing in an impalpable state in combination with other bases, as alumina, potash, iron, &c., which combinations are called clays; and any analysis of soils for agricultural purposes should always show the amount of this Silica as distinct from the Silica present as sand in the uncombined state.

Lime is another prominent constituent of the ashes of plants. While it varies from 7 to 12 per cent. in cereals and root crops, it is found in large quantities in all leguminous plants, as pease, beans, &c., in the ashes of which it is present to the extent of 30 per cent. Tobacco is also essentially a lime plant.

Magnesia is always found more or less present with lime, and either seems capable of taking the other's place ; they form part of the soil in combination with carbonic, sulphuric, and phosphoric acid ; and as these salts are insoluble in pure water, but are taken up in small quantities by water containing carbonic acid, we see here one of the reasons why the presence of decomposing vegetable matter in the soil tends to a most luxuriant growth of crops.

Lime seems to have a similar duty to fulfil in vegetable as it has in animal life ; it supplies, conjointly with Silica, the necessary strength to the cellular tissue ; it forms the bones of vegetable life, just as it forms, in combination with phosphoric acid, the bones of animal life.

Sulphuric Acid is generally found in the soil in combination with lime, from which plants extract the quantity necessary for their existence.

The last of the inorganic elements which it is necessary to consider is a mineral acid—*Phosphoric Acid.*—When we incinerate the seeds of cereals, as wheat, barley, rice, &c., or the seeds of leguminous plants, we find a great difference between their ashes and those which remain after the combustion of other parts of the plant, such as stalks or leaves. The ashes of the latter invariably contain a large proportion of the carbonates of the alkalis and alkaline earths, and consequently effervesce with acids, while the fresh ashes of seeds will not effervesce. On closer chemical examination, we find that these ashes consist of alkaline phosphates which are soluble in water, and of the phosphates of lime and magnesia, with a little iron, which are insoluble.

Phosphoric acid forms fully 50 per cent. of the ashes of all the edible grains; and an idea of its importance can be formed when it is known that it has been demonstrated by practical experiments that not a grain of corn can be formed in its absence, and that, as a natural consequence, the quality and quantity of the seed will stand in proportion to the available store of this plant-food.

Now, it is a well-known fact that phosphoric acid is one of those substances the restoration of which to the fields has been totally neglected in India. For centuries it has been withdrawn from the soil, it must be in thousands of tons; the grains containing it have served as food for millions of human beings and animals, but the restoration of this most essential requisite for all our grain crops has been almost *nil*. Thousands of tons of this substance, instead of being utilized with immense benefit and advantage to the country, have been converted into a public nuisance and a fruitful source of disease by being thrown into the sea along with other valuable fertilizers, where they lie polluting our harbours and contaminating our atmosphere ; and this wasteful and abominable practice is still continued, occasioning irreparable loss to the commonwealth of India. Enormous quantities of phosphoric acid can be found in the innumerable foul heaps of refuse in all native villages, emitting miasmatic vapours that lay the germs of contagion and malaria. Thousands of tons can be found lying all over the country in the shape of bones, unused, uncared-for by the native cultivator.

The restoration of this substance, then, has been systematically neglected, and the soil has become impoverished in consequence. It is, however, not too late in the day for reparation ; it is still in our power to avert the impending evil— the inevitable sterility of our fields. But the culpable indifference which has so long been manifested with regard to everything relating to this vital question, must be removed before the disastrous consequences of former neglect can be averted by counteracting beneficial measures.

The public must be aroused to the knowledge

that the laws of nature cannot be disregarded for any length of time without severe retribution, and that the poverty of the agricultural classes of India is a just though severe punishment for the sins of their fathers, who have squandered the resources of the soil in the reprehensible manner I have shown.

It may not be out of place here to draw attention to the export of bones from India, which is steadily on the increase. It is really a matter of deep regret that India's stores of this most important manure, which she herself needs so sadly, should be thus gradually withdrawn to fertilize the soil of a foreign country which has to spend now several millions sterling annually in order to repair the agricultural waste that preceding generations have been guilty of. It is a matter of deep regret that the native cultivator, in his profound ignorance, is not yet aware of the immense importance of bones to agriculture, and therefore never utilizes them; but it is a matter of still deeper regret that the exportation of bones, now going on, will deprive India of a treasure which could repair the culpable waste of the past. India, I say, cannot afford to lose a particle of this most essential aliment for her grain crops; she has already lost enormous quantities, and will want every grain of it ultimately returned.

An analysis of rice grown in Salsette gave the

following result :—100 grains of rice left, after combustion, 1½ grain of ashes, which consisted of 52 per cent. of phosphoric acid, 19 of potash, 6 of soda, 5 of magnesia, 7 of lime, the rest being silica and a little oxide of iron. From this analysis we find that in 1,000 lbs. of rice there are present nearly 8 lbs. of phosphoric acid ; and supposing that the average annual yield of an acre cultivated for the last 2,000 years has been at the rate of 1,500 lbs. of rice (although I am convinced that the same land must have yielded originally nearer 3,000 lbs. per acre, for a good soil in Burmah yields even now this quantity), we have withdrawn not less than 24,000 lbs. of phosphoric acid alone from an acre in the shape of rice ; and what restoration has been made up to this time ? What has become of the grain ? and what has become of its ashes, of its phosphoric acid ? The grain has served as food for mankind ; and its ashes, its phosphoric acid, which we find in the refuse and in the bones of man and beast, have been recklessly wasted—an irrecoverable loss to the commonwealth of India, which, if continued, must assuredly and inevitably lead to the eventual sterility of the soil.

The richest soil of the Deccan contains at present only ¼ lb. of phosphoric acid in every 100 lbs. of soil ; the withdrawal, therefore, of 24,000 lbs. of this important plant-food from one acre, cannot have occurred without seriously diminishing the quantity and deteriorating the quality of the grain which requires this indispensable substance in such large proportions.

I have no hesitation in saying that, as parenthetically remarked above, two thousand years ago these same fields must have yielded something near 3,000 lbs. of rice per acre, while now the yield has dwindled down to 800 lbs. Soils which have supplied food for generations—the soil of the low-lying lands of Lombardy and South Germany for instance—are yielding over 2,500 lbs. of rice per acre, simply because the fields are well cared for, and the soil is nourished with the necessary plant-food. Here in India, with proper care and judicious treatment, that yield could be far exceeded, for the cosmic conditions are especially favorable. A powerful sun, excessive moisture during the monsoons, and an atmosphere heavily laden at that period with carbonic acid and ammonia—all contribute and tend to a most luxuriant growth of vegetable life, and an abundant harvest.

From two analyses of rice grown in Italy and South America which I have before me, I find that both their ashes contain 63 per cent. of phosphoric acid, while those of rice which was grown near Bombay, on what is considered an average fertile soil, yielded me only 52 per cent. It would appear from this that the comparative sterility of our fields is, to a great extent, due to the want of phosphoric acid—a substance which has been taken away year after year without any restoration whatever. To ensure a good and abundant crop of rice, the plant should be able to take up 63 per cent. of phosphoric acid from the soil, the roots must find within the radius of their assimilating powers 63 per cent., while my analysis shows that only 52 per cent. are available.

We cannot be surprised, therefore, that India's acres yield so little in comparison with those of other countries, despite the advantages of its climate. The rice-plants of the Concan look most luxuriant, have a superabundance of leaves and flowers, but the yield of the grain is scanty. Now, we can easily account for this; for rice-straw is developed with only 4 per cent. of phosphoric acid, while the seed requires 63 per cent. for its full development.

The outturn of a field is regulated by *that* constituent of the soil which is present in least comparative quantities. Nature has provided potash, lime, and silica in unlimited quantities, which are further daily increasing by the disintegration of rocks, clays, &c. Soils deficient in any of these minerals can easily be supplied with them from extraneous sources. But the sources from which we can obtain phosphoric acid are so few, that it is necessary to draw more attention to that inorganic constituent of plant-food than to any of the others.

We possess considerable quantities of this valuable substance in guano, the deposits of sea-birds, which have been accumulating for ages on several islands where rain is scarcely known. These deposits are truly treasures reclaimed by nature from the depths of the ocean, the food of these birds being entirely derived from it; they are treasures which we can use with a clear conscience for restoring the fertility of our soils. But they are not inexhaustible; they are diminishing year by year, and will be consumed before long; and what then?

We will then have to recognize the necessity of utilizing what lies at our very doors, and consider the chief sources of phosphoric acid which are available to us, and whence it must ultimately reach the soil. These sources are—firstly, the bones of man and animal, the frame-work of their bodies which nature constructs from the minute quantities of lime and phosphoric acid contained in their food; and secondly, their refuse, solid and fluid, which, when they arrive at maturity, contains to the minutest portion of a grain the ashes of the food consumed. So that every ounce we neglect to gather, every gallon we throw away, is so much total loss to the capital which nature has so wisely provided for our maintenance in the arable soil of our fields.

The waste of these natural fertilizers is, as I have

shown, enormous, but it would almost appear as if Nature, in her unfathomable wisdom, had foreseen the wanton and reckless waste of which man in his ignorance would be guilty; and just as she has displayed this foresight and wisdom in storing up for him, in the remains of a bygone vegetable world, treasures hidden in the bosom of the earth, in order that he may find them only when extreme need would compel him to seek for them, when the consequences of the recklessness with which he wantonly destroyed forests of timber without replanting part of it would awaken him to a sense of his misdoings, and would begin to make him careful of what was left—so Nature has evinced the same wisdom and forethought in preserving the remains of a bygone animal world, and in the fossil bones of antediluvian animals we find partially the means to repair the lamentable waste which we have noticed.

Immense strata of petrified bones have been discovered of late in Europe, and are said to exist also in India in the Sewalik Range, the Nerbudda Valley, and somewhere near Umballa. Nature, in providing these stores, lays it in our power to return to the soil part of the phosphoric acid which has been so wantonly wasted, and these remains of a bygone animal generation will serve to restore the fertility of our fields, and provide for the wants of an increasing population. But the existence of these stores does not justify us in disregarding the fertilizing material before our very doors ; it justifies us as little in wasting the phosphoric acid contained in animal refuse, as the existence of coal does in destroying our forests.

It has been thought very necessary by Government to have a conservancy department for the vegetable world ; then why should we not also have one for the animal world ? Conservancy in the animal kingdom, to which we ourselves belong, is quite as essential—indeed, more so—than in the vegetable kingdom.

The importance of drawing especial attention to phosphoric acid will be acknowledged from the foregoing, but it occupies no such particularly prominent place if the *general necessities* of the plant are only regarded ; for each constituent of plant-food is equally indispensable to the existence and development of plants.

Under the several heads of the inorganic substances of plant-food, I have essayed to give an idea of the manner in which they are assimilated and absorbed by the vegetable system. It has been mentioned that all the mineral or inorganic substances which enter into the system of plants, do so in a state of solution in water. Only those parts of the soil which are either capable by themselves of being dissolved in water, or may become so by the agency of certain solvents, as carbonic acid, the alkalis, &c., can be assimilated and utilized as food by plants ; and it is impossible that any particle of solid matter, however minute, can under any circumstances enter into the system of the plant.

All the different organs of plants consist chiefly of a series of sexagonal cells, separated from each other by a thin membrane or cuticle. This cuticle possesses a property, peculiar also to animal membrane, which is called *Endosmose*, and by which we understand a body that is permeable by a liquid without being dissolved in it.

If a pig's bladder containing a dense liquid—say syrup—is suspended into a vessel containing pure water, a peculiar interchange will take place between the two liquids. Being of different specific gravities, both will exert themselves to bring about a balance of their respective densities; the water will enter through the minute pores of the bladder to dilute the syrup, and *vice versâ*—the syrup will percolate into the pure water; and this interchange will continue until the density of the two liquids is the same, or, in other words, until an equilibrium between the lighter and heavier liquid is established. It will, however, invariably be found that the quantity percolating into the denser liquid is far in excess of that which percolates into the lighter liquid; and it would appear that this wise law of nature has been expressly framed to suit the requirements of vegetable life. For if we consider now the rootlets of plants, consisting of a number of these cells filled with a liquid which is considerably denser than the surrounding moisture, holding only a minute quantity of solid matter in solution, we can understand that, by the principle of "Endosmose," just explained, that is, attraction to inwards, the moisture contained in the soil enters into the most contiguous cells of the root, whence it proceeds to the extremities of the plant.

In the leaves the fluid is exposed to the action of heat, light, and air ; then chemical reaction and decomposition take place under these three powerful agencies, the crude fluid is converted into nutritious sap, and descends by the principle of Exosmose, or the flow to outwards, to the stem, depositing in the various cells through which it passes the different nutriments it contains, and eventually discharges the useless or superfluous substances through the cells of the rootlets into the soil. In this way, a continual rise of crude sap and a continuous fall of nutritious juice occur in the system of the plant, by which the necessary material for the construction of its different parts is supplied.

Some very exact and interesting experiments have been made by Prince Salm Horstmar, proving how essential all inorganic substances are to vegetable life, and how the absence of any single one seriously interferes with the growth and development of plants. He grew oats in a series of artificial soils, each wanting one of the several inorganic substances which constitute the mineral food of plants ;

with the following result :—The oat-plant, grown in the soil containing all the necessary substances except *Silica*, was weak, and incapable of supporting itself, thus proving what has been said of Silica—that it forms, in combination with lime, the bones of the vegetable kingdom. In the soil containing no *Lime*, the plant died just when producing the second leaf ; the absence of *Magnesia* in another case had the same effect as the absence of Silica— the plant could not support itself ; and in the soil that was without either *Sulphuric* or *Phosphoric Acid*, the plant, though but slightly weak, and otherwise normal and upright, formed no seed whatever.

These experiments prove that the absence of but *one* of these substances affects the whole organism of the plant, and prevents the development of certain organs. Thus we can understand why some plants in an apparently good soil do not arrive at perfection, as the cause may sometimes be solely due to the insufficiency or entire absence of a single mineral. The non-production of seed in the absence of Phosphoric Acid demonstrates the great importance of this substance, and its absolute necessity for all our grain crops.

As different species of plants contain these inorganic substances in various proportions, they are distinguished according to the preponderating constituent of the ashes—as *Potash plants*, under which designation we class beetroot, turnips,

Indian corn, coffee, &c.; *Lime plants*, to which all leguminous plants, as beans, pease, &c., belong, as likewise tobacco; and *Silica plants*, including wheat, barley, rice—in fact, all cerealia and grasses.

These different species of plants will, of course, flourish best in soils in which the principal mineral element required is present in largest proportions in an assimilable state; hence, *Potash* plants thrive best in a clayey soil containing a large quantity of Potash, *Lime* plants flourish in a calcareous soil, while all the cerealia and grasses require a rich, silicious earth for their profitable cultivation. Those plants which have a wider dissemination, and are known to grow and thrive in almost any soil, belong to none of these classes in particular; that is to say, the different parts and organs of the plants belong to different categories, as, the leaves and stem to the one, the seeds, &c., to the other.

Classification of some of the principal Plants.

		Salts of Potash and Soda.	Salts of Lime and Magnesia.	Silica.
Silica Plants.	Oat Straw with Seeds	34·00	4·00	62·00
	Wheat Straw	22·50	7·20	61·50
	Barley Straw with Seeds	19·00	25·70	55·30
	Rye Straw	18·65	16·52	63·89
	Good Hay	6·00	34·00	60·00
Lime Plants.	Tobacco	24·34	67·44	8·30
	Pea Straw	27·82	63·74	7·81
	Potato Plant	4·20	59·40	36·40
	Meadow Clover	39·20	56·00	4·90
Potash Plants.	Maize Straw	72·45	6·50	18·00
	Turnips	81·60	18·40	—
	Beetroot	88·00	12·00	—
	Potatoes	85·81	14·19	—

CHAPTER IV.

THE SOIL AND ITS FUNCTIONS.

The soil is the supplier of the inorganic constituents of plants.—The condition in which these inorganic substances must be present.—Their mere presence does not prove the fertility of a soil.—The fallacy of judging by a chemical analysis of the capabilities of a soil.—Tables to "measure" the fertility of a soil.—The injury done to scientific agriculture by hasty conclusions drawn from imperfect experiments.—The constituent parts of the soil are in their original form insoluble in water.—The action of moisture, heat, and atmospheric air renders them soluble.—The peculiar absorptive power of the soil to abstract the elements of inorganic plant-food from their solutions.—The capillary absorbing power of the soil.—Its bearing upon vegetable life.—The physical force of attraction of the soil is stronger than the solvent power of water; but yields when "Endosmose" comes into play.—To judge of the capabilities of a soil, it is necessary to distinguish between the assimilable and unassimilable portion of inorganic plant constituents present in it.

Inorganic plant-food in physical and chemical combination.—Inorganic plant-food necessary in physical combination for the immediate requirements of the soil, in chemical combination for its lasting fertility.—A sufficient quantity of plant-food in the first state indispensable for the purposes of husbandry.—Fallowing.—Its meaning, purport, and action upon the component parts of the soil.—An analysis of a soil should exhibit the physical condition as well as the chemical composition of its ingredients.—Necessary details of a soil analysis to render it useful and interpretable for the purposes of agriculture.—Surface and subsoils of the Concan.—Their relative bearing power.—Subsoils, at first sterile, become fertile.—The subsoil of India contains sufficient inorganic plant-food to make it, if judiciously treated, once more "the Garden of the East."—Surface and subsoils of Salsette.—Difference of chemical composition.—The improvement of the soil by heat, moisture, and atmospheric air.—A knowledge of the condition of his soil necessary to the farmer.—The means to change the inorganic plant-food from the unassimilable to the assimilable state.—The mechanical operations of agriculture.—Their meaning and purport.—The results depend upon the amount of inorganic plant-food present.—The help of science to ascertain what is wanted.—Drainage.—The use of manures to aid the mechanical operations of agriculture.—Lime.—Common salt, saltpetre, ammonia.—Colonel Corbett adding to the evidence of the exhausted nature of India's soil.—Irrigation, with constant cropping, hastens the impoverishment of the soil: wheat-lands degenerate into rice-lands, rice-lands are abandoned to reeds and rushes.—Irrigation will impoverish the soil unless a different system of cultivation is adopted, and the balance of inorganic plant-food more carefully preserved.—The *Oriental* on irrigation-works in India, and manures.—The natural state of the plant compared with its artificial or cultivated state.—The difference between soils bearing a natural growth of plants and those under cultivation by mankind.—The enrichment of the one and the impoverishment of the other.

THE general functions which the soil has to fulfil in vegetable life have already been pointed out in the foregoing pages: it has been shown that the incombustible or inorganic constituents of plants are exclusively derived from it. The great importance of these constituents, and the powerful influence they exercise upon vegetable life, render an intimate knowledge of the chemical and physical properties of their source very necessary before we can fully understand the various operations of husbandry, and their relation to the nutritive processes of plants.

A soil, to be capable of developing vegetable life, must, of necessity, not only contain all those substances which we have found to constitute the inorganic parts of plant-food, but must contain them in a certain condition in which alone they can be assimilated by the plant. For the mere presence of inorganic plant-food in the soil is not sufficient to make it fertile, even though the quantity may suffice for a thousand harvests; it is only when these inorganic substances, through the powerful action of heat, moisture, and atmospheric air, have assumed a certain form and condition, that they are able to serve as plant-food. A rock, even when pulverized, will be unable to support vegetable life, although its chemical composition may be the same as of a fertile soil.

A mere chemical analysis of a soil, therefore, cannot enable us to judge of its quality, and the figures of such analysis can have no value in the eyes of the practical husbandman; for plants depend for their development upon the physical condition of the soil, and upon a certain physical form of its constituents which is but imperfectly revealed by chemical analysis. This fact cannot be made too widely known, for a firm belief still prevails among educated farmers, and others who profess to be acquainted with the principles of agricultural chemistry, that a simple chemical analysis of a soil which exhibits the different constituents and their proportion, shows its quality, and reveals all defects which have simply to be remedied in order to obtain the highest yield with the smallest outlay. Several scientific agriculturists have even attempted to formulate certain tables and figures by which the farmer could, so to speak, "measure" the quality of his land. A soil containing a certain quantity of phosphoric acid, lime, potassa, &c., was made a standard of fertility applicable to all climates and to all soils.

The hasty and erroneous conclusions which these gentlemen drew from imperfect experiments have done immense harm to the cause of scientific agriculture, and it will be long before the distrust now engendered in the minds of the majority of farmers can be removed. For when the farmer, acting on the advice of these men, forwarded samples of the different soils of his fields to be analyzed, the result in many cases was that a poor and almost sterile soil yielded to chemical analysis the same substances in almost the same proportion as a soil which had yielded most luxuriant crops year after year. The physical condition of the soil and its constituents was but rarely examined, a classification was adopted which proved fallacious in practice, and in consequence the farmer began to doubt the truth of the new theory, and, labouring under disappointment in his expectations, came to view with distrust all other teachings of scientific Agriculture.

In very rare cases can we rely upon the figures of a chemical analysis for gauging the capabilities of a soil; it is a test which can be turned to good account only by the most initiated, and even then great discrimination must be observed. Much light has of late been thrown on this subject, and we are beginning to understand more and more the important *rôle* which the physical or mechanical condition of the soil plays in connection with its chemical composition.

The constituents of the soil are in their original form, as parts of rocks, insoluble in water; they form chemical combinations of a powerful nature, and are in this state incapable of serving as plant-food. By the disintegrating action of moisture, heat, and atmospheric air, the rock crumbles to pieces, the pieces to powder; the chemical combinations of its constituents are severed, and the constituents themselves become soluble in water. Corresponding with this progress of disintegration, the soil now acquires peculiar absorptive powers. For if we allow water, containing a certain quantity of each of the mineral constituents of plant-food in solution, to percolate through a stratum of arable soil, we fail to recover from the water, after its passage through the soil, the elements which it contained in solution. This power of the soil to abstract from their solutions the elements of plant-food, is ascribed to a peculiar force of attraction, which may be called the *capillary absorbing power* of the soil.

This faculty is of the greatest importance, and seems to be specially bestowed on the soil for the purposes of agriculture. For, were it otherwise, all the elements of plant-food which became soluble in water would be carried away into the subsoils, and thence into the rivers, leaving the soil itself incapable of supporting vegetable life. According, then, to this provident law of nature, the pores of the surface-soil attract the elements of plant-food immediately they become soluble.

Each particle of earth has a certain point of saturation; when this is attained, it loses all further absorptive power, and passes the unchanged solution on to the next particle; but it regains this power when the nutritive processes of plants diminish the store of these elements. The action of water as a solving power ceases as regards these absorbed elements of plant-food; the physical force of attraction prevents their being dissolved again, until another and stronger power counteracts this attraction and restores them to a state of solubility in water; and this power we find in the vitality of plants.

The delicate fibres of the roots consist of a number of minute cells which press against the surrounding soil. The contents of these cells, the sap, is divided from the particles of earth enclosing it by a thin permeable membrane only, and, contact being established by the moisture in the soil, "Endosmose" comes into play. This is the power which overcomes the physical force of attraction; the mineral plant-food, being thus restored to its previous state of solubility in water, permeates through the thin membrane of the root-cells, and enters the system of the plant.

Now, to judge correctly of the capabilities of a soil, we have to distinguish into two great classes those of its constituent parts which serve as food for plants. The first includes all those minerals which, by the disintegrating action of moisture, heat, and atmospheric air, have been converted into a state of solubility in water, and are retained in *physical* combination with the soil only by the slight force of, what has been termed, its capillary attractive power. To the second class belong all those constituents which are still in a state of *chemical* combination; as, insoluble silicates of potassa, phosphates of lime, &c.

The first of these classes is most important if we regard the immediate wants of agriculture; it is this portion which we have chiefly to consider when the capabilities of a soil are in question, for only those parts of a soil which exist in physical combination are available as plant-food, and it follows that the fertility of a soil will be proportionate to the amount of this portion.

It is quite immaterial, for the *immediate* requirements of husbandry, how much potash, or phosphoric acid, or lime a soil may contain, if these substances are present only in chemical combination, in which condition they are, as it were, locked up, and cannot be assimilated by the plant. A large store of these substances is necessary to ensure the *lasting* fertility of a soil; but in the absence of sufficient mineral plant-food in a state of physical combination, the soil will be as barren as pulverized rock.

The advantage derived by allowing fields to lie fallow for some time to recover their original fertility, has been known to the husbandman from the most remote times; but the causes which effected this change from sterility to fertility have, even in the present century, been but imperfectly understood. The late Baron von Liebig was the first who gave a satisfactory explanation of this phenomenon, by explaining that the improvement of the soil by what is called fallowing, especially when well ploughed during that time, is solely due to the action of moisture, heat, and atmospheric air, which decomposes the different constituent parts of the soil, separates them from their chemical combinations, and converts them into that state in which alone they are available for plants. In other words, the inorganic plant-food passes from a chemically combined state to one of physical combination with the porous soil.

An analysis of a soil, therefore, which does not show the number and quantity of its different constituents present in the available form of plant-food, nor exhibits them separate from those which may become available in course of years by appropriate manures or the disintegrating influence of external agencies, is entirely useless to the practical agriculturist.

To arrive at correct conclusions of the comparative sterility or fertility of a soil, and of its suitability for certain crops, as well as of the means to effect permanent improvements, an analysis of a soil, representing the average of the uppermost ten inches, should exhibit the following particulars :—

(1) The percentage of stones and sand, as distinct from clay and other impalpable matter.
(2) The percentage of water it can absorb.
(3) The percentage of water it will evaporate within a certain time when exposed to the atmosphere.
(4) The percentage of organic matter.
(5) A chemical analysis of the mineral constituents which are dissolved out of the soil by digesting it for twenty-four hours in

diluted hydrochloric acid—the nearest representation of inorganic plant-food in *physical combination*.

(6) A chemical analysis of what is not dissolved by the above process.

(7) A chemical analysis of the subsoil.

Mr. W. E. Ivey remarks with regard to soil analysis:—"In forwarding samples of soil for analysis, great assistance may be rendered to the chemist in many cases, and value added to his report, if they are accompanied with as full particulars as possible upon all points likely to throw light upon any observed features of the soil, especially when examination is desired for the purpose of ascertaining the cause of the peculiarity. The samples should be 3 to 4 lbs. in weight, and should be taken from the surface to a depth of about 6 inches. Samples of the subsoil should always accompany them, and the following information should be given :—

1st.—Situation and origin. Thus, if the soil is from hill-country, its aspect should be given ; or if from level country, swamp, or alluvial lands, the geological formation from which it is derived.

2nd.—If it is virgin forest soil, information should be given as to the character of the trees and undergrowth ; and of the grasses, if it is open country.

3rd.—If the land is arable, it should be stated how long it has been in cultivation, &c.

4th.—Peculiarities of climate should in all cases be given.

5th.—If any peculiarities are observed in the soil, the particular features it is expected that analysis will aid in elucidating should be stated."

In order to ascertain the relation between soils and subsoils in India, I have analyzed a number of rice-bearing soils in the vicinity of Bombay and in the Concan, and found that the subsoils contain, on an average, 30 per cent. more of the elements of inorganic plant-food than the surface-soils. I demonstrated their relative bearing powers by growing, during the rainy season of 1872, a number of rice-plants in surface-soils and an equal number in subsoils. None of the soils was prepared in any way, and no manure was used. The rice growing in the surface-soils yielded 16 fold, in the subsoils only 5 fold. In February 1873 both kinds of soils were thoroughly tilled with a small spade, and this was repeated after the first shower of rain in June, after which some rice was sown again. The yield was now from the surface-soils 17 fold, from the subsoils 40 fold. The experiment was, for want of time, not continued; but I have no doubt that the yield of the subsoils would have been even larger in the following year.

After what has been stated, it is scarcely needful to explain the causes of this sudden change of the subsoil from comparative sterility to fertility. Chemical analysis showed that the subsoil contained a far greater proportion of the constituents of inorganic plant-food than the surface-soil; but the practical results of its cultivation proved their unfitness to serve as such. A year afterwards, however, we observe entirely different results, the subsoil being then the more fertile of the two. It was exposed for a whole year to the action of the weather; and a portion of the potash, phosphoric acid, silica, &c., was rendered soluble by the disintegrative powers of the climatic influences, and a store of available plant-food thus prepared.

From personal knowledge and from various communications I have received, I am induced to believe that the subsoil of India is very fertile, and contains a most abundant store of inorganic plant-food, especially phosphoric acid, which is the chief element wanted in the surface-soil. The soil has never been stirred or broken up to a greater depth than eight inches—indeed, on an average only half that depth—so that very little below the surface we find an almost virgin soil, which will become a most important item in restoring the fertility of India's fields. To increase, and even double, the present outturn, it will only be necessary to turn up every year a portion of the subsoil (nature doing the rest), which will act as a powerful fertilizer of the now exhausted surface-soils. Thousands of square miles could be treated in this way, the only requisite being a deeper-furrowing instrument than the primitive plough of the ryot.

The following analysis of a surface and subsoil in Salsette shows the large store of inorganic plant-food still available in the subsoil :—

	Surface.	10 inches deep.
Insoluble Silica	59·26	53·71
Soluble Silica	2·63	3·96
Alumina	3·12	3·27
Iron	6·10	7·15
Lime	5·36	8·85
Magnesia	0·02	0·21
Soda	0·93	1·02
Potash	1·53	1·89
Carbonic Acid	7·00	10·36
Phosphoric Acid	0·13	0·49
Sulphuric Acid	0·63	0·94
Chlorine	1·20	1·32
Organic matter	12·09	6·83
Total	100·00	100·00

It has been asserted that deep-ploughing is unnecessary in India, the reason advanced being that the soil in the lower strata is exposed to the action of the atmospheric air by the deep cracks which in the hot weather intersect the ground in all directions. It is really surprising that such an assertion was ever made, for it should be well known that, in the absence of moisture, no disintegration can occur which would benefit the plant.

The beneficial effects of exposing the soil as much as possible to the influence of the weather, have been well known at all times; that the fertility of an exhausted soil could be restored by rest, and repeated ploughing and turning the soil, was a well-recognized fact, long before the causes which effected this restoration were understood.

India then, as I have stated, still possesses in the subsoil of her fields sufficient fertilizing materials to regain the lost fertility of her surface-soil, and it will become the duty of Government to urge the use of deeper-ploughing instruments in order to enhance the scanty yield.

It will be clear from the foregoing how essential it is for the practical farmer to know the condition of the inorganic plant-food present in his soil, and to be acquainted with the means by which the ineffective portion can be converted into that form in which alone it can be assimilated by the plant. It is by no means necessary that he should call in the aid of science to gain this information; a few simple experiments, and a careful observation of their results, should be sufficient for his guidance. If extra ploughing and careful tillage are attended by a corresponding increase in the outturn, it will be evident that there is ample nourishment in the soil, and that the condition of his field can be improved by such means as will destroy the *chemical combinations* of the nutritive substances present, and change their state into that of *physical combination.*

We can obtain these results either by *mechanical* or *chemical* means. Among the former are included all the ordinary operations of husbandry, such as draining, ploughing, harrowing, &c.; among the latter we include the application of lime, marl, ammonia, common salt, which are not intended so much as an augmentation of the fertilizing material present in the soil, as to render such material available for the nutritive processes of plants.

The mechanical operations of agriculture purpose to prepare the soil so as to offer the least resistance to the extension of the root; and to mix it thoroughly, in order that plants may find sufficient nourishment equally distributed throughout the field.

The plough every year exposes a new surface of soil to the action of moisture and atmospheric air, which renders a fresh portion of chemically combined plant-food available for the next crop. To prove the importance of ploughing, it is sufficient to state that of two soils of equal fertility, the best ploughed one will always yield the highest return, and moreover a poor but well-tilled soil will often yield as much as a far more fertile but not so well-tilled soil. The ancient Romans recognized this principle fully, for, as we have already seen, Cato says that the first commandment of Agriculture is to plough; the second, to plough again; and the third, to plough a third time.

But, as a matter of course, no degree of ploughing will avail the practical agriculturist if his land is deficient in any of the substances constituting plant-food, in which case such deficiency must be supplied, whether it be potash or soda, lime or magnesia, silica or phosphoric acid; and, to ascertain the element that is so wanting, the agriculturist should seek the aid of the chemical analyzer.

Drainage is another mechanical improvement of the soil adapted for dry crops. It removes from the subsoil all the stagnant water that is so injurious to our edible crops; it causes the atmospheric air to penetrate deeper through the pores of the soil; and, following the air, the roots penetrate into the lower strata of the soil, and furnish additional nourishment to the plant from a fresh and abundant source.

But although these mechanical operations are most important, and will effect marvellous improvements in neglected soils, the action of chemicals in effecting a decomposition of the chemically combined food elements, and distributing them in the soil, is still more powerful. The addition of lime, for instance, has a most wonderful effect on all clayey soils, as it changes their character entirely. It renders the soil porous, decomposes the clay silicates, sets their alkalis free—in short, it effects in twelve months a change in the condition of the soil that perhaps a hundred years of thorough exposure to climatic influences could not have produced. Organic matter decaying in the soil, assists also in its disintegration by the carbonic acid which it evolves, and which possesses the remarkable property of dissolving the phosphates of lime and magnesia. This property of acting as a solvent of phosphates otherwise insoluble in water, is shared likewise by other chemical substances, such as common salt, nitrate of potash, sulphate of ammonia, &c.

The increased yield, due to the use of these materials as manures, must therefore be considered as owing partly to their solvent actions on otherwise insoluble food constituents, and partly to being elements of plant-food themselves, and therefore augmenting the existing supply in the soil. When the cause of the nutritive powers of the soil is once known, it becomes an easy matter to explain and remedy sundry unaccountable occurrences and defects which but too often have been misunderstood and misinterpreted.

Lieutenant-Colonel Corbett, in a small pamphlet against irrigation, mentions several injurious effects which he asserts water has on the soil. "Lands," he says, "which formerly produced wheat, are now said to grow only rice, and previous rice-plantations to produce no other crops than reeds and rushes." We have no reason to doubt this statement, and in fact have thus another lamentable proof of the exhausted nature of India's soil.

Before irrigation was introduced, the ryot obtained from the soil one crop annually, which shielded him from starvation, while the soil was suffered to lie fallow for a great part of the year, and a fresh portion of the food elements was thus converted from the chemically to the physically combined state, and, by the time another sowing season arrived, the soil had recovered its power to yield another crop. But on the introduction of irrigation, the ryot began to raise two, and even three, crops a year, thus increasing the call upon the resources of the land, while no time was allowed to prepare the necessary plant-food.

No restoration whatever, or at best only of a most inadequate character, was made of the fertilizing substances withdrawn. What marvel, then, that the soil should yield a diminishing quantity every year, and in time cease to yield a remunerative wheat crop, and compel the ryot to grow an inferior crop—rice? The soil refuses ultimately even to grow that crop, reeds and rushes take its place; and thus the fatal descent is accomplished.

A spoliation of the soil such as has been effected

by the mode of Indian Agriculture, must inevitably lead to the results Colonel Corbett mentions in his pamphlet. It is a most dangerous delusion—and we must not deceive ourselves and others by it—to think that, because the fields of India have for centuries past yielded sufficient food for millions, they will continue to do so for centuries to come, under the present system of cultivation.

Ample proofs have been given of the almost exhausted state of the soil, and the facts Colonel Corbett mentions show how near we are to the end. The present system of stimulating the soil by irrigation, to make it yield its utmost, will inevitably result, as has already been the case, in the more speedy exhaustion of the soil: the larger the crop, the sooner the ruin of the land and all depending on its fertility.

The extensive irrigation-works contemplated by Government will, if carried out, contribute towards the more speedy ruin of the fields irrigated, unless proper means be adopted *to give back to the soil what is taken from it*, or, in other words, unless the ryot lives on the interest of the capital stored up in the soil, instead of drawing an annually diminishing percentage from the stock itself.

The *Oriental*, in an article on "Irrigation-works in India," aptly remarks :—" Water alone will not help the land to produce crops that would, after paying the land-tax and heavy water-rates, support the agriculturists ; the land is poor and pretty well exhausted, and, until manures are introduced and the agriculturists are taught and induced to use them, the land will not yield much more than it does now."

The only reliable foundation of our knowledge of the laws of nature is based upon observation : by observing the works of nature, we can form correct conclusions as to the laws which govern them ; and this remark applies also to vegetable life. We must observe plants in their natural state, that is, when undisturbed and untended by the hand of man, to arrive at a correct knowledge of the general laws which govern their growth, existence, and decadence, and by which laws we should be guided in their cultivation, or, more correctly speaking, in the artificial rearing of once wild plants.

A plant in its natural state, if perennial, returns constantly a portion of what it had withdrawn from the soil and air, by shedding its leaves, which become decomposed into their constituent parts, and serve again as food, perhaps to the same plant which had shed them. Eventually it dies on the spot where it had grown, and all the inorganic substances withdrawn from the soil are returned, together with all those substances which it had derived from water and atmospheric air. For immediately upon the sustaining power of life becoming extinct, in vegetable as in animal life, the general laws of nature reassert their influence, which had partly been checked by vital power ; decomposition sets in, the organic compounds separate themselves into their constituent parts, the inorganic parts return to the soil whence they were derived, and the organic parts are restored to the atmosphere ; new life, new plants, spring up, perhaps upon the decomposing remains of their very parent; and thus the amount of food necessary for the requirements of vegetable life is constantly maintained— nay, even increased—by the additional storage of organic substances in the soil.

These observations explain to us the cause of the luxuriant vegetation in virgin forests, of the astoundingly productive capabilities of a soil newly recovered from nature's hands. But does not the process of artificial vegetation, and the Indian mode of cultivation in particular, differ most materially from these Rational Principles of nature's actions ? The ryot tills and sows, and, when his crops have ripened, he removes them from the soil to serve as food, partly for himself and partly for the cattle which assist him in his work, without the slightest regard to the necessities of the soil.

The only conclusions which can be drawn from these two facts, the great natural law and rational principle of Agriculture to which they point, are patent. The plant in its natural state, on the one hand, dies on the spot where it grew, it decomposes there, returns to the soil what it had taken from it, *viz.*, the elements of inorganic plant-food, and transmits to its descendants the fruit of its activities in the shape of organic and inorganic food available for their immediate consumption. The plant in its artificial state, on the other hand, is taken away from where it grew, and not only leaves virtually nothing for its successors, but, on the contrary, takes away a certain quantity of fertilizing substances from the soil which nature is unable to restore. Water, carbonic acid, and ammonia, the three great suppliers of organic food for the vegetable kingdom, are brought to the plant by nature herself, by rain and by the constant circulation of our atmospheric air; but not an ounce of potassa, lime, or silica, not a grain of phosphoric or sulphuric acid, can nature ever restore to the soil whence the plant, which had been removed by human hands, had derived it.

Mention has been made in the preceding pages that soils are divided into different classes, named after the preponderating constituent; thus we speak of clayey, sandy, calcareous, and humous soils. The following classification by M. Schübler is the most complete we possess, and will enable the agriculturist to determine himself the description of any particular soil by aid of the hints given on the page following the tables.

Schubler's Classification and Nomenclature of Soils as recommended by Dr. DAUBENY.

(From the Journal of the "Royal Agricultural Society" of England, Vol. III., page 156.)

Names of the different Descriptions of Soils.			Proportions of Ingredients in every 100 Parts.				Agricultural Designations and General Relations with reference to their Produce.
Classes.	Orders.	Species.	Clay.	Lime.	Humus.	Sand.	
1. *Argillaceous or Clayey Soils.* Above 50 per cent. of Clay.	Without Lime	Poor	Above 50	0	0·0 to 0·5	The Remainder	*Land for Wheat and Spelt.* The calcareous kinds, not too rich in clay and not too poor in sand and humus, give good returns. Wheat, spelt, barley, rape, beans, flax, and clover flourish in it especially. Those poor in humus are still suited for oats.
		Intermediate	,, 50	0	0·5 to 1·5	,,	
		Rich	,, 50	0	1·5 to 5·0	,,	
Not more than 5 per cent. of Lime	With Lime	Poor	Above 50	0·5 to 5·0	0·0 to 0·5	,,	
		Intermediate	,, 50	0·5 to 5·0	0·5 to 1·5	,,	
		Rich	,, 50	0·5 to 5·0	1·5 to 5·0	,,	
2. *Loamy Soils.* Not more than 50 nor less than 30 per cent. of Clay.	Without Lime	Poor	30 to 50	0	0·0 to 0·5	,,	*Land for Barley.* The soils which are rich in humus, and contain lime, are well suited even for wheat and spelt, and often approach nearly to the foregoing kinds. They are, moreover, suited for Triticum dicoccum (Emmer), one-grained wheat (Einkorn), rye, oats, rape (Raps), flax, and clover.
		Intermediate	30 to 50	0	0·5 to 1·5	,,	
		Rich	30 to 50	0	1·5 to 5·0	,,	
Not more than 5 per cent. of Lime	With Lime	Poor	30 to 50	0·5 to 5·0	0·0 to 0·5	,,	
		Intermediate	30 to 50	0·5 to 5·0	0·5 to 1·5	,,	
		Rich	30 to 50	0·5 to 5·0	1·5 to 5·0	,,	

Names of the different Descriptions of Soils.			Proportions of Ingredients in every 100 Parts.				Agricultural Designation and General Relations with reference to their Produce.*
Classes.	Orders.	Species.	Clay.	Lime.	Humus.	Sand.	
3. *Sandy Loams.* Not more than 30 nor less than 20 per cent. of Clay Not more than 5 per cent. of Lime	WithoutLime	Poor	20 to 30	0	0·0 to 0·5	The Remainder	*Land for Barley and Oats.* Less suited for wheat and spelt than the former soil, but even better adapted for Triticum dicoccum and T. monococcum, as well as for rye. Potatoes, turnips, and other roots thrive well in it.
		Intermediate	20 to 30	0	0·5 to 1·5	,,	
		Rich	20 to 30	0	1·5 to 5·0	,,	
	With Lime	Poor	20 to 30	0·5 to 5·0	0·0 to 0·5	,,	
		Intermediate	20 to 30	0·5 to 5·0	0·5 to 1·5	,,	
		Rich	20 to 30	0·5 to 5·0	1·5 to 5·0	,,	
4. *Loamy Sands.* Not more than 20 nor less than 10 per cent. of Clay Less than 5 per cent. of Lime	WithoutLime	Poor	10 to 20	0	0·0 to 0·5	,,	*Land for Oats and Rye.* Barley thrives well in those rich in humus. They are also well suited for buck-wheat. Wheat, spelt, and clover do not succeed.
		Intermediate	10 to 20	0	0·5 to 1·5	,,	
		Rich	10 to 20	0	1·5 to 5·0	,,	
	With Lime	Poor	10 to 20	0·5 to 5·0	0·0 to 0·5	,,	
		Intermediate	10 to 20	0·5 to 5·0	0·5 to 1·5	,,	
		Rich	10 to 20	0·5 to 5·0	1·5 to 5·0	,,	
5. *Sandy Soils.* Not more than 10 per cent. of Clay Less than 5 per cent. of Lime	WithoutLime	Poor	0 to 10	0	0·0 to 0·5	,,	*Land for Rye.* Of less value; often cultivated only every third year, and the poor land not at all. Those containing humus are chiefly fit for buck-wheat, oats, hemp, tobacco, potatoes, and spergula arvensis.
		Intermediate	0 to 10	0	0·5 to 1·5	,,	
		Rich	0 to 10	0	1·5 to 5·0	,,	
	With Lime	Poor	0 to 10	0·5 to 5·0	0·0 to 0·5	,,	
		Intermediate	0 to 10	0·5 to 5·0	0·5 to 1·5	,,	
		Rich	0 to 10	0·5 to 5·0	1·5 to 5·0	,,	

* This of course chiefly applies to the soil and climate of Germany.

Schübler's Classification and Nomenclature of Soils—(continued).

Classes.	Orders.	Species.	Proportions of Ingredients in every 100 Parts.				Agricultural Designation and General Relations with reference to their Produce.
			Clay.	Lime.	Humus.	Sand.	
6. Marly Soils. More than 5 but not more than 20 per cent. of Lime	Argillaceous {	Poor Intermediate Rich	Above 50 " 50 " 50	5 to 20 5 to 20 5 to 20	0·0 to 0·5 0·5 to 1·5 1·5 to 5·0	The Remainder " "	Chiefly suited for wheat and spelt, together with lucern and sainfoin.
	Loamy {	Poor Intermediate Rich	30 to 50 30 to 50 30 to 50	5 to 20 5 to 20 5 to 20	0·0 to 0·5 0·5 to 1·5 1·5 to 5·0	" " "	Less suited for wheat and spelt, more so for barley, Triticum dicoccum and T. monococcum, but are among the most fertile soils.
	Belonging to the Sandy Loams {	Poor Intermediate Rich	20 to 30 20 to 30 20 to 30	5 to 20 5 to 20 5 to 20	0·0 to 0·5 0·5 to 1·5 1·5 to 5·0	" " "	Barley and oats.
	Belonging to the Loamy Sands {	Poor Intermediate Rich	10 to 20 10 to 20 10 to 20	5 to 20 5 to 20 5 to 20	0·0 to 0·5 0·5 to 1·5 1·5 to 5·0	" " "	Oats and rye.
	Humus {	Clayey Loamy Sandy	Above 50 30 to 50 20 to 30	5 to 20 5 to 20 5 to 20	Above 5·0 " 5·0 " 5·0	" " "	The humous and argillaceous marly soils are amongst the best that exist.

Names of the different Descriptions of Soils.			Proportions of Ingredients in every 100 Parts.				Agricultural Designation and General Relations with reference to their Produce.*
Classes.	Orders.	Species.	Clay.	Lime.	Humus.	Sand.	
	Argillaceous	Poor	Above 50	Above 20	0·0 to 0·5	The Remainder	The argillaceous soils often approach in value to the argillaceous marls; the remaining orders of both these classes equally correspond one with the other; to the most valuable belongs, as in the former case, the humbus. Those wanting in humus require much manure. Those rich in clay are well suited for spelt and wheat. Oats, Triticum dicoccum, lucern, and sainfoin thrive in them. Their value is much decreased by containing an excess of lime.
		Intermediate	" 50	" 20	0·5 to 1·5	"	
		Rich	" 50	" 20	1·5 to 5·0	"	
	Loamy	Poor	30 to 50	" 20	0·0 to 1·5	"	
		Intermediate	30 to 50	" 20	0·5 to 1·5	"	
		Rich	30 to 50	" 20	1·5 to 5·0	"	
	Belonging to the Sandy Loams	Poor	20 to 30	" 20	0·0 to 0·5	"	
		Intermediate	20 to 30	" 20	0·5 to 1·5	"	
		Rich	20 to 30	" 20	1·5 to 5·0	"	
	Belonging to the Loamy Sands	Poor	10 to 20	" 20	0·0 to 0·5	"	
		Intermediate	10 to 20	" 20	0·5 to 1·5	"	
		Rich	10 to 20	" 20	1·5 to 5·0	"	
	Sandy	Poor	0 to 10	" 20	0·0 to 0·5	Any portion less than 80 per cent.	
		Intermediate	0 to 10	" 20	0·5 to 1·5		
		Rich	0 to 10	" 20	1·5 to 5·0		
	Pure	Poor	0	" 99	0·0 to 0·5	None.	
		Intermediate	0	" 98	0·5 to 1·5	"	
		Rich	0	" 94	1·5 to 5·0	"	
	Humus	Clayey	Above 50	" 20	Above 5·0	The Remainder	
		Loamy	30 to 50	" 20	" 5·0		
		Sandy	20 to 30	" 20	" 5·0		

7. *Calcareous Soils.* Containing more than 20 per cent. of Lime.................

* This of course chiefly applies to the soil and climate of Germany.

Schubler's Classification and Nomenclature of Soils—(*continued*).

Names of the different Descriptions of Soils.			Proportions of Ingredients in every 100 Parts.				Agricultural Designation and General Relations with reference to their Produce.*
Classes.	Orders.	Species.	Clay.	Lime.	Humus.	Sand.	
8. *Humous Soils.* Containing more than 5 per cent. of Humus	Soluble Mild Humus	Clayey	Above 50	With or without Lime.	Above 5·0	The Remainder	The value of these soils is greatly augmented by admixture with lime. Those which contain lime and clay are suited for wheat, spelt, barley, and oleaginous plants; the loamy and sandy are especially adapted for oats, and in most places for wheat. The peaty and acid humous may be made fruitful by admixture with lime, **sand, and clay.**
		Loamy	30 to 50		,, 5·0	,,	
		Sandy	20 to 30		,, 5·0	,,	
	Insoluble Carbonized or Acid Humus.	Clayey	Above 50	With or without Lime.	,, 5·0	,,	
		Loamy	30 to 50		,, 5·0	,,	
		Sandy	20 to 30		,, 5·0	,,	
	Insoluble Fibrous Vegetable matter.	Bog and Peat Earth	With Lime. Without Lime.		,, 5·0 ,, 5·0	,, ,,	

* This of course chiefly applies to the soil and climate of Germany.

Now, to determine the class of any soil does not require any very profound knowledge of analytical chemistry. A few readily ascertained facts suffice, and the following directions will be useful to those unable to consult a trained chemist :—

1. Take 100 or 1,000 grains of a soil, after well drying it in an oil-bath at 250° F., and heat it to redness in a platinum crucible, keep up the heat for half-an-hour, stirring the mass occasionally. Cool, and weigh. The loss of weight is *Humus*.

2. Digest what remains in the crucible in a phial with cold, diluted muriatic acid ($\frac{1}{2}$ oz. acid to 10 oz. water to 100 grains soil) for about an hour, shaking it from time to time. Filter through a weighed filter, and wash with pure water until the liquid passing through ceases to be sour. Dry the whole at 250° F.; weigh, and deduct the weight of the filter. The loss of weight represents the amount of *Lime*.

3. The contents of the filter are now carefully removed into a tall glass cylinder, and the impalpable matter separated from the sand and coarser particles by repeated washing with water. Stir well, let subside for a minute, and pour off the supernatant liquid. The impalpable matter thus separated represents the *clay*. Collect in a filter, dry as before, and weigh.

4. The remainder is *Sand*.

It must be understood that the results obtained by the above method will be only approximate, but still reliable enough for the purposes of classification.

CHAPTER V.

MANURES.

History of using manures.—First **manure, animal** and vegetable refuse.—A farm in ancient times returned to the field what was taken away from it.—A decrease in **the outturn** first perceptible when the farmer exported his **produce.**—Rotation of crops forced upon the farmer by **the declining fertility** of the soil.—Fallowing the next step.—The **soil** ceases to be remunerative and requires rest.—The **rational solution of the difficulty.**—The importation of manure **as an equivalent for the** exportation of produce.—Artificial **manures; their use** and abuse.—Different manures for different **crops and soils.**—**Special** manures; their nature, and relation to the soil.—The disappointment which must follow their indiscriminate **use.**—**Monetary** waste in supplying phosphoric **acid to a soil already** containing it in abundance.—An intimate **knowledge of a soil** necessary **in order** to obtain the highest results by the smallest outlay.—**Liebig on manures** in their relation **to** crops and soils.—**The Minimum Theory.**—An analysis necessary to point out the Minimum.

An instinctive though vague comprehension of the requirements of plants induced cultivators from the earliest times to spread refuse, animal and vegetable, over their fields, in order to maintain their fertility; and this procedure we call manuring.

Reverting to the farming of those times, we find that the description of manure first employed was naturally all the animal and vegetable refuse which accumulated on the farm—the refuse of the food consumed by the cultivator, and by the animals which assisted him in tilling the ground, as also the litter and grass which collected on the farm. As these ancient agriculturists cultivated almost exclusively for their own consumption, we may fairly suppose that the refuse of their farms represented nearly all what had been withdrawn from the soil ; this refuse, then, was restored to it, and in this way the fertility of the land was maintained, and may even have increased, crops being raised year after year in rarely diminishing quantities.

But when arts and manufactures were introduced, when fields were deserted for towns, when mankind began to congregate in masses for which the adjoining fields were unable to provide sufficient food, and it had to be supplied from remote districts, when farms thus began to grow their products for exportation and not only for self-consumption—from that time the fields commenced to exhibit a gradual decrease in the outturn of the crops—an inevitable result ; for thenceforth, year after year, a large quantity of inorganic substances, essential to the successful cultivation of our food-plants, was removed from the soil, and never, or at best but imperfectly, restored—in fact, a portion of the soil was exported.

As a palliative, the system called "rotation of crops" then came into practice, the soil refused to grow the same description of crop year after year without receiving back the elements of plant-food it had been deprived of; it was temporarily exhausted of available substances constituting the inorganic plant-food; it required a period of rest to be able to recover and reproduce them in an assimilable form from the material stored up in it, and nature effected this by the action of moisture, heat, and atmospheric air. In the meantime, different crops were grown which derived their plant-food from the soil of a lower stratum, inaccessible to the roots of the first description of crop, or which required somewhat different plant-food; but finally it was found necessary to allow the land to remain idle altogether for a season, after certain intervals, in order to restore the capability of the soil of yielding remunerative harvests. This system has been called "fallowing."

Notwithstanding all these expedients, however, the yield of the crops became perceptibly smaller, and the farmer was compelled to resort to other means to avert the impending ruin, and the importation of manure for the use of farms, as an equivalent for the crops and other products which had been exported from them, then first came into vogue; here the farmer had at last arrived at the only rational principle on which farming for exportation can be carried on for any length of time without assuredly and infallibly impoverishing both the land and its owner. This is the period when artificial manures first came into use and, I may add, *abuse*.

The all-important question which every intelligent agriculturist desires to solve is, how to stimulate the soil so as to obtain, with the smallest outlay and least labour, the most abundant harvests, without any detriment to the soil, and without injuring the resources of the land. This question can only be solved, and the desired result obtained, by using *appropriate* and sufficient manure, and by tilling the soil after each harvest in such a manner as to ensure a thorough mixture of it.

All intelligent agriculturists agree now that, as the constituent parts of the ashes of different kinds of plants vary considerably in their proportions, so the manures best adapted for their successful cultivation must differ accordingly, and specific manures were therefore manufactured and sold. Thus we had manures for wheat, potato, turnips, coffee, tea, &c., which were strongly recommended by well-known scientific men. The satisfactory results obtained on some particular soil were greatly extolled, and the manures were advertised as being the most perfect that could be applied, and peculiarly adapted to the specified crops. No attention was directed to the fact that the success depended entirely upon the constitution of the soil. Numberless disappointments were the natural consequence of this indiscriminate application of manures without any regard to the particular requirements of the soil. For of all the varieties of matter on this globe, there is none perhaps that exhibits such a diversity, that differs so much in its constituent parts, as the soil of our arable fields. There are scarcely two fields—nay, scarcely two spots on the same field—which contain their mineral constituents in exactly the same proportion; and to recommend, therefore, the indiscriminate use of specific manures to the agricultural public, must be regarded as nothing short of wilful deception.

To use, for instance, the specific coffee manure, which consists chiefly of potassa, for the fertilization of a soil containing already an excess of potash, would be a mere waste of time and money, when a small addition of lime and magnesia would have the desired effect. Again, what benefit can accrue by manuring with superphosphate of lime a soil containing a large amount of phosphoric acid, out of proportion to some of the other constituents? Or who would use lime as a manure for a calcareous soil?

If a soil contains an abundance of potash, lime, phosphoric acid, &c., while only a small quantity of available silica is present, it follows that, to make the soil yield a remunerative crop, of cereals for instance, it would be of no advantage whatever to supply any additional potash, lime, or phosphoric acid ; they would not tend to increase the yield ; for, in the absence of silica, the plant cannot make use of the large store of the other inorganic food constituents, so that any additional supply of these substances would be simply throwing away money and labour ; but were a proportionate quantity of available silica, the defective element, supplied, we would then be giving the only substance necessary to make the soil yield most abundant harvests.

The particular manure, then, required for a certain crop, can only be determined by the most intimate knowledge of the natural condition and requirements of the soil on which it is to be grown.

Most soils contain one or another of the inorganic substances required by plants in minutest quantity, out of proportion to the others ; and it has been mentioned that the experiments made by Prince Salm Horstmar showed that, in the absence of any single mineral in the soil, plants, after having exhausted the small quantity contained in the seed, will either perish after making a feeble attempt to grow, or, as in the absence of phosphoric and sulphuric acid, will not bear any seed ; so that we can conclude from these experiments that an insufficiency of any of these inorganic plant constituents in the soil will most seriously interfere with its capability of yielding remunerative harvests.

Liebig, in his "Natural Laws of Husbandry," says with regard to this subject:—

"A manure will exercise its beneficial action upon a field in the most marked manner, when it establishes a more suitable relative proportion between the several mineral constituents in the soil, because upon this proportion the crops are dependent. No special argument is needed to demonstrate that where a wheat soil contains just so much phosphoric acid and potash as will suffice to afford the quantity of these two substances required for a full wheat crop, and no more (accordingly for every part by weight of phosphoric acid, two parts by weight of potash), any additional supply of one-half more, or even of double the quantity of potash, cannot exercise the slightest possible influence upon the crop of corn. The wheat-plant requires for its full development a certain relative proportion of both nutritive substances, and any increase of one beyond this proportion makes the other not a whit more effective, because the additional supply exercises by itself no action.

"An increase of phosphoric acid alone has just as little influence in making the returns greater, as an increase of potash alone: this law applies equally to every nutritive substance—potash, magnesia, and silicic acid; no supply of these substances beyond the requirement of the wheat-plant, or its capacity of absorption, will have any effect upon its growth. The relative proportions of the mineral substances which the plants draw from the soil, are easily determined by analyzing the ashes of the produce. It is found by analyses that wheat, potatoes, oats, and clover receive the following proportions of phosphoric acid, potash, lime, magnesia, and silicic acid:—

	Phosphoric Acid.	Potash.	Lime and Magnesia.	Silicic Acid.
Wheat (corn and straw)	1	2·0	0·7	5·7
Potatoes (tubes)	1	3·2	0·48	0·4
Oats (corn and straw)	1	2·1	1·03	5·0
Clover	1	2·6	4·0	1·0
Average	1	2·5	1·5	3·0

"Supposing wheat, potatoes, oats, and clover to be cultivated in a field for four years in succession, each of these plants will absorb from the soil the proportion of mineral constituents which it requires; and the sum total, divided by the number of years, *viz.*, four, shows the average relative proportion of all the nutritive substances which the soil has lost.

If in the formula...... $n\,(1\cdot0 \quad 2\cdot5 \quad 1\cdot5 \quad 3\cdot0)$

we determine the value of n, which is meant here to designate the number of kilogrammes of phosphoric acid which the four crops have received from the soil, we find for the wheat crop 26 kilogrammes of phosphoric acid, for the potato crop 25 kilogrammes, for the oat crop 27 kilogrammes, and for the clover crop 36 kilogrammes. Altogether 114 kilogrammes; multiplying the above proportional numbers by this number, we obtain the sum total of all the nutritive substances extracted from the soil by the four crops. With the help of these proportional numbers, we are better able than before to give some more accurate explanations.

"Suppose that the soil of a certain field contains, in an available state, the requisite quantities of phosphoric acid, potash, lime, and magnesia to supply the four crops stated above, but that it is deficient in the proper proportion of silicic acid—containing, for example, for 1 part by weight of phosphoric acid, only $2\frac{1}{2}$ parts of silicic acid, in an available condition—this deficiency will, in the first place, be felt in the crops of cereal plants, whilst the potato and clover crops, on the contrary, will not be at all diminished. It will depend upon the weather to determine whether this deficiency in the crop of cereal plants extends both to corn and straw, or is confined to the straw alone. A want of potash, in proportion to all the other constituents, will barely affect the wheat and oat crops, but it will reduce the potato crop; in like manner, a want of lime and magnesia will impair the clover crop.

"If the ground can furnish one-tenth more potash, lime, magnesia, and silicic acid than corresponds to the given proportion of phosphoric acid—thus, if

	Phosphoric Acid.	Potash.	Lime and Magnesia.	Silicic Acid.
Instead of	1	2·5	1·5	3·0
The ground should be able to furnish	1	2·75	1·65	3·3

the crops would not turn out larger than before. But if, in such a field, the quantity of phosphoric acid is increased, the produce will increase, until the right proportion is restored between the phosphoric acid and the other mineral constituents.

"The additional supply of phosphoric acid serves in this case to increase the amount of potash, lime, and silicic acid in the produce; but if this additional supply exceeds one-tenth of the phosphoric acid present in the soil, the quantity in excess remains ineffective. Up to this limit, every pound—nay, every ounce—of phosphoric acid supplied, has, in this case, a fully determinate action.

"If potash or lime alone is wanted to restore the right proportion among the nutritive substances in the soil, a supply of ashes or lime will increase the produce of all the crops—the additional supply of lime effecting, in this case, an increase in the amount of phosphoric acid and potash in the augmented produce.

"If we find that a soil will not bear a remunerative crop of cereal plants, though it remains fruitful for other plants, such as potatoes, clover, or turnips, which require just as much phosphoric acid, potash, and lime as the cereals, we may assume that the soil had the latter substances in excess, but was deficient in silicic acid. And if in the course of two or three years, during which other produce is cultivated on it, the land recovers its fertility for cereals, this must be because it contained, though unequally divided and distributed, an excess of silicic acid also, which, during the fallow season, migrated from the places where it was in excess to those where it was deficient; so that when the subsequent period of cultivation began, there was in all these places the right proportion of all the nutritive substances needed by cereal plants. For similar reasons, if peas or beans can be cultivated on a given field only at certain intervals—and experience shows that skilful, industrious tillage is usually more effective than manure in shortening these intervals—we may infer that in such cases the nutritive substances were not deficient in total quantity in the whole field, but in proper proportion in all parts of the field."

It is the *minimum* quantity of what may be a single constituent which regulates the outturn of a field and determines its fertility; and it is by supplying this minimum constituent—it may be potash or soda, lime or magnesia, phosphoric or sulphuric acid, iron or silica—that we can raise any soil to the highest degree of fertility it is capable of attaining. The means to gain this end are within the reach of every one, and the chief question which a farmer must solve, after having selected that crop which practical experience and theoretical knowledge convince him as being best suited for his fields, is, whether the available inorganic substances which serve as plant-food are present in the proportion in which they are required by the plant. To gain this information, a complete analysis, exhibiting all the details I have mentioned, should be made, which will show any deficiency, by supplying which the farmer will induce his lands to yield the highest crops they are capable of producing; and all that remains for him to do thenceforward, to maintain this fertility, is simply to conscientiously restore year after year the small quantity of inorganic substances withdrawn with each harvest.

CHAPTER VI.

MANURES AVAILABLE IN INDIA.

Mr. R. H. Elliot on the future prospects of agriculture in India, the want of manure, and the degeneration of man and animal.—The fertility of a soil-depends upon the quantity of inorganic plant-food which it contains in physical combination.—The chief object of agriculture should be to maintain this fertility.—The progressive exhaustion of the soil, under the present system of agriculture in India, expressed in figures.—Man and animal part of the soil.
The total consumption of food-stuffs by the Indian subjects of Great Britain.—The ashes, or inorganic parts of these food-stuffs, are to be found in human refuse.—The welfare and ultimate existence of nations depend upon the proper utilization of this fertilizing matter.—The calculations of Liebig—730 crores of rupees the value of food-stuffs consumed annually in British India.—The loss to the commonwealth by the waste of the inorganic constituents contained in the refuse of food, which, if carefully restored, would have enabled the soil to yield another crop worth 730 crores.—Public opinion awakening to a knowledge of the enormous waste going on.—The *Times* on the River Pollution Commission.—The conservation of human and animal refuse in India offers no difficulties.—The project of a system adapted for all small towns and villages.—Mr. Buck on the utilization of town-refuse at Furrukhabad.—Experiments made in the Deccan with human refuse as manure give remarkable results, more than doubling the outturn.—Town-refuse adopted as manure for all food-stuffs.—Its approximate composition.—Its mode of application.

As an introduction to the chapter on Manures, I quote *in extenso* a letter from Mr. Robert H.

Elliot, published in the London *Times* of the 2nd February 1875. This letter paints the future of Indian Agriculture in very dark colours indeed, and cannot be said to exaggerate existing facts; but it will be shown in the following pages that, besides the hitherto untouched stores of fertilizing substances in the subsoil, Indian agriculturists have many indigenous manures available, but are ignorant of their nature and value. The future is therefore not quite so gloomy and hopeless as would appear, but no time should be lost in introducing a different and more rational system of agriculture.

" To THE EDITOR OF THE *TIMES*.

" SIR,—Will you allow me to direct attention to the very serious question of the miserable condition and melancholy future prospects of agriculture in India, and, at the same time, indicate such remedial measures as have been suggested by my practical experience as an Indian planter ?

" As to the facts of the existing condition of Indian agriculture, I may observe that they are too well-known to require my entering into any lengthened particulars, and may be briefly and accurately described by saying that, with the exception of land irrigated by rich river-water, and of certain wooded tracts where the feed for cattle is abundant and the agricultural area very limited, the people have been living for a very long period, not on the interest, but very largely on the capital of the soil. Nor does it require many words to show how this must be the case; for if, for instance, you go into the interior of the province of Mysore—a province generally admitted to be above the average of Southern India—and examine the scanty manure heaps, you will find that they consist almost entirely of the dung of lean cattle, and of the ashes of such part of the dung as has been used for fuel; and the value of this manure may be estimated by stating that even the dung of grass-fed cattle only, contains, out of every 1,000 lbs., about 11 lbs. of valuable matter. Whence, then, asks the practical agriculturist, is to be supplied the phosphoric acid, lime, potash, and nitrogenous matter which is carried off the land, partly to be eaten by the farmer, and partly to be exported to enable him to pay his rent; and whence that vegetable matter which is entirely consumed by cattle, but which is so necessary, not only for its constituents, but for the effect it has in maintaining the texture as well as the radiating and absorptive powers of the soil? The answer is that there are no means of adequately supplying them at all. The land, as we have seen, is deprived of its vegetable matter because that is needed to feed cattle, and from the absence of trees there is no means of procuring leaves; nor is there any practicable means of supplying vegetable manure. It is deprived of its phosphoric acid, lime, and nitrogenous constituents, which are but very partially replaced by the infinitesimal quantities of these substances to be found in the dung of lean cattle, and it is deprived of its potash and other mineral constituents, which can hardly be said to be replaced at all. And what is true of the interior of Mysore is true generally, as far as our information goes; and were I not afraid of wasting your space, I could easily bring ample evidence to show that the soil of all India is, with few exceptions, bordering on exhaustion.

"Now let us look at the future agricultural prospect. We have seen that the manure at command is both poor in quality and small in quantity; but, as the population increases, even these paltry resources must steadily diminish; for, as more and more of the grazing-lands are broken up, it is evident that fewer and fewer cattle can be kept in proportion to the cultivated area. Even already complaints have been made as regards that extension of cultivation which, to persons unacquainted with the agricultural circumstances of the country, seems to be a sign of steady progress. And if that is the case now with a population of only about 240 millions, what will the state of things be in 20 years, when the people will have increased to 293 millions, or, to look a step further, in 40 years, when we shall have a population of 357 millions? It would seem ridiculous to look on to a further period, but the question as to whether the Government should take over the Indian railways now or 80 years hence, makes it worth while to point out that, by that time, these exhausted soils will have to support about 530 millions of persons.

"In conclusion, let me state what is practicable, in order, not to raise Indian soils to a fair state of fertility—for, unless some undreamt-of manurial resources be discovered, this would be impossible—but at least to prevent matters going from bad to much worse than they are at present.

"In the first place, then, the grazing-lands attached to, or in the vicinity of, each village, must not be encroached on, unless it can clearly be shown that they are far in excess of the requirements of the community. In the second place, wherever it is practicable, each village should be compelled to plant, fence, and maintain a considerable block of forest trees, partly to improve the climate and the grazing by sheltering it from drying winds, partly for wood for building and firewood, but mainly for the supply of that great want in the plains of India, a sufficiency of leaves, which, by being used as bedding for cattle, would absorb the most valuable constituents of the manure, and especially of that liquid portion of it which is now entirely lost.

" One word more. It is grievous to see how much we have failed to accomplish in India owing to the fact of our officials knowing nothing about agriculture. Take Mysore for instance. We have governed it for about 43 years, and, if some of our most intelligent Scotch factors—acting, of course, in conjunction with the advice and co-operation of the most able natives in the country—had been employed and allowed to have their way, the whole face of the country might now have been altered, and its climate largely modified for the better. At a very trifling expense it might have been studded with woods and plantations, its manurial resources and grazing capabilities largely increased, and its agricultural area kept well and evenly within the bounds of its manurial resources. Does any proprietor here allow moor and grazing-land to be enclosed and broken up without seeing that suitable plantations are formed both for wood and shelter, that the cultivator has the means of doing it justice, and that such restrictions are imposed as will fairly protect him from having his land run out and utterly destroyed? Why, then, should the greatest landed proprietor in the world—Her Majesty the Queen—have her Indian estates managed on principles exactly at variance with those which are generally accepted here?

       Obediently yours,

Clifton Park, Kelso." ROBERT H. ELLIOT.

But though the above letter proves the great want and the importance of manures in this country, it would be useless to discuss in a book specially written for India the advantages of manures that are not available to the Indian agriculturist, and I will therefore confine my observations to such materials only as are easily accessible to him.

It must be remembered that the fertility of a soil depends upon the quantity of fertilizing elements which it contains in physical combination, and that it should be the chief object of agriculture to maintain a balance of these substances in sufficiently large quantities to enable the soil to yield remunerative crops. The average yield of wheat-lands in India is 660 lbs. of grain and about 1,650 lbs. of straw per acre; and the loss sustained by the soil will amount to about 8 lbs. of phosphoric acid, 15 lbs. of potash, and 50 lbs. of silica, besides the other minor mineral constituents. If we now assume that the soil contains within reach of the plant a thousand times this quantity of mineral plant-food, the roots of the plant will find, in the following year in every part of the soil, a thousandth part less of nourishment; and supposing climatic influences to be exactly the same, the soil will naturally yield a smaller crop in the next year, the proportion to the previous year's outturn being 999 : 1,000. That is to say, 250 years hence the outturn would be reduced by one-fourth. But it having been assumed that all the fertilizing ingredients are in a state of physical combination—while, in fact, only a small portion of them are so—the declension will be more rapid. To keep, therefore, a sufficient working balance in the soil, we have to return every year the amount of mineral constituents we withdraw with the crops.

The soil sustains by its produce man and beast; and the connection between the fertility of our fields, and the residue of the consumed food raised therefrom, is so intimate, that we cannot safely and rationally regard the one without the other. The total population of India under direct English administration amounts to about 200 millions. If we allow now only 2 lbs. a head per day of food-stuffs, and value it at the rate of 20 lbs. per rupee, we find that 400 millions of pounds of food-stuffs a day are consumed in British India, representing a value of 2 crores of rupees, or 730 crores per annum.

The ashes, the mineral constituents of this enormous quantity of food, that have been withdrawn from the soil, are almost entirely contained in the refuse of the food, in the excrements of man and animal; and it is to this valuable manure, which has been so universally neglected (except in China and Japan), that I would draw the chief attention of my readers. For it is upon the proper utilization of the enormous quantity of this fertilizing matter, that the welfare and existence of all countries depend ; and it is to the reckless and lamentable waste of human refuse that India owes the exhaustion of her soil.

Liebig says with regard to this subject:—"If we could collect, without the least loss, all the solid and fluid excrements of all the inhabitants of towns, and return to each farmer the portion arising from the produce originally supplied by him to the town, the productiveness of his land might be maintained almost unimpaired for ages to come, and the existing store of mineral elements in every fertile field would be amply sufficient for the wants of the increasing populations. At any rate, that store is at present still sufficient to do so, although the number of farmers who take care to cover, by an adequate supply of suitable manures, the loss of mineral matters sustained by the land in the crops grown on it, is but small in proportion to the whole agricultural population. However, sooner or later the time will come when the deficiency in the store of these mineral matters will be important enough in the eyes of those who are at present so void of sense as to believe that the great natural law of restoration does not apply to their own fields ; and the sins of the fathers in this respect will also be visited upon their posterity. In matters of this kind, inveterate evil habits are but too apt to obscure our better judgment. Even the most ignorant peasant is quite aware that the rain falling upon his dung-heaps washes away a great many silver dollars, and that it would be much more profitable to him to have on his fields what now poisons the air of his house and the streets of his village; but he looks on unconcerned, and leaves matters to take their course, because they have always gone on in the same way."

Food-stuffs worth 730 crores are, we have estimated, annually consumed by the Indian population, being entirely the produce of India's soil; and more than 20 crores of rupees was the income Government realized in 1875 as land-revenue. The mineral constituents of all these food-stuffs have been wasted for centuries, and are irrecoverably lost to the soil, which has received virtually nothing in return for all it gave, and the total loss which the Indian Empire and the commonwealth of its people have suffered in consequence up to the present time must be stupendous.

The careful restoration of human refuse to the soil, such as is practised in China and Japan, would have the effect of annually returning to the soil a quantity of fertilizing matter sufficient to raise a crop worth 730 crores of rupees, while non-restoration would, on the contrary, result in so much loss to the commonwealth. The *Times*, in an article on the River Pollution Commission and on the importance of human fertilizers, expresses itself as follows :—

"Every well-wisher to England, who reflects upon the great sewage question and its present condition, must feel humiliated by our national and willing helplessness and shortcomings as regards the disposal and utilization of this our vast food-producing treasure. The blundering from beginning to end has been immense. Our sanitary reformers, in their laudable desire to preserve our health, abolished our cesspools, poisoned our rivers, and deprived us of the only cheap and effective means for fertilizing our fields and filling our stomachs.

"A jury of Chinamen would pronounce us guilty of suicidal insanity, for in China their 400 millions of people depend mainly on human sewage for the production of their food; they do not, like us, purchase bird's dung from Peru, or import the antiquated dust and ashes of foreign men and animals. Every one in Britain believes in the sheepfold, but about the manfold, which is superior in its effects and results, there has been complete apathy."

No elaborate and expensive schemes, no extraordinary ingenuity, is required to make the utilization of human fertilizers practicable. It has been brought to perfection in China and Japan, and I have no doubt that a careful study of the method adopted in those countries could enable us to introduce it into India without any considerable alterations.

In villages and small towns especially, the conservation of all refuse matter for agricultural purposes is really a very simple matter, and attended with very little trouble. I would select a high-lying, dry piece of ground at a convenient distance from the village or town, and have three pits dug, each of sufficient dimensions to contain double the estimated amount of human refuse and sweepings that could be collected during a year. All the refuse of the village—nightsoil, house-sweepings, street-scrapings, garbage, ashes of fuel (which, consisting mostly of dried cow-dung, is a valuable straw-producer)—in short, refuse of all kinds— should be thrown into these pits, and a layer of dry earth put over so as to cover each day's collection. A simple, inexpensive shed erected over the pits would enable this disposal being continued during the monsoons. When a pit is full, it should be covered with a layer of earth six inches thick; and the refuse should then be allowed to remain there a whole year in order that it be totally decomposed, after which it will be available for use, having the appearance of black mould; there will be nothing left which could be repugnant even to the most sensitive nerves.

There can be no doubt that the ryots would but only too gladly avail themselves of this manure, and they should be allowed to carry away as much as they liked, in exchange for an equal quantity of earth. After a couple of years a trifling charge could be made upon each basket, the revenue thus derived going towards defraying the expenses of the establishment maintained for this purpose. Having three pits, each holding fully a year's collection, there would be one pit in use, another containing the refuse of the previous year in process of decomposition, while the third contains available manure.

There are some towns in India where the utilization of human refuse is carried on systematically; Furrukhabad for instance. From a report of Mr. E. C. Buck I abstract the following, which will confirm what has been repeatedly advanced, that the value of human refuse as a manure cannot be over-estimated. He says:—

"The Kachies are a well-known class of cultivators in the Doab, and correspond to the class known as market-gardeners in England. They are seldom found except in the vicinity of large villages or towns, in which manure is plentiful and easily accessible, because the crops which they are skilled in producing are all crops which require a large supply of manure. By this system three crops can be produced on the same ground every year:—Mukka, or Indian corn, is grown in the rains; potatoes at the commencement, and tobacco at the end, of the cold weather. The gross outturn of these three crops is valued at between 300 and 400 rupees in some years. A potato crop sometimes weighs 150 maunds to the acre, and sells for 1 or $1\frac{1}{2}$ rupee a maund; on the other hand, the cost of cultivation is great. The area under this triple crop in one year in the vicinity of the city was 1,312 acres. Land under such heavy cropping as this requires to be sustained by a very large supply of manure. The Kachies obtain the necessary manure from the city, whence it is generally brought in sacks by buffaloes or bullocks, and deposited on the fields at the end of the rains, just before the potatoes are planted. The bullock-loads were counted in a very large number of fields during one season. The number per acre was seldom less than 400, never less than 300, and often much in excess of 400. Assuming that the number of the loads per acre is on an average 350, the amount of manure required for 1,312 acres is reckoned, in bullock-loads, $350 \times 1{,}312 = 469{,}200$. The manure deposited can hardly have been less than 400,000 loads.

"A different rent is charged for land to which manure is accessible, and for land to which it is not accessible. The land close to the village site, which is frequented by the villagers for purposes of nature, is rented at three times the rate at which land near the boundary of the villages is rented, and land which is out of the reach of such adventitious manure. For manured land round village sites, Kachies generally pay from 15 to 20 rupees an acre.

"Now, at Furrukhabad there is a well-marked rise in the rates as the city is approached, which rise is due to the supply of manure and the presence of Kachies. The rates spring from 5 and 6 rupees an acre outside the manure line, to 10 and 12 rupees within it. Within the city, where manure is most abundant and accessible, they rise to 20 rupees, and in a limited number of fields lying on either side of a drain from which liquid sewage is baled out on the land, they rise to 30 and 40 rupees an acre. The difference between the rental calculated at manured rates and at ordinary rates, in and around the city, cannot be less than 40,000 rupees. That this estimate is not an improbable one, may be proved by a similar calculation for one of the district pergunnahs.

"Mr. Elliott, Settlement Officer of Furrukhabad, found that the following were the prevailing rent-rates for good irrigated land in the pergunnah of Kanouj :—

Fully-manured land, close to site, Rs. 10-8 per acre.

Partially-manured, further from site, Rs. 7-8 per acre.

Little or never manured land, distant, Rs. 5-4 per acre.

"Mr. Elliott expressly states that the difference between these rates is due to difference in the supply of manure, and in distance from the village site, and not to difference in natural soil.

"I may state, as an example of the way in which the rent of land may be enhanced, that some fields which were trenched and manured some four or five years ago at Cawnpore, and which belong to the Municipality, are now rented to Kachies for 40 and 50 rupees an acre, whereas previously they had only fetched 10 and 12 rupees an acre."

From other parts of India also, statistics are available of the utilization of town-refuse, but the quantity used is only a drop in the ocean when compared with the total annual loss :—

Mr. Halsey reports that town-refuse was highly efficacious for sugarcane, jowar, sorghum, Indian corn, melons, cabbages, and many other garden crops.

The Assistant Commissioner of Cotton, East Berar, says that at the Umroota farm, soil, manured with town-refuse, yielded 101 lbs. of clean Hingunghat cotton per acre, against an outturn of 25 lbs. from unmanured land.

The Commissioner in Sind says of this manure that "the gardeners of Sind, who are almost invariably Banians, are well acquainted with its use."

In Surat, nightsoil, mixed with ashes, has been sold to

Hindu and other cultivators, and is used by them without the least prejudice as the best manure for cultivating jowari, vegetables, and fruit-trees.

In the Deccan, nightsoil has long been utilized under the name of *sonkhud*, 'golden manure.'

In Barabunki, the public latrine refuse is sold, in a semi-moist state, to cultivators who use it chiefly for their sugarcane and wheat-lands. It is used also by Murans cultivating cabbages and cauliflowers, for which it is regarded as the best of manures.

The results obtained by the utilization of human fertilizers have been so remarkable, that it is a matter of surprise that the subject has not attracted public attention before. Some experiments made with village sweepings and nightsoil on the black soil of the Deccan, showed the following remarkable results :—

"The ground had been slightly manured the year previous; in 1873 the ground was prepared by ploughing several times and laying up in ridges, as is the custom for planting sugarcane in the country; plots were marked off ten yards wide, and the manures applied to every alternate plot, the alternating plots being left without manure. Artificial manures and guano were applied at the rate of 4 cwts. per acre—estimated cost per acre Rs. 28; nightsoil, 10 tons per acre—estimated cost Rs. 20; village sweepings, 20 tons per acre—estimated cost Rs. 20. The results are as under :—

    Land with no manure yielded per acre 19 tons by weight of sugarcane.

    Land manured with village sweepings, per acre 41 tons 5 cwts. by weight of sugarcane.

Land manured with crude nightsoil, per acre 48 tons 2 cwts. by weight of sugarcane.

Land manured with nightsoil supplied in irrigation water, per acre 49 tons 6 cwts. by weight of sugarcane."

The use of nightsoil produced an increase of 29 tons 2 cwts. over the unmanured plot; and when we consider that this increase represents something like Rs. 150 while the outlay on manure was only Rs. 20, we cannot but admit that rational agriculture with inexpensive manure ought to be one of the most remunerative undertakings for a capitalist.

Nightsoil and village sweepings are suited as manure for all crops and food-stuffs consumed by mankind, as they contain all the mineral constituents of plant-food. The composition of a manure consisting of human and animal refuse, village sweepings, and dry earth prepared in the manner detailed before, would almost equal that of farm-yard manure, the ashes of which have been shown by an analysis by Liebig to consist of the following percentages :—

Potash	2·7
Soda	2·7
Lime	8·2
Magnesia	1·0
Oxide of Iron	1·8
Chloride of Sodium	2·7
Phosphoric Acid	6·4
Sulphuric Acid	3·6
Carbonic Acid	4·5
Sand and Silica	66·4
	100·0

If, in addition to these mineral fertilizers, we consider that the organic matter present in such a compound would average about 20 per cent., and contain a high percentage of nitrogen, we cannot value it too highly. From the results of careful experiments made in Europe with farm-yard manure and poudrette, I estimate that an application of 10 cart-loads of this village manure to an acre would increase the outturn of wheat by about 250 lbs., of rice by about 300 lbs.—*i.e.*, the present outturn would be increased by about one-third.

This manure should be applied broadcast over the field as top-dressing, either shortly before or shortly after the seed has been put into the ground, and will have an immediate effect upon the crop, as all its component parts are always in a high state of fitness to serve as plant-food.

CHAPTER VII.

EARTHY PHOSPHATES AND LIME.

The importance of phosphoric acid as the predominating mineral constituent of the seed.—Bones are the principal source of phosphoric acid.—Their composition.—Bones the chief necessity of high agriculture.—Their behaviour to pure water, and to water containing carbonic acid.—Their comparative solubility depends upon their state of division.—The solvent action of carbonic acid upon bone phosphates in solutions of common salts, saltpetre, and ammonia.—Superphosphate of lime.—Coprolites—Phosphoric acid, the chief loss sustained by the soil of India.—Its application to the soil will double the outturn.—The use of phosphoric acid in Cheshire.—The action of superphosphate is immediate, and chiefly confined to the upper layers.—Bone-dust, on the contrary, penetrates deeper, and requires some years before the maximum result is obtained.—Mr. Robertson's experiments with bone-dust.—Soils most profited by bone-manure.—The action of phosphates on soil and plant.—Quantity used per acre.

Lime.—Its extensive use as a manure.—Its composition.—*Kunkur.*—Quicklime.—Action of lime on clay and soils in general.—The liberation of alkaline silicates from their unassimilable compounds.—Lime a powerful aid to the mechanical operations of agriculture.—Shell-sand.—Its extensive use in Ireland and France.—Quantity used per acre.—Lime increases the assimilable store of inorganic plant-food, resulting in a corresponding increase of the outturn.—Its use must go hand in hand with a careful restoration to the soil of what is withdrawn.—If not, lime will enrich the father and impoverish the son.—Experiments of lime-manuring at Oberbobritzsch.—Mr. Robertson's experiments on the Madras Model Farm.—Quicklime has the greatest effect on stiff, clayey, or marshy soils.—The permanent improvement of the soil effected by lime, and its effects upon different crops.—The action of lime on soil and plant.

THE importance of phosphoric acid as an essential and predominating constituent in the seed of all our grain crops, has been amply discussed in previous pages, and will doubtless be fully recognized. Any substance which contains this mineral acid in appreciable quantities, must, therefore, be considered a most valuable manure, and specially adapted for India's soil, which, by the existing system of agriculture, has lost more of this constituent than of any other.

Bones, the frame-work of human beings as well as of animals, are the chief source of phosphoric acid available to the agriculturist. Their composition varies within certain limits, but the following table given by Dr. Thomson represents a fair average constitution:—

	Ileum of a Sheep.	Ileum of an Ox.	Vertebræ of a Haddock.
Organic Matter	43·3	48·5	39·5
Phosphate of Lime	50·6	45·2	56·1
Carbonate of Lime	4·5	6·1	3·6
Magnesia	0·9	0·2	0·8
Soda	0·3	0·2	0·8
Potash	0·2	0·1	0·8
	99·8	100·3	100·8

The great value of bones, then, as powerful fertilizers is evident from the above, and their use as such has long been recognized in Europe, especially in England, where they have been greatly instrumental in maintaining the high returns.

Earthy Phosphates, being insoluble in pure water, could not assist in the nourishment of plants, were it not for their peculiar property of becoming soluble in water containing carbonic acid; but even then their solubility is very small (four thousand parts of water containing carbonic acid dissolving only one part of finely-divided Phosphates), and depends upon the fineness of their division; so that the finer the bones are broken up, and the larger the percentage of carbonic acid in the soil, the more rapid will be the decomposition.

A whole bone, or even coarse fragments, will remain several years in the soil without their volume being reduced to any appreciable degree. The organic substances will, of course, be decomposed, but they will be distributed over the field before the carbonic acid, the result of their decay, can exert any great solvent action upon the bones, the contact surface of which is not very great.

But if bones are finely pulverized, they not only permit a much more uniform distribution over the field, but the contact surface is so great—every particle of the powder being exposed to the solvent action of carbonic acid and moisture—that even in the first year of application the plant receives the full benefit of the increase in the available amount of this plant-food. This solvent action of carbonic acid shows us the importance of decaying organic matter in the soil ; and, as a consequence, a soil containing 10 per cent. of organic matter will dissolve double as much phosphate of lime as one containing only 5 per cent. This peculiar property of carbonic acid is shared also by other substances, the principal of which are common salt, nitrate of potash, and ammonia salts. The presence of these salts in the soil is therefore conducive to its fertility not only by virtue of being themselves elements of plant-food, but chiefly by possessing digestive powers, as it were, to convert other inorganic food-elements into a fit state for assimilation by the plant.

It is, however, often very desirable to obtain the earthy Phosphates contained in bones in a soluble form at once, and for that purpose crushed bones are subjected to the action of sulphuric acid, which converts the insoluble phosphate of lime into a soluble salt. This preparation is called superphosphate of lime, and contains generally 25 per cent. of phosphates soluble in water.

The use of bone-dust or superphosphate of lime is entirely unknown among native agriculturists, while the high prices of English manufacture must have deterred many of the more enlightened landholders, who were convinced of its advantages, from trying it. But both **bone-dust** and **superphosphate** are now prepared in **Bombay** by the Western India Chemical Works Company, and can be obtained from them, I believe, **at Rs. 60 per ton for** bone-dust and Rs. 80 for superphosphate.

Another source of phosphoric acid is available to the Indian agriculturist, namely, the deposits of fossil-bones, the remains of bygone animal generations, which have been discovered in several parts of India. These coprolites, as they are termed, contain **a vast** store of phosphoric acid, and will become **very** important in course of time when their agricultural value will be duly recognized.

Fossil-bones, even when finely divided, are very little acted upon by the usual solvents of earthy phosphates, and therefore require to be converted into Superphosphate before being applied to the land.

It has been shown that the chief mineral plant constituent lost by the soil of India has been phosphoric acid. The system of manuring with the ashes of grass, straw, leaves, and similar matter, has always restored to the soil a small quantity of potash, lime, silica, and magnesia ; but the store of phosphoric acid has been continuously reduced year by year, partly by the total non-utilization of human refuse, partly by the custom of using dried dung as fuel—a practice which has for centuries deprived the soil of one of its most legitimate manures.

The great fertilizing value of earthy Phosphates, containing, as they do, the chief mineral element wanted for our grain crops, will therefore be clearly apparent. The majority of soils under cultivation are deficient in this inorganic plant-food, so that every pound now added will stimulate the soil, and have an immediate effect upon the outturn.

We may safely maintain that bone-manure has contributed more to the large outturns of the soils in Europe, than any of the other improvements that science has recommended to the agriculturist. Its application to soils deficient in phosphoric acid doubled the outturn there as if by a miracle; and the effect is not spasmodic and temporary, for, under a judicious treatment and a close observance of the Principles of Rational Agriculture, this fertility has been preserved up to the present day.

Among some of the earliest applications, the use of bone-manure in Cheshire is worthy of particular remark, it having been applied there to pastures, exhausted by having supplied for centuries milk, butter, and meat, the mineral constituents of which —phosphoric acid being the principal—have regularly been consigned to the sewers of London, and were thus irrecoverably lost.

An application of 30 cwts. of bone-dust per acre increased the value of these pastures from 10*s.* or

15s. to 30s. or 40s. per acre, and the effect of this single application was felt even after the lapse of twenty years, when the rent was still two or three times the amount paid before its application.

The practical agriculturist, in choosing between bone-dust and superphosphate of lime, will be guided by the objects he has in view—whether, that is, he wishes immediate or prospective results, and intends growing plants that are surface or subsoil feeders. For the action of superphosphate is immediate (and, as it can be obtained in a coarse powder, it is most advantageous to sow it with the seed), and has the greatest effect upon plants that are surface-feeders, for it never penetrates deep into the soil; it is specially adapted for all cereals and garden vegetables, the effect of it being equal to the best Peruvian guano. Bone-dust, on the contrary, is most effective two or three years after application, and penetrates far into the subsoil before it is decomposed and retained by the capillary attractive power of the soil; hence it is best suited for root-crops (such as turnips, &c.), all subsoil feeders, and fruit-trees.

The expenditure incurred in the purchase of bone-manure will be repaid the farmer many fold in the increased outturn, and its pecuniary advantages will be evident from the undermentioned results of an experiment made and reported to

Government by Mr. Robertson, the well-known Superintendent of Government Model Farms, Madras :—

	Increase due to Manure.		Value of Increase per Acre.	Profit.
	Grain.	Straw.		
	lbs.	lbs.	Rs. a. p.	Rs. a. p.
Expended 18 Rupees per acre on Bone-dust	864	7,560	45 8 3	27 8 3

This is evidently the result of its application in the first year only, but the outturn will, of course, be still greater in the two following years.

Bone-manure will be most remunerative when applied to light or loamy soil; if applied to a clayey soil, care should be taken that the land is well-drained and ploughed, and also that a sufficient quantity of organic matter, such as straw, grass, &c., is present; for this not only facilitates the access of air into the soil, but supplies by its gradual decay the carbonic acid that is so essential a solvent of the Phosphates.

Straw, grass, and similar other matter should never be burnt on a clayey soil, but always ploughed-in whole. As calcareous soils already contain large stores of phosphoric acid, the addition of bone-manure to such is unnecessary, and will cause no perceptible increase in the outturn. The best manure for such soils is the compost Town-Manure.

A reference to the table showing the average composition of bones will explain their powerful action upon vegetable organism; for they not only contain some of the most essential inorganic plant-constituents, such as phosphoric acid, lime, and magnesia, but also contribute greatly to the development of the plant by the large quantity of organic matter they contain, nitrogen alone amounting to over 5 per cent. Its effect in so largely increasing the outturn of all nitrogenous food-stuffs, especially cereals, is therefore due partly to its supplying the soil with phosphoric acid, the chief mineral plant-food required by the seed, and partly to the large quantity of ammonia the plant derives from it in addition to that obtained from the atmospheric air. The amount to be applied to an acre will depend upon the means of the farmer; but generally one to two tons of bone-dust at first, and then an addition of half a ton every tenth year, will give the best results, for it must always be remembered that the more liberally the soil is treated, the larger will be the returns.

Lime.

One of the most important and extensively-used mineral manures is undoubtedly Lime. Properly speaking, it can scarcely be called a manure, in the narrow sense of its meaning, as the chief advantage in its use consists in its powerful action upon silicates. Lime—*kunkur*, as it is called in India—is the common denomination of a mineral more correctly spoken of as carbonate of lime, which is met with in all parts of the world in a more or less pure state.

The purest carbonate of lime contains in a caustic state 56 per cent. of lime and 44 per cent. of carbonic acid. Such a pure mineral is, however, seldom found in India. Carbonate of lime is generally met with in the state of nodules, called *kunkur*, which contain a large proportion of foreign matter, chiefly silica, alumina, phosphates, iron, and magnesia. If these nodules of impure carbonate of lime are exposed to a great heat, the carbonic acid will separate from the lime and be driven off into the air, leaving the lime in what is called its caustic state, commonly known as quicklime.

Quicklime, when sprinkled over with water, or otherwise exposed to the influence of moisture, begins to swell, breaks up spontaneously into small pieces, and falls finally into an impalpable powder, called " slaked lime." If, in this state, it is added to clay, diffused through water, the mixture thickens almost instantaneously, and, if suffered to remain for some time, muriatic acid will dissolve the clay, previously unacted upon by that medium, into a gelatinous mass. The caustic lime had combined with the elements of the clay, and liberated the alkalis and silicates from their powerful chemical combinations.

We will understand now its action upon the arable soil, the clay of which represents the greater portion of inorganic plant-food in chemical combination. The action of moisture and atmospheric air, as we have seen, converts yearly a percentage of this store into that state of physical combination in which alone it is available to the plant, and all the mechanical operations of agriculture have as their principal object the facilitation of this natural decomposition.

But the addition of Lime to the soil will liberate in a single year more inorganic plant-food from their chemical combinations, than moisture, atmospheric air, and the mechanical operations of agriculture can in a century. Carbonate of lime in its unburnt state possesses the same property as quicklime, namely, it decomposes the alkaline silicates; but as it acts much slower than quicklime, and must be finely powdered to have full effect, it is generally much more economical to burn *kunkur* and slake it into an impalpable powder.

Another important source of lime available to the Indian farmer is the shell-sand which abounds on the sea-coast. Some of the shell-sand near Bombay, I have found, contains as much as 70 per cent. of pure carbonate of lime in the shape of small fragments of broken shells, an appreciable quantity of animal matter, and small quantities of soda, potash, and magnesia ; 25 per cent. only being sand.

We learn from Johnston that shell-sand is not only extensively utilized in Ireland and on the coast of Cornwall, whence it is transported to some distance into the interior, but that on the coast of France also it is procured in large quantities, and is in great demand by inland farmers, who use it at the rate of 10 to 15 tons per acre.

The shell-sand found on the coasts of India will prove a cheap and valuable manure for all heavy soil, which it will not only decompose, but render more porous, and thus better fitted for higher cultivation. All clay soils will be largely benefited by it ; and, being so cheap and easily obtainable, I have no doubt but that its utility has only to become known to ensure its extensive use.

Shell-sand will prove a most useful manure for grass-lands, and, where available, I would recommend its use largely, for it will extirpate all weeds, all sour and harsh grasses, and produce a sweet herbage which will well repay the trifling additional outlay.

Several other Indian sources of carbonate of lime might be mentioned, but I am not sufficiently acquainted with their nature or the extent of their existence to mention anything more than the fact that they exist.

Reverting to *kunkur*, it has been said that it can

be applied to the soil in two different ways—either in a finely powdered state, when its effect is slow, arriving at its maximum perhaps five or six years after application ; or in the burnt state, when it will, as slaked lime, have an almost immediate effect upon the outturn.

The quantity to be used per acre depends greatly upon the peculiar nature of the land. Clayey soils, for instance, will require lavish treatment, as also wet or marshy lands ; but some circumspection is necessary when light and sandy soils are in question, as an excessive quantity is very often productive of temporary sterility.

The depth of the soil will also regulate the quantity : the deeper the arable soil, the more lime will it bear. A clayey or marshy soil will require about 8 tons, or 25 candies, of quicklime, while on a lighter soil 5 to 6 tons will be sufficient. This will serve as the first application, but every fourth year an additional quantity should be supplied, when 2 tons, or 6 candies, will be sufficient for a heavy, wet soil, and $1\frac{1}{4}$ or $1\frac{1}{2}$ ton for lighter soil.

The application of lime-manure on a large scale *must* be attended by a more rigid observance of the natural Laws of Agriculture, and it especially demands an adequate return to the land of the elements it is deprived of. For should lime be used, and such restitution not be made, almost all the remaining store of mineral fertilizers would be rendered available under the powerful influence of lime; the soil would yield magnificent harvests for about twenty years, exhausting its entire resources in the effort, but followed by a reaction that would **permanently** incapacitate it from yielding remunerative harvests, and there would be nothing left but to abandon it as hopelessly sterile. Experiments have been made in Europe with the above results, and it thenceforward became a proverbial saying that lime enriches the father and impoverishes the son.

But when the soil is liberally treated, and a careful restoration of the elements withdrawn is substituted for the present system of wanton waste, the application of lime will always be followed by the highest results, permanent in their nature. Some experiments made in Saxony, by Traeger of Oberbobritzsch, show the following very remarkable result in favor of quicklime:—

Lime Manuring (110 *cwts. Quicklime*).

	Produce per Acre Unmanured.		Produce per Acre Manured with Lime.	
	Corn.	Straw.	Corn.	Straw.
	lbs.	lbs.	lbs.	lbs.
1851—Rye	1,453	3,015	1,812	3,773
1853—Oats	1,528	1,812	1,748	2,320
1852—Potatoes	9,751	......	11,021	......
1854—Clover Hay	911	......	2,942	......

Equally good results have been obtained in India by lime-manuring, as the following experiment by Mr. Robertson at Madras shows :—

Financial Result.	Increase due to Manure.		Value of Increase per Acre.	Profit.
	Grain.	Straw.		
	lbs.	lbs.	Rs. a. p.	Rs. a. p.
18 Rupees per Acre expended on Carbonate of Lime............	702	5,922	36 9 10	18 9 10

Quicklime should be used for all clayey and marshy soils as soon as slaked, spread equally over the field, and then ploughed in at least three months before the next crop. For use on grass-lands and on light soils, quicklime should be allowed to fall to powder by the moisture of the atmospheric air alone ; only when the air is too dry may it be slaked with water, but it should be exposed to atmospheric action at least a couple of months before use, as otherwise it will destroy the herbage, and deprive the light soils of their organic matter in too great a ratio. But no such precautions need be observed when carbonate of lime is employed.

The advantages attending the use of Lime-manure consist not only in an increase in the outturn, but in the improvement of soils to such a degree as to enable them to grow superior crops; an average rice soil will then yield an abundant crop of wheat, a wheat soil will become capable of growing tobacco, &c. The soil will become more grateful for manures, and maximum results will be obtained with a minimum of outlay.

It is said that the grain of the cerealia are especially benefited by a lime-manure. The husk is stated to be thinner, the grain heavier and yielding more flour, which is richer in gluten. Also potatoes have been found to be more mealy. In fact, such favorable accounts are numberless. But on flax lime appears to have a deleterious action, as some have stated that it injures the fibre of the stem.

Slaked lime, being an impalpable powder, is apt to be washed into the subsoil, and limed lands should therefore be deeply ploughed every third or fourth year.

The different properties of lime, to which we must ascribe all the favorable results of its application, are of a complicated nature, and it is difficult to say to which of them it owes most of its repute. Its mechanical action of rendering heavy soils lighter and more porous, and therefore more permeable to the influence of moisture and atmospheric air, may sometimes be as important as its chemical action, which may briefly be said to consist—first, in its being an important ingredient of inorganic plant-food; secondly, in its decomposing the insoluble silicates, and liberating the alkalis and other mineral food constituents from their unassimilable combinations, and converting them into available plant-food ; thirdly, its decomposing rapidly any inert organic substances which may be present ; and fourthly, in its neutralizing all acids or other compounds injurious to healthy vegetation.

CHAPTER VIII.

GYPSUM, NITRATE OF POTASH, AND AMMONIA.

Gypsum allied to lime in its composition and general effects.—Preferable for green crops and grass-lands.—Dr. Pinkers' experiments.—How Gypsum is applied.—Its effects upon leaves and stems.—Highly appreciated in Europe.—Aden pumice.—Mr. Smith's experiments on clover and wheat.—Mr. Robertson's experiments.—Refuse of soda-water manufactories.

Nitrate of potash.—*Sora Khar.*—Mr. Robertson's experiments.—Consumption of nitrates steadily increasing.—Quantity per acre, and mode of application.—Effect on the plant.—Common salt checks the tendency of saltpetre to make the crop run into grass.—Ammoniacal liquor of gas-works.—Its usefulness for kitchen plants, and mode of application.

Gypsum, or native sulphate of lime, is closely allied to lime in its effects, as also in its general usefulness as a mineral manure. In Germany it is applied, in the burnt and unburnt state, to all kinds of grass and green fodder-lands, but its use is now extending to all descriptions of lands. In America it is used chiefly for grain crops, and the results are said to be extremely satisfactory.

Gypsum is found in abundance all over India, but I would recommend its use for the improvement of grass-lands only, until its action upon grain crops is fully established by experiments. Dr. Pinkers, of Insterburg, has given us some valuable and carefully prepared figures with regard to this manure. He ascertained its effect upon clover, and established the fact that it will raise the outturn of clover hay by one-half.

The best mode of applying it, is to dust it over the young plants at the rate of about 5 to 10 cwts. per acre. Its effect is chiefly confined to the increased production of leaves and stems, and woody fibre in general; its application would therefore benefit cereals by increasing the food-absorbing surfaces, and consequently increase to some extent the assimilation of nourishment and the outturn in seed.

Its use in Europe has of late been increasing greatly, and the results appear very satisfactory. In a London letter to the *Times of India*, special attention has been drawn to this manure, which is highly spoken of. I extract the following as most interesting :—

" The notice in your Overland Summary of the 17th ultimo, of the Aden pumice-beds, has attracted considerable attention here. If the strata contain gypsum in large quantities, the pumice is good for other purposes than those of making hydraulic mortar, though for this purpose alone the deposits must be very valuable. We often hear and read of the great want of manure in India. Now, here—I am writing from Kent, the garden of England—

gypsum is highly prized as a fertilizer. On a farm at Holkham it was spread on sainfoin lays, at the rate of four bushels per acre, and the crop in some instances was doubled. It has been employed with great advantage in calcareous sandy loam, and even on stiff soils which had been previously limed or chalked, the result being to increase lucern and clover crops threefold, and it was found equally beneficial to leguminous crops. Mr. Smith, of Funstal, near Sittingbourne, by using powdered gypsum at the rate of five bushels to the acre, obtained the following results from a field of red clover when first mown for hay, and afterwards cut for seed :—

	Hay crop. cwt.	Seed. qrs. lbs.	Straw. cwt. qrs. lbs.
Gypsum	60	3 21	22 3 12
No Manure	20	0 20	5 0 0

"The cost of the gypsum was then 5s. 1d. per bushel, and the difference between the two experiments £16-2-9. Cattle show a remarkable predilection for gypsumed clover. Wheat also shows marked improvement when treated to a top-dressing of this manure, and produced thirty-eight bushels to the acre against twenty bushels off the same land. Gypsum is to be found in many parts of India, and I confidently recommend it to the attention of all interested in the advancement of eastern agriculture. Egypt alone would take all that Aden could produce. The soils best suited to it are the light, dry, sandy, gravelly, and chalky, and it produces the best results when applied in dry weather. Upon exhausted land, or on land containing little vegetable mould, it is useless, unless ploughed-in with dung or a green crop."

The results of its application in India are also very encouraging, as appears from the following results of an experiment made by Mr. Robertson of Madras :—

Financial Result.	Increase due to Manure.		Value of Increase per Acre.	Profit.
	Grain.	Straw.		
18 Rupees per acre expended on Sulphate of Lime.........	lbs. 648	lbs. 4,914	Rs. a. p. 32 9 1	Rs. a. p. 14 9 1

The action exercised by gypsum upon the soil has not yet been sufficiently ascertained, it being of a very complicated nature. But we have every reason to believe that its chemical properties of absorbing ammonia, and disengaging magnesia and potash from their insoluble combinations, are the chief agencies to which we must attribute the undeniable improvement of the soil which follows a judicious application of this manure. Gypsum should always be powdered previous to use, which can be very easily effected by half-burning the gypsum, as the tenacious nature of the natural crystals is thus destroyed.

The refuse of soda-water manufactories, consisting of sulphate of lime, is one of the cheapest sources of this manure, and, on account of its fine state of division, preferable to native gypsum.

Nitrate of potash, the *sora khar* of the native of India, is a manurial agent procurable all over the country, and, though commanding a high price, the agriculturist should not hesitate to purchase it, as he will receive back more than twice its value in the increased crop.

In the series of experiments with chemical manures made on the Madras Model Farm, the application of saltpetre gave the following high results :—

Financial Result.	Increase due to Manure.		Value of Increase per Acre.	Profit.
	Grain.	Straw.		
	lbs.	lbs.	Rs. a. p.	Rs. a. p.
18 Rupees per acre expended on Saltpetre..................	900	7,380	46 7 6	28 7 6

It will thus be seen that a dose of about one cwt. per acre nearly doubled the crop, and gave the farmer a clear profit of nigh thirty rupees per acre—a result entirely due to the use of this manure.

Similar results have been obtained in Europe, and the utilization of this mineral manure is therefore steadily increasing. It should be used in quantities of one to two cwts. per acre, and applied as a top-dressing when the plants are a couple of inches high; it will be well to mix it with double its volume of dry earth or fine sand, so as to ensure its more equal distribution.

Saltpetre should never be used on a soil already apt to produce luxuriant foliage, or containing a large store of organic nitrogenous matter; for then an application of this manure will only result in an increased growth of stems and leaves at the expense of the seed.

It is remarkable that a small addition of common salt checks this tendency of saltpetre to make the produce run into grass, and as the common *sora khar* contains chloride of sodium as one of its chief impurities, the agriculturist will prefer the cheapest quality procurable. Nitrate of potash, as a chemical manure, is chiefly adopted for cereals and grasses, to which it supplies potash and ammonia—the latter by the decomposition of its nitric acid.

The ammoniacal liquor of gas-works is another excellent manure, and should be utilized wherever obtainable. A gallon of ammoniacal liquor of the Bombay Gas-works I found to contain $5\frac{1}{2}$ ounces of dry ammonia. At present all this ammonia of the gas-works is wasted, and the Company would be glad to have it taken away. Ammonia is specially adapted for all kitchen plants, and is therefore invaluable to the market-gardener. Before use, it should be diluted with about five times its volume of water, as it injures the rootlets in its concentrated form.

Several other manures available to the Indian ryot could be mentioned in addition to the above, but a sufficient number has been enumerated to enable the intelligent farmer to select what is best adapted for his soil and crop.

CHAPTER IX.

JAPANESE HUSBANDRY A MODEL FOR INDIAN FARMING.

EXTRACTS FROM THE REPORT TO THE MINISTER OF AGRICULTURE AT BERLIN ON JAPANESE HUSBANDRY; BY DR. MORAN, MEMBER OF THE PRUSSIAN EAST ASIATIC EXPEDITION.

The climate of Japan.—Cotton and rice, buck-wheat and barley.—The soil of Japan; its fruitfulness the artificial product of proper cultivation.—Advantages of soil and climate turned to good account by an industrious people.—Agricultural questions yet unsolved in Europe have long been settled in Japan.

The Japanese axiom of agriculture: "Without continuous manuring, no continuous harvest."—Kind of manure, and mode of collecting and storing it.—Way of using it.—Japanese compost-manure.—Manuring with every crop.—"Fallow" not known in Japan.—Export of farm produce and import of manure.—The Japanese lives truly on the *interest of the capital of the soil.*—Tillage.—Deep cultivation.—Drill-cultivation brought to perfection in Japan.

SOIL AND MANURING.

THE Japanese Empire extends from the 30th to the 45th degree of north latitude. The average temperature and distribution of heat constitute a climate embracing all the gradations between those of Central Germany and of Upper Italy. A solitary tropical palm, not fully developed, grows beside the northern pine, rice and cotton with buck-wheat and barley. Everywhere on the chains of hills, which cover the whole country like an irregular fine network, the pine predominates, imparting to the landscape that homely northern character which affords so cheering a view to the northern traveller after passing through the sultry and luxuriant regions of the tropics. In the valleys, on the other hand, the burning south holds sway, covering the earth with a rich vegetation of rice, cotton, yams, and sweet-potatoes. Hundreds of footpaths and little ravines lead to charming transitions between pine and cotton, hill and dale; everywhere is a gay assemblage of laurels, myrtles, cypresses, and, above all, shining camelias.

The land is of volcanic origin, and the entire surface belongs to the tafa and the diluvium formation. The soil on the hills consists of an extremely fine, yet not over-fat, brown clay; whereas that of the valleys is, throughout the country, with some trifling modifications, of a black, loose, and deep garden-mould, which, upon trial in different places, I found extended to a depth of 12 to 15 feet, being throughout of the same quality, though somewhat more compact in the deeper layers. An impermeable stratum of clay probably underlies this arable crust. As the clay strata of the mountains, in consequence of the frequent and copious falls of rain, give rise to numberless springs which are everywhere at hand, and may thus easily, and without any great skill, be turned to account for the purpose of irrigation, so the impermeability of the stratum underlying the surface-soil in the valleys enables the Japanese husbandman to turn the soil at pleasure into a swamp for the cultivation of rice.

Whichever way one may feel inclined to decide the question—whether the present fruitfulness of the soil is simply the artificial product of cultivation continued for several thousand years, or whether this fertility existed from the beginning, making this people cherish and prize the labours of agriculture—this much must be granted however, that the clay of the diluvium, the mild climate, and abundant water, afforded all the conditions, and the most convenient means, for a thriving cultivation.

All these natural advantages have been most carefully turned to account by an industrious, ingenious, and sober people; and husbandry in Japan has become a truly national occupation. The Japanese have thoroughly mastered the difficulty of maintaining agriculture in a state of the highest perfection, although the pursuit is entirely confined to peasants and yeomen, who take rank in the sixth (and last but one) class of the social scale; and no Japanese gentleman is a farmer. There are no agricultural institutions for instruction in husbandry, no agricultural societies, no academies, no periodical press to disseminate the teachings of science. The son simply learns from the father, and as the latter knows quite as much as *his* father and grandfather before him, he pursues exactly the same system of husbandry as any other peasant in any other part of the Empire; it is a matter of perfect indifference where the young agriculturist learns his business. The young pupil in husbandry will always be able to master a certain amount of information which the experience of ages has shown to be true, so that it may be looked upon as positive knowledge and a sort of hereditary heirloom.

I must confess, says Dr. Moran, that I experienced a feeling of deep humiliation on many occasions, when in the face of this simple knowledge, and the safe and uncontested practical application of it in husbandry before my eyes, I thought of home.

We boast that we are a civilized nation; in our land, men of the highest intellectual attainments devote their best energies to the improvement of agriculture; we have everywhere agricultural institutions and agricultural societies, chemical laboratories and model-farms, to increase and diffuse the knowledge of husbandry. And yet how strange that, despite all this, we still go on disputing, often so vehemently and acrimoniously, about the first and most simple scientific principles of agriculture; and that those who earnestly search after truth are forced to admit the infinite smallness of their positive and undisputed knowledge! How strange, also, that even this trifling amount of positive knowledge has as yet found so little application in practice!

Among the great questions which still remain in dispute with us (whilst in Japan they have long since been settled in the laboratory of an experience extending over thousands of years), I must mention, as the most important of all, that of manuring.

The educated sensible farmer of the old world, who has unconsciously come to look upon England, with its meadows, its enormous fodder production, and immense herds of cattle, and withal its great consumption of guano, ground bones, and rape-cake, as the *beau ideal* and the only possible type of a truly rational system of husbandry, would certainly be considerably surprised to see a country much better cultivated, without the advantages of meadows, fodder production, or even a single head of cattle, either for draught or for fattening, and without the least supply of guano, ground bones, saltpetre, or rape-cake. This is Japan.

I cannot refrain from a smile when I remember how, on my passing through England, one of the chief leaders of agriculture in that country, pointing to his abundant stock of cattle, endeavoured with an assuming air to impress upon my mind the following axioms as the great secret of true wisdom: —' The more fodder, the more flesh; the more flesh, the more manure; the more manure, the more grain!' The Japanese peasant knows nothing of this chain of conclusions; he simply adheres to one indisputable axiom, *viz.*, '*without continuous manuring there can be no continuous production. A small portion of what I take from the soil is replaced by nature* (the atmosphere and the rain), *the remainder I must restore to the ground.*'

How this is done is a matter of indifference. That the produce of the land has first to pass through the human system before it can be returned to the soil, is, as far as manuring is concerned, simply a necessary evil, which always involves a certain loss. As to the intermediate stage of cattle-feeding, which we deem so requisite in our system, the Japanese farmer cannot at all see the necessity. He argues, in his way, that it must cost a great deal of unnecessary and expensive labour to have the produce of the field first consumed by cattle, so troublesome and expensive to breed, while it must involve more loss of matter than his own. How much more simple it must be to eat the corn yourself, and to produce your own manure!

Far be it from me, however, because of the widely differing results to which the development of agriculture has led in the two lands, to pass judgment upon our system of husbandry, and to exalt unduly that of the Japanese by attributing superior intelligence to that nation. Circumstances have brought about the results in question, and the following more especially have exercised a decided influence in the matter. The religious belief of the two great sects in Japan, the Sintoists and the Buddhists, forbids the consumption of flesh, as also of everything derived from animals (milk, butter, cheese), and this prohibition, of course, disposes of one of the principal objects for which cattle are bred. Even sheep, if kept for the wool alone, would be unremunerative, as our farmers begin to find out even in Germany.

The very limited area of homesteads in Japan also renders the maintaining of cattle superfluous. The smallness of the farms must not be attributed, however, to any excessive tendency to sub-division of landed property, but to the fact that the land belonged to the great princes or Daimios of the country, who bestowed it in fee upon the lower nobility. The latter, again, being precluded by the institutions of the country from farming their own estates, parcelled out the land, apparently from time immemorial, on perpetual leases, among the peasantry of the country. The size of these farms varies from two to five acres, the limitation having been most likely determined either by their natural position, or from the course of some brook or rivulet. Now, as this limited area is intersected moreover by drains and ditches, it will be readily seen that there is hardly a plot of ground to be found where beasts of burden might be profitably employed.

Now, with us, matters are very different in these respects. We have a notion that we could not possibly exist in health and vigour without a considerable consumption of animal flesh, although we have the fact constantly before our eyes that our labourers, who undeniably require as much strength as any other class of society, are, for the most part, involuntary Buddhists. Our farms are always sufficiently large to preclude the notion of working them by hand, even though we leave out of consideration the important circumstance that the price of labour is rather too high, in proportion to the value of the produce, to admit of such a system of farming. But that the culture of the soil is all over the world in direct ratio to the division of the land, is a well-established fact, of which the reality and significance are made most clearly apparent to the traveller who passes from the north of Germany to Japan *viâ* England.

The only manure-producer, therefore, in Japan, is man; and we need not wonder that the greatest care should be bestowed in that country upon the collection, preparation, and application of his excrements. Now, as the entire course of procedure of the Japanese contains much that is highly instructive for us, I consider it my duty to give as detailed a description of it as possible, even at the risk of offending the delicate feelings of the reader.

The Japanese does not construct his privy as we do in Germany—in some remote corner of the yard, with half-open rear, giving free admission to wind and rain; but he makes it an essential part of the interior of his dwelling. As he ignores altogether the notion of a 'seat,' the cabinet—which, as a general rule, is very clean, neat, and in many cases well prepared, or painted and varnished—has a simple hole in the form of an oblong square running across and opposite to the entrance-door, and serving to convey the excrements into the lower space. Squatting over this hole, with legs astride, the Japanese satisfies the call of nature with the greatest cleanliness. I never saw a dirty cabinet in Japan, even in the dwelling of the poorest peasant. It appears to me that there is something very practical in this form of construction of a closet. We in Germany construct privies over our dung-holes and behind our barns for the use of our farm-servants and labourers, and provide them with seats with round holes. With even only one aperture, they are too often found, after a few days' use, more like pigsties than closets for the use of man, and this simply because our labourers have a decided, perhaps natural, predilection for squatting. The construction of the Japanese privies shows how easy it would be to satisfy this predilection.

To receive the excrements, the Japanese places below the square hole a bucket or tub, of a size corresponding to it, with projecting ears, through which a pole can be passed to carry the vessel. In many instances, a large earthen pot, with handles, is used, for the manufacture of which Japanese clay supplies an excellent material. In rare instances in the towns, I found a layer of chopped straw or chaff at the bottom of the vessel, and occasionally also interspersed among the excrements—a course which, if I mistake not, has of late been recommended also in Germany. When full, the vessel is taken out and emptied into one of the larger dung-vessels which are placed either in the yard or field. They are large casks or enormous stoneware jars, in capacity of from 8 to 12 cubic feet, let into the ground nearly to the brim. It is in these vessels that the manure is prepared for the field. The excrements are diluted with water, no other addition of any kind being made to them, and stirred until the entire mass is worked into a most intimately intermixed fine pap. In rainy weather the vessel is covered with a portable roof to shield it from the rain; in dry weather it is removed to admit the action of sun and wind. The solid ingredients of the pap gradually subside, and fermentation sets in; the water evaporates.

By this time the vessel in the privy is again ready

for emptying. A fresh quantity of water is added, the whole mass is again stirred and most intimately mixed together—in short, treated exactly like the first process; and this is repeated till the cask is full, when the mass is left, according to the state of the weather, for two or three weeks longer, or until required for use; *but under no circumstance is the manure ever employed in the fresh state.*

This entire course of proceeding clearly shows that the Japanese are no believers in the nitrogen theory, but care only for the solid ingredients of the dung. They leave the ammonia exposed to decomposition by the action of the sun and volatilization by the wind, but take the greater care to prevent the solid ingredients from being wasted or swept away by rain, &c.

As the peasant, however, pays his rent to his landlord not in cash, but in a certain stipulated percentage of the produce of his fields, he argues quite logically that the supply of manure from his privy must necessarily be insufficient to prevent the gradual exhaustion of his soil, notwithstanding its marvellous richness, and despite the additional supply of manuring matter derived from the water of the brook or canal which irrigates his fields. He places, therefore, wherever his field is bordered by public roads, footpaths, &c., casks or pots buried in the ground almost to the rim, with a request to the travelling public to use them.

To show how universally the economical value of manure is felt and appreciated in all classes of society in Japan from the highest to the lowest, I need simply state the fact that, in all my wanderings through the country, even in the most remote valleys, and in the homesteads and cottages of the very poorest of the peasantry, I never could discover, even in the most secret and secluded corners, the least trace of human excrements. How very different with us in Germany, where it may be seen lying about in every direction, even close to privies!

I need not mention that the manure thus left by travellers is treated exactly in the same way as the family manure.

But the excrements of the peasant contain also some other matter—not derived from the soil of his fields, and which may be said to represent an additional importation of manure. The river, brooks, and canals, and the numerous little bays, abound in fish, which the religion of the Japanese permits him to eat—a permission of which he most largely avails himself. Fishes, crabs, lobsters, and snails are eaten in quantities, and these ultimately afford a most valuable item of contribution to the privy, and consequently to the fertilizing field manure.

The Japanese farmer also prepares compost. As he keeps no cattle to convert his straw, &c., into manure, he is obliged to incorporate this part of his produce with the soil without 'animalization.' The method pursued to effect this object consists simply in the concentration of the materials. Chaff, chopped straw, horse-dung, excrements gathered in the highways, tops and leaves of turnips, peelings of yams and sweet-potatoes, and all the offal of the farm, are carefully mixed with a little mould, shovelled up in small pyramidal heaps, moistened, and covered with a straw thatch. I also often noticed in this compost, heaps of shells of mussels and snails with which most of the brooks and rivulets abound, and which in all parts close to the seashore may be obtained in considerable quantities. The compost heaps are occasionally moistened, and turned with the shovel, and thus the process of decomposition proceeds rapidly, under the powerful action of the sun. I have also often seen the shorter process of reduction by fire resorted to, when there was plenty of straw, or when the manure was required for use before it could have been prepared by the fermentation process. The half-charred mass was in such cases, so far as my own observation enabled me to judge, strewed directly on the seed sown in the ground.

I consider the treatment of this compost another proof that the Japanese farmer does not care for the azotized matters, and that he strives to destroy all organic substances in his manure before making use of it. *His great object in all these is to turn his manure to account as promptly as possible.* To attain this object, besides preparing his manures in the way described, he has recourse also to the following means :—

1. He applies his manures, and particularly his chief manure, human excreta, invariably as much as possible in the liquid form.

2. *He knows no other mode of manuring than that of top-dressing.* When wishing to sow, he furrows the land as more fully described further on, and strews the seed by hand, covering it with a thin and even layer of compost, over which very dilute privy manure is poured.

The manure is diluted in the buckets in which it is carried from the preparing tub or pots to the seed-furrow, this being the only way to ensure uniform intermixture of the materials. This manure being fully fermentated, it could without danger be brought into immediate contact with the seed, and thus materially assist the first radiation.

It may be that this Japanese system of manuring cannot as yet be introduced into Europe in its entirety. But with such excellent results to show for their proceedings, we might surely take a few lessons from these old practical men, and employ them with such modifications as our social relations require. At all events, we might adopt in principle the following :—

1. The greatest possible concentration of

manures, which must necessarily lead also to a material reduction of cost. When I stated that the Japanese does not trouble himself about the azotized matters in his manures, and that his land is notwithstanding in a most flourishing state of culture, I do not mean to urge it as a proof that it might not even be better to endeavour to fix the nitrogen too. If a more practical system can be devised—of which, however, I have my doubts—combining the advantages of both, of course so much the better! But till something better is discovered, we might surely adopt that which experience has proved to be good.

2. Top-dressing, which is, of course, necessarily connected with cultivation in drills or furrows.

3. Liquid manuring: not to the extravagant extent, however, in which it was sought to be carried out in England, but in accordance with the present condition of German agriculture.

4. Manuring with every crop. The Japanese never cultivates a crop without manuring it, but he gives each crop or seed exactly as much manure, and no more, that is required for its full development. He does not care about enriching the soil for future crops. What he demands is simply a full crop in return for each sowing. How often do we hear our farmers talk about this manure being preferable to that manure on account of its fertilizing action being 'more

lasting'; yet with all our wise provision for the future, how far are we now behind the Japanese, who seem to calculate always upon the next harvest only! As they manure for each fresh crop—and the term 'fallow' in our acceptation is entirely unknown to them—they are forced to distribute their yearly production of manure equally over the entire area of their land, which can be accomplished only by sowing in drills or furrows, and by top-dressing.

The contrast between this rational system, and the profuse application of our long straw manure over the entire field, is truly glaring.

I may also add here that manure in Japanese towns is never artificially converted into guano or poudrette, but is sent every night and morning in its natural form into the country around, to return after a time in the shape of beans or turnips. Thousands of boats may be seen early every morning laden with high heaps of buckets full of the precious stuff, which are carried from the canals in the cities to the country. These boats come and go with the regularity of the post; it must be admitted, however, that it is a species of martyrdom to be the conductor of a mail-boat of this kind. In the evening, long lines of coolies are seen on the road, who, having carried the produce of the country to the town in the morning, return each with two buckets of manure, not in a solid, concentrated form, but fresh from the privies. Caravans of packhorses, which often have brought manufactured articles (silk, oil, lacquered goods, &c.) a distance of 200 to 300 miles from the interior to the capital, are also returned with baskets or buckets of manure. In such cases, however, care is taken to select solid excrement.

Thus in Japanese agriculture we have before us the representation of a perfect circulation of the forces of nature ; no link in the chain is ever lost ; one is always interlaced with the other.

I cannot here refrain from drawing a comparison in this respect between the Japanese and our system. In our large farms we sell a portion of the productive power of our soil in the shape of corn, turnips, or potatoes ; but the carts conveying the products to the town or factory bring back no compensation. One of the links of the chain is thus lost. Another portion of our produce is devoted to the feeding of large herds of cattle, of which a considerable amount is sent forth in the form of fat cattle, milk, butter, or wool ; this also is never returned, and a second link of the chain is lost. Another small portion we and our labourers consume. *This* last portion at least might be turned to proper account, if we only saved and used it as carefully and wisely as the Japanese do. Will any one venture to assert that the privy manure of our farms is of the least real importance ?

I verily believe that, under the present system, the privy manure of an estate of a thousand acres would be barely sufficient for half an acre of ground. There remains, then, from our present agricultural system, out of the entire productive power withdrawn by the crops from the soil, only that portion which is returned by our cattle—an insignificant part, indeed, of the whole, if we take into consideration its bulk, and reflect in what a concentrated form we have disposed of the rest of that power in the shape of grain, milk, or wool.

But, it may be remarked, it is strange our system of keeping large stocks of cattle is conducive to a high state of cultivation and abundant produce. I admit the fact, only let us ascertain first its true significance. It is, above all, necessary to settle about the true acceptation of the term 'culture.' For if by 'culture' is meant the capability of the soil to give permanently high produce, by way of *real interest on the capital of the soil*, I must altogether deny that our farms, with perhaps a few exceptions, can properly be considered as in a satisfactory state of culture. But we have, by excellent tillage and a peculiar method of manuring, put them in a condition to make the entire productive power of the soil available, and thus to give full crops for the time being. It is not, however, the interest that we obtain in such crops, but we draw upon the capital of the soil itself. The more largely our system enables us to draw upon this capital, the sooner will it come to an end. The term 'culture' applied to such a proceeding is a misnomer.

The peculiar method of manuring alluded to consists merely in our endeavouring to feed the soil of our fields with the largest possible supply of azotized matter. Now, ammonia and the other azotized compounds may doubtless be looked upon as excellent agents to rouse the hidden and slumbering forces of the soil, but, after all, they may be regarded somewhat in the light of a banker who kindly exchanges the pound we wish to spend for thirteen shillings; and then we can spend the change fast enough. This accounts for the large party amongst us, thriftless and careless, who love and cherish the obliging banker.

This is the great difference between European and Japanese culture. The former is simply a delusion that will be detected sooner or later. Japanese cultivation, on the other hand, is actual and genuine; the produce of the land represents truly the interest of the capital of the soil's productive power. As the Japanese is aware of the necessity of living upon that interest, his chief care is devoted to preserving the capital intact. He withdraws from his soil with one hand only when he can compensate with the other; and never takes more than he can return. He never tries to force the production by large supplies of azotized matters.

The fields in Japan do not therefore, as a general rule, present that luxuriant aspect which gratifies the sight occasionally at home. We see no impenetrable forests of straw from six to eight feet high, nor turnips weighing 100 lbs. (with 99 lbs. of water in them). There is nothing extravagant and superabundant in the sight of Japanese crops; but what distinguishes them most favorably as compared to ours, is their certainty and uniformity for thousands of years. The real produce of land can be calculated only by the average crops of a series of years.

If additional proof were needed to show that the state of cultivation is very superior, and that the land yields abundant produce, I would point to the fact that the Japanese Empire, which covers an area similar to Great Britain and Ireland, but of which one-half at the most (because of the hilly nature of the country) can be looked upon as fit for tillage, not only contains a greater population than those countries, but maintains them without any supply of food from other parts. Whilst Great Britain is compelled to import corn to the extent of many millions annually, Japan, since the opening of its ports, actually *exports* no inconsiderable quantities of food.

Tillage of the Soil.

Deep cultivation of the soil has come to be

recognized by our modern writers as inseparable from agriculture, and the principle of the system is at least fully admitted on all hands, the only objection occasionally raised against it being that it requires a large supply of manure. But the most enthusiastic admirer of the system in Europe can hardly conceive how universally, and in what high perfection, it is carried on in Japan.

The Japanese husbandman treats his field as a plastic material, to be turned to account in any way or form he pleases, just as a tailor may fashion, out of a piece of cloth, cloaks, coats, trowsers, or vests, and occasionally makes the one out of the other. To-day we find a plot of ground covered with a wheat crop; eight days hence the wheat is reaped, and half the field is transformed into a swamp thoroughly saturated with water, in which the farmer, sinking knee-deep, is busy planting rice; whilst the other half is a broad and dry plot, raised two or two-and-a-half feet above the rice-swamp, and ready to receive cotton, or sweet-potatoes, or buck-wheat, or anything else the farmer chooses to grow. It often happens also that a square plot in the centre is turned into a dry bed, surrounded by a broad rice-swamp; and as the water must cover the surface of the latter only slightly, it is evident the levelling must have been effected with great care, and with the use of instruments.

This entire work is done by the farmer and his small family in very little time—a proof of the great depth of the loose arable soil, even after a harvest ; and that the farmer could venture it without troubling himself about the next crop, is a sign of the boundless wealth of the soil in mineral constituents. It is only when great depth of the loose arable soil is combined with a plentiful store of mineral constituents, that deep tillage of the ground should be resorted to.

The description here given is not a mere fiction or creation of the imagination, but a faithful statement of facts which I have witnessed hundreds of times. Considering that rice requires at least from 1 to $1\frac{1}{2}$ feet of a cultivated soil, and adding to this half the height of the raised bed, *viz.*, 1 to $1\frac{1}{4}$ feet, this gives a cultivated depth of arable soil of from 2 to 3 feet. This system of working the land at pleasure, either as a raised dry plot or as a swamp, is indeed at present in Japan simply a proof of the existence of deep tillage ; but it is clearly evident that at one time it must also have been the means of effecting it. If we always wait till we collect a sufficient excess of manure (at the best but a very relative term) before proceeding to deepen the arable crust of our land, we may predict with certainty that the system will but very rarely make any progress with us. We cannot learn to swim without going into the water.

The introduction and improvement of the system of deep tillage has been powerfully assisted in Japan by the practice, pursued from time immemorial, of growing all crops in drills. With the advantage of this method we also have long been familiar. Among the favorable features presented by the cultivation of root-crops, our agricultural books always place in a prominent position the fact that it enables the farmer to deepen the arable soil of his land. All our gardeners, at least, have adopted it long ago.

I was not fully aware of the true importance of growing crops in drills until I saw it carried out to the fullest extent in Japan. We in Europe are as yet far from having adopted this plan as an essential part of our system of husbandry; we look upon the question still in a very one-sided way—only in reference to the particular crop which we wish to grow. But the Japanese farmer has raised it to the rank of a system, by which he has fully relieved himself of the slightest necessity of regarding, as we are compelled to do, the rotation of crops. By its means he has practically become master of his land. He has not only succeeded in growing crops at one and the same time which formerly followed each other in rotation, but has carried to the highest degree of perfection the principle of mixed cultivation, which begins now to find favour with our European farmers also : he has, in this respect, put an end to our confused and haphazard way of mixing crops on the same field, having, by the method of drill-planting, introduced order and regularity into the system. The following description of the Japanese system may serve by way of illustration.

We have a Japanese field before us, in the middle of October, with nothing but buck-wheat upon it. The buck-wheat is planted in rows 24 to 26 inches apart ; the intervening, now vacant, space had been sown in spring with small white turnip-radishes which have already been gathered. These intervening vacant spaces are now tilled to the greatest depth attainable by the implement. A portion of the fresh earth is raked with the hoe from the middle up to the buck-wheat plants, which are now in full flower : a furrow is thus formed in the middle, in which rape or the grey winter pea, is sown, the seed being manured in the manner already described ; and seed and manure are then covered with a layer of earth. By the time the rape or the pea has grown one to two inches high, the buck-wheat is ripe for cutting. This done, a few days after the rows it occupied are dug-up, cleared, and sown with wheat or winter turnips. Thus crop follows crop the whole year through. The nature of the preceding crop is a matter of indifference, the selection of the succeeding one being determined by the store of manure, the season, and the requirements of the farm. If there is a deficiency of manure, the intervening rows are allowed to lie fallow, until a sufficient quantity has been collected for them.

This system, as a whole, has also this great advantage, that the manure may be used at all times, and need never lie idle as a dead capital bearing no interest; and moreover, perhaps, the most important point of all is, that a direct ratio is thereby secured between the power of the soil, as shown in the crops, and the stock of manure on hand—a ratio not disturbed here by artificial means or by any *tour de force*. Expressed in other words, the income and expenditure of the soil are always kept evenly balanced.

I have witnessed this system carried out to the fullest attainable degree in the vicinity of large towns, such as Yeddo, also in particularly fertile valleys, and on fields bordering on the great highways. Here crop succeeded crop, manure followed manure. Here the plot of ground produced much more than could be consumed on it, but the great city and the privies on the highroad returned a supply of manure to balance the export of produce.

I have, however, also visited farms situated on hilly parts at great distances from the highroad, and only recently reclaimed and cultivated. (But the Japanese farmer, as a general rule, prefers the valleys to the hilly ground, the supply of manure here being more restricted and difficult, and any addition to it from towns or by travellers being almost altogether out of the question.) Here I found occasionally only one crop on the ground; yet the rows were so wide asunder that another crop could have found ample space between them.

With this system it is at least possible to till properly and repeatedly the intervening spaces intended to receive the next crop; besides, the constant supply by raking, of fresh earth to the present crop, places a larger store of soil at its disposal than could be done otherwise. In this manner, only half the field (corresponding to the limited supply of manure) is actually cultivated; but the system of planting the crop in drills wide apart always returns a much more abundant yield than could possibly be obtained if half the field as a continuous plot were completely sown, the other half being allowed to lie fallow. As the home production of manure, or its importation from other parts, increases, the farmer proceeds to fill part also of the vacant rows, which thus leaves only the third or fourth part of the field fallow, until ultimately every row is planted.

How wide the difference between this system and ours! When we break up and till a plot of ground, we begin by extracting from it three or four harvests, without bestowing a particle of manure, but apply it only when we find the soil exhausted. The Japanese husbandman never breaks up a plot of land unless he possesses a small stock of manure that he can invest in the ground; and even then he cultivates the new plot to the extent only that his supply of manure will permit. This rational proceeding shows the deepest insight into the nature of the system of agriculture to be pursued with a reasonable prospect of securing a constant succession of remunerative crops. No other illustration can so clearly show the difference between our European way of viewing the matter, and the Japanese.

We in Europe cut down the trees on a forest plot, sell the timber, grub up, plough, and till the ground, and then proceed to dispose of the productive power of the new soil in three cereal crops obtained without the least supply of manure; or we may possibly assist in accelerating the exhaustion of the ground by a small dose of guano. All that this course of proceeding is calculated to accomplish is, that we have now to distribute the manure, hitherto produced on our state, over a somewhat more extended surface than formerly. But when the Japanese husbandman breaks up a plot of ground, he finds a virgin soil, the productive power of which he has no intention of impairing. He therefore, from the very outset, takes care to establish a proper balance between crop and manure, expenditure and income, maintaining thus intact the productive power of the ground, which is all that can reasonably be attempted by any rational husbandman.

PART II.

THE STAPLE PRODUCTS OF INDIA.

CHAPTER I.

RICE.

Rice, the principal food of one-third of the human race, chiefly cultivated in Asia.—The varieties of rice.—Mode of cultivation in Salsette and the Concan.—Ploughing, sowing, and transplanting.—An improved culture resulting in an improved staple.—The superior quality of Carolina rice attributable to superior cultivation.—The endeavours of the Court of Directors to introduce this variety into India. —Mr. Kittredge's instructions.—History of Carolina rice. —Mode of cultivating it in South Carolina.—The importance of Carolina rice as a subsoil-feeder.—Experiments made by the Indian Government to acclimatize this variety.—The general advantages of its cultivation.—The improvement of indigenous rice equally important.—Careful cultivation the means of accomplishing it.—Rice soils, and the means of improving them.—Limeing.—Cultivation in furrows.—Deep-ploughing.—Selection of seeds.—Manuring.

RICE, the principal product of the fields of India, is one of the most extensively cultivated of all our grain crops, and forms the principal food of more than a third of the human race. It is the seed of Oryza sativa; the plant belonging, as do most of our other edible grains, to the species of grasses.

Its cultivation, though chiefly carried on in Eastern and Southern Asia, is far from being confined to that Continent, but extends to Egypt, the southern countries of Europe, some parts of

Western Africa, and America. The principal countries, however, in which this great staple food is grown, are India, China, Japan, Ceylon, Madagascar, Eastern Africa, Italy, South Carolina, and Central America.

The varieties of this plant which have been originated by different climates and different modes of cultivation, are more numerous than those of any other grain crop; for while in the Bombay Presidency alone we count nearly fifty varieties, Bengal can show several hundreds. The plant is undoubtedly a native of India, for Alexander von Humboldt mentions that a wild variety of it was found growing in some of the valleys of the Himalaya Mountains.

Rice, in common with most of our field and garden products, owes its superiority of seed and straw over the wild variety to the careful cultivation it has received for centuries, and it has formed the principal food of the natives of India from time immemorial.

The chief variety of this plant flourishes best in low marshes, or in a soil flooded, during the greater part of its growth, either by heavy rains or the inundations of rivers. Any one visiting Salsette or the Concan during August or September, will see, as far as the range of vision extends, countless fields covered with the luxuriant green of young rice-plants, growing in a soil which, by the continuous and heavy rains of our monsoons, is for the most part inundated.

The general mode of rice-cultivation in the vicinity of Bombay is as follows :—Before the approach of the rains, the remaining stubble of the previous crop is burnt, as also leaves, grass, and other vegetable products of the like description, the ashes of which serve as manure for the coming crop. The ploughing of the land is generally deferred till the first burst of the monsoon has moistened the earth; the plough used is a most primitive instrument, doubtless familiar to most of my readers ; the soil is stirred up by this to the depth of three or four inches ; and as this procedure of ploughing (or, more properly speaking, of scraping) the earth takes place very often when the fields are inundated, the soil is left in an irregular, uneven state, which is anything but advantageous for the coming crop.

In the meantime, paddy, as the rice in husk is called, is sown thickly in nurseries, and, when the plants have attained a height of four or five inches, they are transplanted out into the fields in small bunches of three or four. One hundred pounds of paddy are generally used up as seed for one acre of land, and the yield is on the average seven to eight fold—rarely exceeding, in fact, 900 lbs. per acre. The crop takes from four-and-a-half to five months to ripen.

A careful cultivation of the rice-plant for consecutive centuries, has been the means of developing an insignificant grass into one of the most important of our food-grains; but the plant is far from having reached the limit of improvement, for it will be shown that a still more careful cultivation will produce a still superior food-grain.

India is, no doubt, the native habitat of rice, but its cultivation has gradually spread to other countries —to Egypt, Madagascar, the south of Europe, and America. In this last-mentioned country its culture has been improved to an extent that raises it above all other descriptions grown elsewhere; and while the best Patna rice realizes in the London market 13s. to 16s. per cwt., American or, as it is more commonly called, Carolina rice is quoted from 35s. to 37s. per cwt.

Such difference in price—indicating, as it does, the superior quality and nutritive power of Carolina rice—did not fail to attract the attention of the Indian Government at an early period. When, therefore, in 1845, the Directors of the East India Company sent Captain Bayles to America, to procure American cotton-seed, gins, and overseers, for the purpose of ascertaining the practicability of raising cotton by the American method in India, they gave him especial instructions to initiate himself thoroughly into the American system of rice-culture.

The Carolina rice-plant is essentially the same

as that cultivated in India, but European energy has subjected it to such a careful cultivation in the rich soil of young America, that the result is the production of a grain which excels in its nutritive and other qualities the best Patna rice, as much as the latter may be said to excel the wild variety. The grain of Carolina rice is larger, whiter, better flavored, and more nutritious on account of the greater percentage of gluten present. The Jury of the Industrial Exhibition in London, in 1851, pronounced it as "magnificent in size, colour, and clearness," and awarded it a prize-medal.

Various attempts have been made by the different Governments to introduce this variety into India. Seed was ordered out from America; but, instead of a suitable centre for its cultivation and gradual acclimatization being selected, it was distributed all over the country, and the experiments were entrusted to officials whose ignorance of agriculture in general, could only be equalled by their ignorance of rice-culture in particular.

The results of such unsystematic proceedings were naturally not very encouraging; the failures were attributed to floods, excessive rains or drought, birds, insects—everything, in short, seemed to have conspired against the successful introduction of this new variety into India; but, I am afraid, the non-success was due more to the carelessness and indifference with which the experiments were conducted.

It was Mr. Kittredge, I believe, who five or six years ago furnished the Government of India with particulars as to the mode of rice-cultivation pursued in America, but they appear to have been entirely ignored, for they do not seem to have been adopted in any of the experiments instituted since. Individuals were left very much to their own resources and notions, and Carolina rice was consequently sown on high land and on low land, was sown broadcast and was transplanted from nurseries—in fact, was cultivated indiscriminately, and in every possible way but the right way.

The superiority of Carolina rice is, as I have said, due to the peculiar mode of cultivation to which the plant has become accustomed for nearly two centuries ; and if we intend to successfully introduce this important plant into India, and preserve its valuable qualities, we must observe as closely as possible the American method of cultivation.

But, before detailing this method, it will interest most of my readers to know how rice came to be introduced into South Carolina; the particulars are related in Ramsay's "History of South Carolina" as follows :—

" Landgrave Thomas Smith, who was Governor of South Carolina in 1693, had been at Madagascar before he settled in America, and, while there, paid some attention to the cultivation of rice, and observed the peculiarities of soil and climate under which it came to perfection.

" Having some ground attached to his garden at East Bay, Charleston, he was persuaded that both soil and climate were well adapted for the cultivation of rice. Communication between Charleston and Madagascar being then very difficult, the opportunities of procuring the seed were very rare; however, just about that time, a vessel from Madagascar, being in distress, came to anchor near Sullivan's Island, and the master, having known Mr. Smith while at Madagascar, inquired after him. In the course of an interview which took place afterwards, the Governor expressed the wish to procure some seed-rice to plant in his garden. The ship's cook had fortunately a small bag of rice fit for the purpose on board, and this was presented to Mr. Smith, who sowed it in a small spot in Longitude lane."

From this small beginning did one of the great staple commodities of South Carolina take its rise, and soon became the chief support of the colony and its great source of opulence, the total rice-crop in 1850 having amounted to nearly 100,000 tons.

It is cultivated in South Carolina in the following manner:—Low-lying or marshy land is selected, and the soil thrown up by a hoe in furrows or trenches twelve inches apart and eight to twelve inches deep. The paddy, or rice in husk, is sown at the bottom of these trenches, a little water being kept in them to assist germination. When the plants are a few inches high, the water is allowed to run off, the weeds are eliminated, and the rice-plants thinned where they stand too thick, any vacant spots being filled with such spare plants. Water is then turned on again, and is kept in the trenches to the depth of six or seven inches, or, when strong winds are blowing, even within an inch or so of the top, as that tends to keep the stem steady. When the plant begins to ripen, the water is allowed to run off altogether.

The whole process, it must be acknowledged, is very simple, and offers no great difficulties ; and provided the land is well drained and the subsoil sound, there is nothing that should hinder the acclimatization of this variety. It will well repay any land-owner to undertake the cultivation of this superior grain.

The importance of its introduction into India cannot be over-estimated, and it justly deserves the high consideration of Government, for it will confer a lasting benefit on the masses whose existence depends upon the products of the soil.

It has been mentioned that the superior qualities of the grain, and its proportionately high price, were the causes that attracted the attention of the Government of India to Carolina rice ; but there is another and extremely weighty reason why it should command the earnest consideration of every educated farmer and land-owner, whom we must expect to take the lead in initiating its growth.

The rice-plant of India is a surface-feeder ; its roots are lateral, and rarely penetrate further than three or four inches into the ground; while the Carolina rice-plant, on the contrary, extends a straight, vigorous root, six to eight inches long, through the surface into the subsoil, whence it obtains the greater portion of its mineral food.

Now, that the surface-soil of most Indian fields is bordering on a state of exhaustion, is a fact that cannot be contested; but under this surface-soil there are still immeasurable riches buried, there is still an enormous quantity of mineral plant-food available, if only the roots of our rice-plant could reach it. The American variety, therefore—feeding chiefly, as it does, in the subsoil—will be the means of availing ourselves of the riches stored up in the subsoil of India's fields, and, following in the wake of its introduction, we shall begin a new era of productiveness.

For this very reason, Carolina rice, as a subsoil feeder, will sometimes fail in a soil which has yielded fair crops of country paddy; for, unless the subsoil is healthy, and has been reached by the tillage, the Carolina variety will perish for want of proper food.

Mr. Knight, editor of the *Agricultural Gazette of India*, says in a note on this subject—"We have abundant proof that this rice will produce as luxuriant crops in India as in Carolina itself, with a subsoil in healthy condition; and when we remember that it commands nearly three times the price of the Indian **staple, and** that the yield per acre is infinitely greater, the importance of the effort to introduce it into India will, it is believed, be more generally understood."

It has been mentioned that the early attempts to introduce this variety of rice into India did not offer great encouragement to Government, but I am glad to observe that the attempts have not been entirely abandoned, and that fresh seed for further experiments has been sent out from time to time by Her Majesty's Secretary of State for India. The last consignment of nearly 200 barrels arrived here in March 1873; but no portion of it has, to my knowledge, been reserved for distribution in this Presidency, and I was sorry to learn that the Bombay Government had concluded that it would be useless to proceed with the experiments on account of the discouraging reports received.

This conclusion is greatly to be regretted; for, considering that the unsuccessful experiments were not only conducted in a palpably unsystematic and careless manner, but that the seed was bad, the season unfavorable, and the plant subjected to a mode of cultivation totally different to what it was accustomed to, no satisfactory results could have been reasonably expected, but, on the contrary, there was every reason to anticipate failure.

Most of the attempts made in Khandeish, including those conducted under the superintendence of

Mr. Fretwell, are all reported to have failed from the effects of the late floods. In fact, a perusal of the several reports on this subject, submitted to the Bombay Government, would induce one to imagine that the very elements had formed a league against the successful introduction of this new variety. But the fact is, as I have stated before, that the experiments were entrusted to persons who, while possessing scanty knowledge of the subject, further contributed towards the failures by a most careless and indifferent procedure, and then attributed them to natural defects. We can therefore scarcely blame the Bombay Government in deciding to discontinue the experiments, seeing that that decision was formed on the basis of unsatisfactory reports. But, considering the importance of the subject, it is to be earnestly hoped that the laudable attempts to acclimatize the American rice will be resumed when occasion offers, and be then entrusted to more competent and careful men.

The other local Governments are in the meantime prosecuting their experiments, and success is slowly crowning their labours; but, so long as the American method of cultivation is not followed as far as is feasible in the Indian climate, the results will, even in experienced hands, be always doubtful and untrustworthy.

The reports received from the Central Provinces are generally satisfactory, and some trials made near Jubbulpore showed an outturn of 12½ fold, while the yield from indigenous seed in adjacent fields was only 6 to 7 fold; and this result was attained with seed of which scarcely 50 per cent. germinated. The Chief Commissioner, in a summary of the results, considers that the plant in these trials shewed itself to possess all the advantages which are generally ascribed to Carolina rice.

The experiments made in the North-West Provinces seem to have suffered greatly by excessive rains, and the Board of Revenue, in their report, make due allowance for the circumstance. Some trials, however, especially at Saharunpore and Cawnpore, have been so signally successful, that a report of a detailed description of the method of cultivation adopted has been demanded.

But the most successful attempts to acclimatize this plant seem to have been made in the Madras Presidency, most of the experiments proving decidedly satisfactory. Some trial cultivations in Tellicherry have been very favorably noticed. The yield from a good soil was 160 fold, and the natives were said to have been much impressed with the superior qualities of the rice and straw, and were anxious to cultivate the plant.

In the Kistna district, a Carolina rice-crop, grown alongside one of the best native paddy, and under precisely similar circumstances, yielded one-and-a-half times as much as the latter; and one important point is noticed, showing the estimation in which the American paddy is held, namely, that it realizes now double the price of the native variety. It has further been proved by experiments that, if occasional irrigation is available after the crop has been reaped, a second crop may be obtained from the same roots, the yield of which, although not so large as the first, is still very considerable.

The results of all these trials have established beyond doubt the fact that the introduction of Carolina paddy into India is perfectly feasible, and that common care and some discretion are the only requisites to success.

The advantages which its cultivation offers have been summed up as follows:—

(1) It is a four months' crop.
(2) It requires less water than the native paddy.
(3) For the same area, 24 measures of seed will go as far as 32 measures of native seed.
(4) Each seed that germinates is capable of producing from 10 to 17 plants without any particular care—a productive power not possessed by native paddy to any appreciable extent.
(5) The ears are incomparably longer than those of native paddy grown under the most favorable circumstances.
(6) The largeness of its yield.
(7) Its superiority as food grain.

(8) The larger amount of more succulent and palatable straw than that of ordinary paddy.

All these advantages render the introduction of this variety into India highly **desirable**; but it is still more desirable that we should improve the indigenous rice by more careful cultivation.

It would be superfluous to give here any instructions about the description of soil best suited for rice-culture: the native cultivator knows that from experience; and as rice grows in almost any soil, he will very seldom make any serious mistake in his selection.

The first step necessary for improving all marshy, stiff, and clayey rice-lands is to "lime" them. About 20 candies of chunam, of the kind generally used for building purposes, will be found enough for heavy clay soils, while 12 to 14 candies will suffice for loamy or sandy soils. But care should be taken not to "lime" any lands already containing an abundance of calcareous matter, for a serious falling-off of the outturn, for a couple of years at least, would be the result of "overlimeing" the land. The chunam should be applied shortly after the removal of the crops, or at least three months before a new crop is grown. All "limed" lands will be grateful for any vegetable refuse, leaves, grass, &c., which should be ploughed-in with the lime, and *not burnt*, as is now usually done.

Wherever the flow of water can be regulated or irrigation is available, rice should never be sown broadcast, but always in furrows, following as closely as possible the American method of cultivation. The ground should be ploughed deep, preferable by the hoe, and the seed sown in the bottom of the furrows, four or five grains a foot apart, mixed with bone-dust, or, if not available, cow-dung.

Great care should be taken in the selection of the seed; not a single one should be sown that is not of more than average size and fully developed. Seed from different districts and soils should be preferred to self-grown, as plants are known to degenerate by being cultivated continually in the same soil. From soil thus treated and seed thus selected, we have every reason to expect most satisfactory results.

To maintain the fertility of the soil, the land should be manured each year with as much village refuse as is obtainable, the proper quantity of which can be easily ascertained by a few years' experiments. To commence with, eight or ten cart-loads per acre would suffice on average lands. In addition to this yearly supply of manure, heavy clay soils should receive another dose of lime, of about five to six candies, every fourth year; while for light soils an application of three to four candies every eighth year would be sufficient.

A still higher yield than can be expected by the use of any other manure, can be obtained, especially on poor soils, by giving the land a top-dressing of bone-dust or superphosphate of lime in quantities of about four to five cwts. per acre. A more liberal treatment of the soil will not only result in larger yields, but will improve the grain in quality ; and the gluten, the most nourishing portion of it, will increase in the same proportion as the nourishment of the plant increases in the soil.

CHAPTER II.

WHEAT.

Indian wheat in the European markets.—The exports from Bombay.—The high quality of wheat and the increasing demand.—The successful cultivation of wheat demanding a thorough knowledge of the Principles of Rational Agriculture.—Exhaustion of the soil rendering wheat-plants liable to be attacked by disease and parasites.—Deficiencies in soils on which wheat has been grown for any length of time.—Available silica in its relation to wheat.—How to increase available silica in wheat-soils.—Rotation of crops.—The agricultural advantages of India in connection with irrigation.—The defects of wheat-soils determinable by studying the mineral elements contained in wheat.—Nitrogen and wheat.—Mineral constituents necessary for the development of a long, well-filled ear.—The composition of wheat-ash.—Salt a fertilizer for wheat.—Composition of wheat-straw.—The relation between seed and straw, and the mineral constituents relatively required.—The manuring of wheat-soils to be adapted to the wants of the plant.—The first step of profitable farming in India is the accumulation of the raw material, *i.e.*, manure, for good harvests.—The deepening of the soil.—An acre twelve inches deep is worth more than four acres six inches deep.—General instructions for sowing, ploughing, and manuring.—The Cultivation of Wheat in the Central Provinces by A. C. Elliot.

Not less important than rice, although not so largely consumed by the native of India, WHEAT claims next our attention as another staple product of India.

Indian wheat is beginning to be greatly demanded in the European markets, and there is every probability of the exports of this food-stuff increasing steadily, as they have during the past few years. The exports from Bombay alone have increased in four years from 26,000 to 688,000 cwts., the relative yearly shipments having been as follows:—

	Cwts.
1872	26,000
1873	274,000
1874	741,000
1875	688,000

It is said that the Indian wheat is coming more and more into request, especially in England, and that there is every reason to believe that it will soon rank equal to Californian and second only to Australian wheat. Its cultivation in India is keeping pace with the increasing demand, but we fear that, under the native mode of cultivation, the Indian wheat—as indeed all other grains—will in course of years degenerate and lose its present good repute.

There is perhaps no crop the cultivation of which demands greater observation of all the Laws and Principles of Rational Agriculture, than wheat. A most exhaustive and highly interesting account of wheat cultivation is given by Dr. Lewis C. Beck in a report on the "Bread-stuffs of the United States of America." *There is no crop—we gather

---

* The remarks that follow on the cultivation of Wheat are for the most part quotations from this Report.

from this report—the skilful and successful cultivation of which on the same soil, from generation to generation, requires more art than is demanded to produce good wheat. To grow this grain on fresh land, adapted to the peculiar habits and wants of the plant, is an easy task; but such fields, except in rare instances, fail sooner or later to produce sound, healthy plants that are little liable to attacks from the malady called "rust," and that give lengthened ears or "heads" well filled with plump seeds.

The writer of the report, having long resided in the best wheat-growing district of America, had devoted years of study and observation to all the influences of soil, climate, and constitutional peculiarities which affect this bread-bearing plant, and we have consequently every reason to accept him as an authority on the cultivation of wheat. It seems that wheat is far more liable to smut, rust, and shrink in some soils than in others. This appears to be particularly the case where wheat has been long cultivated. As the alkalis and other fertilizing elements become exhausted in the soil, the crops of wheat not only become smaller on an average, but the plants become impaired in constitutional vigour, and are more liable to diseases and attacks from parasites and destructive insects. Defects in soil and improper nutrition lead to these disastrous results.

Soils that have been under wheat cultivation for long periods are generally defective in the following particulars:—They lack soluble silica, or flint in an available form, with which to produce hard, glassy stems that are little subject to "rust." Cultivated soils never contain soluble flint in great abundance, and, after being tilled some years, the quantity becomes still less. It is not very difficult to accurately learn the amount of silica which rain-water, as it falls on the earth, will dissolve out of 1,000 grains of soil in the course of eight or ten days. Hot water will dissolve more than cold water; and water charged with carbonic acid, more than pure hot water.

What elements of crops rain-water, at summer heat, will render available to the plant out of ten or twenty pounds of soil, in the course of three months, is a point in agricultural science which should be made the subject of numerous and careful experiments. In this way, the capabilities of different soils, and their adaptation to different crops, may be tested in connection with practical experiments in field-culture on the same kind of earth. Few wheat-growers are aware how much available silica an acre of good wheat demands to prevent the plants having coarse, soft, and spongy stems, which are anything but an indication of healthy organization.

In the *Journal of the Royal Agricultural Society,*

vol. 7, there is an exhaustive "**Report on the** Analyses of the Ashes of Plants, **by Thomas** Way, Professor of Chemistry at the Royal Agricultural College, Cirencester," which gives the result of sixty-two analyses of the **ash of wheat,** from as many samples of that grain, **mostly** grown on different soils and under different circumstances. The report gives the quantity of wheat **per acre,** the weight of straw cut near the **ground,** and also that of the chaff. These researches show that from 93 to 150 lbs. of soluble silica are required to form an acre of wheat ; and it would appear from investigations that three-fourths of this silica is demanded by nature during the sixty days preceding the maturing of the crop.

This is the period when the stem acquires solidity and strength, and most of its incombustible earthy matter, the quantity of which varies from three to fifteen per cent. of the weight of the straw. Professor Johnston and Sir Humphrey Davy adduce instances when more than fifteen per cent. of ash was found, **while Professor** Way **states** cases where less than three **per cent. was** obtained. The mean of forty samples **was** four-and-a-half per cent. Dr. Sprengel gives three-and-a-half as the mean of his analyses, while M. Baussingault found **an** average of seven per cent. As silica is truly **the** *bone* of all the grass species, as cane, corn, oat, rye, rice, millet, &c., imparting strength to them, the proportion of this mineral varies as much in wheat-straw as bone does in very lean and very fat swine or cattle.

A young growing animal, whether a child or a colt, that is kept on food that lacks *bone-earth* (phosphate of lime), will have soft cartilaginous bones. Just the same as nature cannot substitute iron or any other mineral in the animal system, out of which to form hard, strong bones, so no other mineral in the soil can perform the peculiar function assigned to silica in the vital economy of cereal plants. To protect the living germs in the seeds of wheat, corn, oat, rye, barley, &c., the cuticle or bran of these seeds contains considerable flint. The same is true of chaff.

The question, then, naturally arises, how is the farmer to increase the quantity of available silica in his soil? This is a question of the highest practical importance. There are three principal ways in which the object named may be attained.

First, by keeping less land under the plough. Land in pasture, if well managed, will regain its fertility, and in the process accumulate soluble silica in the surface-soil. In this way, more wheat and surer crops may be made by cultivating a field in wheat two years than four or six. If the field in the meantime be devoted to wool-growing, butter or cheese-making, or to stock-raising, particular care should be observed to make extensive crops of grass or clover grow on the land, and have all the manure, solid and liquid, applied to its surface. There are many countries in England yielding an average of thirty-two bushels of wheat per acre for ten crops in succession, whereas but few districts in India yield half that quantity while possessing greater agricultural capabilities than Great Britain.

Another way to increase soluble silica in the soil is to grow such crops, in rotation with wheat, as will best prevent the loss of available silica. This remark is intended to apply more particularly to districts growing cotton, tobacco, and opium, as these plants require no considerable amount of silica, while the soil is improved by the tilling which is necessary for them.

Indian-corn, well managed, will extract more silica from the soil than any other plant. As not an ounce of this mineral is needed in the constitutional economy of man or beast, it can all be composted in the stalks, blades, and cobs of, or in the dung and urine derived from, Indian-corn, and be finally incorporated in the stems of wheat-plants.

Indian-corn and wheat culture, if skilfully and scientifically conducted, go admirably well together. Of the two, perhaps the Indian-corn will yield a better-paying crop. But when what is called 'high farming' in England is introduced into India, the crops both of wheat and Indian-corn grown here will demonstrate our poor appreciation of the vast superiority of this climate for the economical feeding and clothing of the human family, over that of the greater part of Europe.

In Europe only one crop of wheat can be raised in twelve months ; but in India, where irrigation is available, wheat sown in December is ready for cutting by the middle of May. A good crop of hay may then be reaped in July, followed by a crop of peas which could be harvested in October, after which the ground may be prepared for wheat, or a rotation of wheat and cotton might be adopted.

Sufficient justice has never been done to the vast agricultural resources of India. While the mean temperature of England is so low that Indian-corn will not ripen, in India a crop of wheat may be grown in the winter, and nearly two crops of Indian corn successively in the summer and autumn, before it is time to sow wheat again.

But there is much of Indian soil that is not rich in the elements of bread. Nothing but the careful study of these elements, and of the natural laws governing them, can remedy defects in wheat-culture anywhere, but especially of course on very poor land.

All alkaline minerals, such as potash, soda, lime, ammonia, and magnesia, hasten the solution of the several insoluble compounds of silica in the soil. This fact should be remembered by every farmer.

Having secured the production of a bright, hard, glassy stem, the next desideratum is to develop a long, well-filled ear. Towards this end, available ammonia or nitrogen, phosphorus, potash, and magnesia are indispensable. Ammonia (spirits of hartshorn) is necessary to the formation of the combustible part of the seed, while the other ingredients mentioned are required to assist in the formation of the incombustible part. In 100 parts of wheat-ash there are the following substances, viz.—

Silica	2·28
Phosphoric Acid	45·73
Sulphuric Acid	0·32
Lime	2·06
Magnesia	10·94
Peroxide of Iron	2·04
Potash	32·24
Soda	4·06
Chloride of Sodium	0·27
Total	99·94

The quantity of ash in wheat varies from $1\frac{1}{4}$ to $2\frac{1}{2}$ per cent., the average being about 1·69. The amount of phosphoric acid in any given quantity of wheat-ash varies from 40 to 50 per cent. Seeds having a thick cuticle or bran, and little gluten, contain a smaller percentage of phosphoric acid, and more silica. About one-third of the ash is potash; in nearly all cases, magnesia varies from 9 to 14 per cent., lime from $1\frac{1}{2}$ to 6 per cent. Peroxide of iron is seldom as abundant as in the ash above given, and the same holds good of soda. Chloride of sodium is common salt, and exists in a small quantity. Salt is beginning to be much used as a fertilizer on wheat-lands in Western New York, as it tends indirectly to increase the crop.

The following may be accepted as about the average composition of the ash of wheat-straw. It is "Specimen No. 40" in the tables of Professor Way, and I reproduce *verbatim* all that is said upon the subject. (Soil sandy; subsoil, stone and clay; geological formation, silurian; drained; eight years in tillage; crop after carrots, 20 tons per acre; tilled, December 1845; heavy crop; mown, August 12th; carried, August 20th; estimated yield, 42 bushels per acre; straw long, grain good, weight 62 lbs. to the bushel.) Length of straw 42 inches.

Relation of Grain, Straw, and Chaff.

	Actual Quantities.	Percentage.
Grain	1,633 lbs.	45.13
Straw	1,732 „	47.89
Chaff	250 „	6.96
Total	3,615 lbs.	

Specific Gravity of Grain	1.396
Weight of Grain per acre	2,604 lbs.
„ Straw „	2,775$\frac{3}{15}$
„ Chaff „	401$\frac{1}{4}$

Mineral matter in an Acre.

Wheat	44$\frac{1}{2}$ lbs.
Straw	113
Chaff	47$\frac{1}{4}$
Total	204$\frac{7}{10}$

Analysis of the Ash of the Grain.

	Percentage.	Removed from an Acre. lbs.	ozs.
Silica	5·63	2	8
Phosphoric Acid	43.98	19	8
Sulphuric Acid	0·21	0	1⅛
Lime	1·80	0	12 4/10
Magnesia	11·69	5	3 3/10
Peroxide of Iron	0·29	0	2
Potash	34·51	15	5 4/10
Soda	1·87	0	13 3/10
Total	99·98	44	6 6/10

Analysis of Straw, with its proportion of Chaff.

	Percentage.	Removed per Acre. lbs.	ozs.
Silica	69·36	111	1 7/10
Phosphoric Acid	5·24	8	6 7/10
Sulphuric Acid	4·45	7	2 3/10
Lime	6·96	11	2 3/10
Magnesia	1·45	2	5
Peroxide of Iron	0·29	1	2
Potash	11·79	18	14
Soda	none	none.	
Chloride of Sodium	,,	,,	
Total	99·54	160	1 1/10

If we subtract the 111 lbs. of silica from the 160 lbs. of minerals in the straw and chaff, the difference between the residue and those in wheat is not great. As the stems and leaves of wheat-plants grow before their seeds, if all the phosphoric acid, potash, and lime available in the soil is consumed before the organization of the seeds begins, from what source is nature to draw her supply of these ingredients to produce a good crop ? Could the farmer reverse the order of nature by growing seeds first and straw afterwards, then of course he would harvest more wheat and less straw. But roots, stems, and leaves grow before nature begins to form the seeds; and every one should know that the atoms in the soil which are consumed in organizing the bodies of cultivated plants, are in the main identical in kind with those required to form their seeds. The proportions, however, differ very considerably. Thus, while 100 parts of the ash of wheat contain an average of 45 parts of phosphoric acid, 100 parts of the ash of wheat-straw contain an average of only 5 parts. The difference is as 9 to 1. In magnesia, the disparity is only a little less striking.

In what are called the organic elements of wheat (the combustible part), there are seven times more nitrogen in 100 lbs. than in a like weight of straw. Hence, if the farmer converts straw into manure or compost, with the view of ultimately transforming it into wheat, it will take 7 lbs. of straw to yield nitrogen enough to form 1 lb. of wheat.

Few are aware of the annual loss in labour and money by the feeding of plants on food not strictly adapted to the peculiar wants of nature in organizing the same. True, most farmers depend on the natural fertility of the soil to nourish their crops, with perhaps the aid of a small quantity of stable and barn manure, distributed only partially. As the natural resources of the land begin to fail, the supply must be drawn from other quarters than an exhausted field, otherwise its cultivator will receive a poor return for his labour.

In Great Britain, where the necessity for liberal harvests and artificial fertilization is far greater than in this country, the yield of wheat is said to be governed in a great degree by the amount of ammonia available as plant-food. This opinion is founded, not on theory at all, but altogether on the teachings of experience. But in England, limeing and manuring are so much matters of constant practice, that few soils are in such an impoverished state as many are in India. With land as naked and sterile as most of India's soil, English farmers could hardly pay their tithes and poor rates, besides other taxes, rent, and the cost of producing their annual crops.

The first step towards making farming permanently profitable in India is to accumulate, in a cheap and skilful manner, the raw material for good harvests in the soil. Over a territory so extensive as the Indian Empire, it would be extremely difficult to lay down any rule that would be even approximately applicable.

There are, however, many beds of marl, gypsum, *kunkur*, saline and vegetable deposits available for the improvement of farm-lands in British India. In addition to these, there are extraneous sources —the ocean with its fish, its shells, its sea-weeds, and its fertilizing salts, which will yield an incalculable amount of animal and vegetable food. In the subsoil and the atmosphere also, every agriculturist has resources, but which are not appreciated at all.

As a general rule, the soil must be deepened before it can be permanently improved. The cultivation of an acre 12 inches deep will be more profitable than four acres 6 inches in depth. Thus, admit that a soil 6 inches deep will produce 14 bushels of wheat, of which 12 bushels will pay all expenses, leaving 2 bushels as profit. Four acres of this land will yield a net income of only 8 bushels. Now double the crop and the depth of the soil: making the former 28 instead of 14 bushels per acre, and the latter 12 instead of 6 inches deep. Fifteen bushels instead of twelve will now pay all annual expenses, and leave a net profit, not of *two*, but of *thirteen* bushels per acre. When small crops pay expenses, large ones will make a fortune; provided the farmer knows how to enrich his land in the most economical way. Paying too dear for the improvement of land is equal to losing money at any other sort of business.

The operator should first acquire all the knowledge within his reach, derived from those who have experienced and practised what he proposes to accomplish himself. Twenty or even fifty rupees, invested in some good agricultural books, may save him thousands in the end, and at the same time double his profits in two years.

A system of tillage and rotation that pays well in a certain locality, on one quality of soil, or in a particular climate, may be found ill-adapted to other localities, different soils and latitudes. Hence, as observed before, no specific rule can be laid down that will meet the peculiar exigencies of a farming country so extensive as the whole of the Indian Empire. For some soils have borne good crops of wheat for centuries, and the produce still remains undiminished, while other soils have declined in fertility so greatly as to cause their abandonment altogether.

Many agriculturists grow peas, beans, turnips, beetroot, and carrots very extensively, as well as clover, Indian-corn, oats, and barley. Peas and beans, both pulse and stems, when well cured, are excellent food for sheep, and on good land are easily grown. They also tend to prepare the soil well for wheat.

All the manure derived from sheep should be husbanded with extreme care by the farmer wishing to enrich his land. On a deep, rich, arable soil, if highly cultivated, a large number of sheep may be kept; for their manure enables the land to produce extensive crops of wheat at small expense. Of all business men, farmers should be the closest calculators of *profit* and *loss*.

Great care should be observed in sowing good and

clean seed on clean land. Previous to putting the seed in the ground (drilling is preferable to sowing broadcast), wheat should be soaked not longer than five or six hours in strong brine, after which a peck or more of recently slaked lime should be added to each bushel, and shovelled over well, in order that the lime may cover each seed. The seed is then ready for sowing. Most good farmers roll the earth after seeding; some before. As a general rule, friable soils need not be ploughed long before the intended crop begins to grow.

Among other fertilizers, wood-ashes, salt, bones, lime, guano, and poudrette have been used in wheat-culture with decided advantage. In Great Britain, manure derived from the consumption of turnips and other root-crops by sheep and neat cattle, is much used in preparing land for wheat. Sheep clover, peas, and Indian-corn rotate well to ensure the economical production of this staple. Manure is usually applied to the crop preceding wheat. *Wheat should always be sown in drills.*

It may be interesting to some of my readers to see here the mean result of several organic analyses of wheat made by M. Baussingault. Wheat, dried at 230° *in vacuo*, was found to contain—

Carbon	46·1
Oxygen	23·4
Hydrogen	5·8
Nitrogen	2·3
Ash	2·4
Total	100·0

Charcoal may be regarded as a fair representative of carbon, and water as the representative of both oxygen and hydrogen. It will be seen by the above figures that over 95 per cent. of wheat is constituted of elements which greatly abound in nature in an available condition, and which nature herself restores by her own processes; and the same is true of all other plants. It is doubtless owing to this circumstance that a comparatively small quantity of mineral fertilizers are able to produce crops five, ten, and even *fifty* times greater than their own weight.

THE CULTIVATION OF WHEAT IN THE CENTRAL PROVINCES.—By A. C. ELLIOT.

The distinctive crop of the district is wheat, and it is the only one respecting the kinds and growth of which I think it worth while to enter into any particulars.

There are five kinds of wheat grown—the *Jelalia*, *Kutia*, *Soharia*, *Bungusia*, and *Pissi*. The *Jelalia* is the finest: it is a large white wheat, and a sample of it, taken from the village of Rehsulpore, obtained the first prize at the Lucknow Exhibition of December 1864, as the "largest and finest" wheat exhibited among a great number of competitors. *Kutia*, however, runs it very hard: it is a first-class red wheat, very little inferior to *Jelalia* in weight, and said to grow better than it in second-class soil. *Jelalia* ripens about ten days earlier than *Kutia*. *Soharia* is a white wheat brought from Bhopa, where it is called *Daoud-Khani*; it is small, but of fine quality, and it is not extensively sown. *Bungusia* is rare, and is only sown east of the Towa. *Pissi* is a very inferior wheat, and is chiefly grown east of the Towa. Its name is derived, on the *lucus a non* principle, from the fact that in the rains it grows so soft and pulpy that it cannot be ground for flour. No beardless wheat is grown here. When the plant is green, *Pissi* may be known by the yellow tinge of its ear, and the grains being a long way apart, but the other wheats are hard to recognize. The *Jelalia* ear, when ripe, has a deep red color, and the beard has a red tinge at the end before it is quite ripe, while the *Kutia* ear is quite white. *Bungusia* has a black beard. In Rajwara and Sohagpore *Pissi* is chiefly sown, either alone or mixed with *Kutia*; in Hoshungabad *Jelalia* and *Kutia* are sown in equal quantities; in Seonee and Hurda *Jelalia* is the most prevalent.

	Jelalia.	Kutia.	Soharia.	Pissi.	Gadurwara Wheat Kutia and Pissi.
	Rs. a.	Rs. a.	Rs. a.	Rs. a.	Rs. a.
Sohagpore......	10 0	10 0	9 8	8 0	....
Hoshungabad ..	13 0	12 8	11 0	10 12	....
Seonee	14 4	..	13 8	12 8	12 0
Hurda	16 0	..	13 8	..	12 8

Pissi fetches a much lower price than *Jelalia* or *Kutia*, ranging generally at Rs. 2 or Rs. 2-8 a *mand* below them in value. The table in the margin shows the price of each grain at the chief marts in the district on the 18th March 1865.

Seed and Produce.

The rate of sowing is as nearly as possible a maund to the acre, or two *pie* to the biswa. It varies slightly for the cultivator will sow less in a moist season than in a dry one, when he knows that many grains will not germinate; and more is sown in light, undulating, than in rich flat soil. But this rate, as a general average, is accepted by the people, and agrees with my experiments. The average number of grains of *Kutia* and *Jelalia* wheat to a rupee is 235, and at this rate 752,000 grains are sown in an acre, and 621 in four square yards. I made a great number of experiments on plots of this size in different parts of the district, and found that the average number of stools is 160, and of ears 339. Thus, of four grains sown, only one comes up, and throws out only two ears—an inability to tiller which seems to me the chief fault of our wheat. The average length of straw is only 2 feet to 2 feet 6 inches. The average produce is a point very keenly debated, but the best native judges are now inclined to put it at fivefold, which, after making allowance for the **loss by reaping**, gleaning, and treading-out, corresponds to a produce of sixfold—*i.e.*, six maunds, or eight and a half bushels, to the acre. This is the general average I have assumed after much careful enquiry. The common cultivators talk of three and fourfold, but I know by experiment how miserably poor a field must be to produce only three fold. On the other hand, ten and twelvefold are not uncommon, and in six places where I cut a biswa in March 1865, I got from fourteen to seventeen-fold. One amusing case happened in a **village** Gurrolie, which I visited when the wheat was young; a cultivator expostulated against my average rent-rates, asserting that his field would only produce threefold. I offered to give him the price of every seer below fivefold if he would give me the same for every seer above, but he declined the bargain. I reaped his field for him. The produce was five *kucha mands* and twenty-one *vooroos*, or fifteen-fold; but then it must be remembered that the harvest of 1864 was a very exceptionally fine one.

Diseases of Wheat.

The chief disease to which wheat is subject is the *gherooa*, a mildew which first attacks the stalk and leaf, turning it yellow and speckled, so that it leaves a yellow stain on the clothes of any one passing through the field, and then affects the ear, shrivelling it up. Some of the grains are merely rudimentary, and blow away with the chaff in winnowing, and all have a wrinkled, withered look. I have heard it said that these grains have not lost vital power, and are as good for seed as any other grains; but the universal native impression is that they are worthless for seed. From the smallness of the grain the disease is called *jirrie*, the grains being almost as small as those of Jeera (cummin). The great and famous year when the wheat was entirely destroyed by this disease was 1831, and the country has had partial visitations of it since. High-lying thin fields appear to be safe from it; it attacks low situations and fields where the wheat has come up very thick. The native idea is that it is caused by the heat thrown back by clouds in the end of January, and they say it is born on the *Bussunt Punchmi;* if within ten days from that time there are no clouds, the wheat is safe. Another disease is the black smut, or *karie;* it attacks single ears, is not contagious, and is supposed to be a sign of richness in the soil, and never does extensive injury. Withering (*oomulfana*) can hardly be called a disease, as it arises solely from dryness. Every stool is generally seen surrounded by dead stalk and leaves, which it has thrown out, but has not been able to keep alive. Irrigation is the obvious remedy for this, but then the fear is generally felt that irrigation would bring on mildew.

Soils.

The soil that prevails is the black alluvial **loam** commonly known as "black cotton soil." It has all the well-known characteristics that distinguish this soil wherever it is met with—the uncommon fertility, the tendency to crack and sink into fissures and holes, which makes it very dangerous for riding, the great powers of absorption, the extreme muddiness and softness in rainy weather, and the retentiveness of moisture. It is of varying depths, from 6 inches to 30 feet, and its average depth is probably about 10 feet; beneath it is found red gravelly clay, **or** sand. The general name for it all **over** the district is *mar*, or *murriar*, but in Rajwara it is usually called *rabur*. Elsewhere *rabur* is considered a more clayey variety of *mar*, quicker to dry, and apter to fissure, mostly found in low bottoms. It is a stronger soil than average *mar* if it gets water enough, but it dries so rapidly that, unless a shower of rain falls during the ploughing, it is as hard as a stone before **sowing** can be begun. The true *mar* should be perfectly flat and level, free from stone or sand, the water running off it by gently-sloping channels, without denuding the land. Where it is undulating, the action of water carries off the top-dressing of good soil, leaving the gravelly clay exposed; or else it cuts deep channels down to these substrata, and spreads their materials over the land. Hence the classification of every description of soil depends on the degree in which it departs from the standard, either undulation, stoniness, or sandiness. If it lies in a hollow, it is called *rabur*. If it undulates slightly, the soil loses its richness, becomes brown in colour, and contains small stones or *kunkur* pebbles; it is then *morin*, or *morund*, or *mouda*. If it undulates still more, and becomes fuller of gravel and pebbles, it is called *rankur*; if it becomes sandy instead of loamy, it is called *sehar* (I presume from the same root which we find in the great "Sahara"); but this is only the case along the banks of rivers, where the sand brought down from the hills has been deposited by floods. If it is a stony hillside, it is called *burrurie*, or *burdie*, or *byrie*, or in some parts *khurrurie* or *khyrie*. Thus flatness and richness go together, and pebbles and light soil are always found where the land undulates considerably, and lies in little hills separated by ravines. There are no great sandy plains or *oosur* tracts, such as are common in Upper India. Every part of the valley is culturable, except where a hill spur stands out into the plain, or a network of ravines leaves no surface for the plough to work upon. From this character of the soils it follows that the best kinds must be given up to rubbee crops, and khureef sown only in the lighter soils. From its richness, its depth, and its capacity for retaining moisture, the *mar* is probably unsurpassed by any soil in India as a producer of wheat; but in this so-called "cotton soil," cotton or any other khureef crop could not grow. When unlimited heat and moisture are supplied, it becomes so rank in its luxuriance that it is absolutely too rich to grow any useful crop; the plant grows up unhealthy, and is choked by the mass of weeds around it. These, in ordinary seasons, it is impossible to clear away, for if hand-hoeing is used, the labourers' feet sink in, and the hoe brings up the sown plant along with the weeds; or if the *kolka* is used, the bullocks' feet sink in. When a break in the rain occurs, and the land gets dry—or *butur*, as it is called—it can be weeded; but the breaks are rare, and in rich soil the weeds would extirpate the plant before the hoe got its chance. A good system of subsoil draining might do something to remedy this, but at present the result is that *mar* and *rabur* lands are devoted entirely to rubbee; the lighter lands produce the khureef crops. There is a debateable class of land, the *morin*, in which either class of crop can be sown, and there rotation can be followed; but for all practical purposes at present, black soil, level land, and land growing rubbee crops, are convertible terms, while undulating, light, and khureef lands convey one and the same idea. The soil round villages is called *khera*, a word which originally meant the raised mound on which a village is placed, and which is applied to mean both the village and the soil of the mound round the village. From its saltness it is good for tobacco, and maize (*mukla*) is also grown on it; but though it is enriched by animal refuse, it is not regularly manured, and has not the same value as the *gowhan* land of Hindustan.

Analysis of Soils.

I submitted three samples of black soil to Mr. D. Waldie, of the Barnagore Chemical Works, near Calcutta, for examination and analysis; and I now proceed to give the results, together with extracts from his report. The samples were taken from Puchlaora, a village in the Rajwara pergunnah; from Rehsulpore, the finest village in the Hoshungabad pergunnah; and from Chewul, a village in the Taptee valley, where the black soil is still almost virgin, and produces a crop of about twelvefold.

After describing the first process of grinding the earth in a mortar, Mr. Waldie goes on to say:—

"Each sample was subjected to a mechanical analysis, by thoroughly softening the soil with boiling water, and elutriating. This was done by subjecting the softened earth, placed in a tall deep glass, to a current of water through a pipe issuing from an orifice of about a sixteenth of an inch in diameter near the bottom of the glass (the column of water in the pipe being about fifteen inches high), till all the finer portions were washed off, the residue being coarse sand. The finer portions being allowed to settle, were again subjected to a gentle current of water, or rather a rapid dropping through the same tube till all the finest particles were washed off. The residue was fine sand. The finest particles settled were the clay. Each portion was dried at 212°, weighed, burnt, and weighed again, and the following were the results :—

No. I.—Black Soil from Puchlaora, Pergunnah Rajwara.

Loss by drying at 212°, 6·8 per cent. moisture.

	Incombustible Earth.	Matter expelled by Ignition.
Coarse Sand and Gravel	4·50	9·04
Fine Sand	18·92	1·68
Clay, or finest particles	68·10	6·76
	91·52	8·48
Loss by ignition	8·48	
Soil dried at 212°	100·	

No. II.—*Black Soil from Rehsulpore.*

Loss by drying at 212°, 5·7 per cent. moisture.

	Incombustible Earth.	Matter expelled by Ignition.
Coarse Sand and Gravel	10·32	0·44
Fine Sand	23·34	1·41
Clay, or finest particles	59·62	5·47
	92·68	7·32
Loss by burning	7·32	
Soil dried at 212°	100·	

No. III.—*Black Soil from Chewul.*

Loss by drying at 212°, 7 per cent. moisture.

	Incombustible Earth.	Matter expelled by Ignition.
Coarse Sand and Gravel	4·03	0·41
Fine Sand	28·14	3·41
Clay, or finest particles	55·57	8·44
	87·74	12·26
Loss by burning	12·26	
Soil dried at 212°	100·	

"The loss of ignition consisted principally of water, the proportion of organic matter being very small. Sample No. III. contained most organic matter; by an approximate trial, No. I. contained rather less than No. II., and No. III. about twice as much as No. II.

"After ignition, to destroy organic matter according to general practice, the soil was digested with moderately diluted muriatic or hydrochloric acid for an hour or two, then diluted, and the soluble portion filtered off the insoluble. In general, the insoluble portion of a soil treated in this way consists of silicious sand, or small particles of quartz mixed with some particles of other minerals in so small a proportion as to make an analysis quite unnecessary. In the present instance, however, the portion insoluble in the acid was evidently a mineral substance composed of silica combined with bases, and it was necessary to analyze it also. The following is the result [to Mr. Waldie's analysis I add, for the sake of comparison, an "Analysis of the Regur, or Black Soil of the Deckan," taken from *Ansted's Elementary Geology*, p. 343"]:—

Constituents of the Black Soil No. II. from Rehsulpore.

	Dissolved by Hydrochloric Acid.	Residue from Hydrochloric Acid.	TOTAL.	Ansted's Black Soil of the Deccan.
Alumina	5·120	9·750	14·870	2·030
Black Oxide of Iron	4·293	2·950	7·243	1·0
Lime	1·386	1·765	3·151	1·6
Magnesia	1·186	0·510	1·696	10·20
Potash	0·595	0·898	1·493	
Soda	0·115	0·167	0·282	
Carbonic Acid, and loss	1·580	......	1·580	
Sulphuric Acid	0·017	......	0·017	
Phosphoric Acid	0·070	......	0·070	
Silica	0·092	61·720	61·812	
	14·454	77·760	92·214	
Humic Acid, dissolved by Alkaline Carbonic 0·374			0·532	
Humus .... 0·158				
Water with a little organic matter			7·254	4·30
			100·	1·00

"It contained almost nothing soluble in water, gave no indication of nitrate or of ammonia, and only very faint indications of any nitrogenized or animal matters.

"The soil consists of trap-rock in process of disintegration, and the two columns of soluble and insoluble in acid shew the process of the decomposition of the rock. The very finest particles of clay obtained by elutriations, when digested with acid, leave a residue of dark-brown particles, differing from the coarser in being more mixed with and incrusted over by the silica separated from the dissolved basis. The largest particles, when washed clean and examined by a magnifier, shew the appearance of the original rock. The black color is due to the original rock. The color is somewhat browner than that of the sample of trap-rock sent with it, owing, no doubt, to the oxidation of some of the black oxide to red oxide. The appearance of extreme blackness in the soil, when it looks blacker than the rock, is fallacious, and is principally due to the presence of water. When powdered and dried, the soil looks browner than the rock, not blacker.

"I have omitted in my analysis of No. II. to notice the presence of chlorine, as the quantity was so minute that it could not be estimated. No doubt it exists as a trace of chloride of sodium, or common salt, which is found in almost all natural waters."

CHAPTER III.

SUGARCANE.

The antiquity of the cultivation of sugarcane in India.—Annual production.—Average outturn per acre.—Composition of sugarcane.—The varieties cultivated in India.—Their relative qualities.—China sugarcane.—Puttaputti producing the best Jaggery.—Otaheite and Bourbon sugarcane.—History of introduction into India.—Soils best suited for sugarcane.—Calcareous matter essential for the production **of superior** sugarcane.—Analysis of soils famed for the **production** of sugarcane.

Manures.—Rotten straw.—Mud from tank-bottoms.—Crushed bones.—Salt.—Preparation of the soil.—Ploughing and planting in the Rajahmundry district.—Watering, manuring, and ploughing in the Mysore and other districts.—Preparation of the fields in general.—The cutting of "sets."—Quantity of tops required per beegah, and average yield.—The planting of sugarcane.—Mr. Vaupell on the most successful mode of cultivating the Mauritius cane in Bombay.—After-culture.—Watering, weeding, and digging.—Draining.—Propping and wrapping the cane.—Harvesting.—Injuries to which the plant is liable.—Effects of different manures upon sugarcane.—Experiments made by the Superintendent of the Poona Botanical Gardens.

THE cultivation of sugarcane in India is of great antiquity, and seems to have been particularly pursued with great success during the Mogul dynasty. The whole annual production of sugarcane in India could not be less than a million tons, and there is every probability of a steady increase, especially if the extensive irrigational schemes in contemplation are carried out.

It is needless to remark of sugarcane, what has been noticed of Indian agriculture generally, that the description of produce, as also the different processes of manufacture, are of the rudest possible description, and a great annual loss is incurred by the clumsy and imperfect mode of extracting the juice.

Sugarcane is composed of water, woody fibre, and soluble matter, or sugar. In round numbers, it may be stated that the proportions are 72 per cent. of water, 10 per cent. of woody fibre, and 18 per cent. of sugar. The average outturn on a good soil is about 25 tons per acre, yielding from 15 to 16 cwts. of sugar.

A thousand grains of sugarcane, on being burnt, yielded $7\frac{1}{2}$ grains of ash, which, on analysis, furnished the following component parts :—

Silica	1·78
Phosphate of Lime	3·41
Alumina and Iron	0·17
Carbonate of Potash	1·46
Sulphate of Potash	0·15
Carbonate of Magnesia	0·43
Sulphate of Lime	0.06
	7·46

During the *regime* of the East India Company, inquiries were instituted relative to the cultivation of the sugarcane in Hindustan, and the information obtained was published in a large folio volume.

I have endeavoured in vain to procure a copy of this very valuable book, and am, therefore, obliged to reproduce the extracts quoted by Mr. Simmonds in his work on "The Commercial Products of the Vegetable Kingdom."

It appears that three kinds of sugarcane are cultivated in India :—

(1) The purple.
(2) The white.
(3) A variety of the white, requiring a large supply of water.

The epitome of the report affords the following information:—

(1)—The purple-colored cane yields a sweeter, richer juice, than the yellow or light-colored, but in less quantity, and is harder to press. Thrives on dry lands. Scarcely any other sort in Beerbhoom; plentiful in Radnagore ; some about Santipore, mixed with light-colored cane. Grows also near Calcutta—in some fields by itself, in others mixed with Pooree or light-colored cane. When sucked raw, is more dry and pithy in the mouth, but esteemed better sugar than the Pooree sort, and appears superior to all others.

(2)—The light-colored cane, yellow, inclining to white ; deeper yellow when ripe and on rich ground. It is the same sort as that growing in the West India Islands ; softer, more juicy than the Cadjoolee, but juice less rich, and produces sugar less strong ; it requires seven maunds of Pooree cane-juice to produce as much *goor* or inspissated juice as six maunds of the Cadjoolee. Much of this description is taken to the Calcutta markets and eaten raw.

(3)—The white variety, which grows in swampy lands, is light-colored, and grows very high. Its juice is more watery, **and yields a weaker sugar,** than the Cadjoolee. However, as a great portion of Bengal consists of low grounds, and as the upland canes are liable to suffer from drought, it may be advisable to encourage the cultivation of this sort, should the sugar manufactured from it be approved in itself without relation to the produce of other canes, in order to guard against the effect of dry seasons. Experience alone can determine the advisability of encouraging cultivation of this description of cane.

Besides the foregoing, several kinds of sugarcane are now known to the Indian planter, of which one, the China sugarcane, was considered by Dr. Roxburgh to be a **distinct** species, designated by him *saccharum sinenses*. It **was** introduced into India in 1796 by Earl Cornwallis, as being superior to the indigenous varieties. It is characterized by a hardness which effectually resists the process of crushing by the country mills ; but this quality is essentially desirable, inasmuch as it enables the cane to withstand the attack of white-ants, swine, and jackals, which are extremely destructive to the common cane.

Dr. Buchanan states that the following four kinds are known in Mysore, two of which are evidently the purple and white, generally known and mentioned already; but as it is not distinctly stated, I have retained the form in which he notes them :—

Restali, which produces the native sugar of Mysore, can be planted only in the last two weeks of March and the two first of April. It completes its growth in twelve months, and does not survive for a second crop. Its cultivation has been superseded by the other.

Puttaputti.—This was introduced from Arcot during the rule of Hyder Ali, and is the only one from which the natives can extract sugar; it also produces the best *Bella* or *Jaggery*. It can be planted at the same season as the *Restali*, as also at the end of July and beginning of August. It takes fourteen months to complete its growth; but the stools produce a second crop, like the ratoons of the West Indies, which ripen in twelve months.

Maracabo and *Cuttaycabo.*—These are very small, seldom exceeding half an inch in diameter; yet in some districts of Mysore, as about Colar, the last-named is the variety usually cultivated, because it requires less water than the larger varieties.

The best varieties are those introduced from the islands of Otaheite and Bourbon. India is indebted for their introduction to Captain Sleeman, who brought them hither from the Mauritius in 1827, and committed them to Dr. Wallich, under whose care they have flourished at the Botanical Garden, and have been the source whence the benefit has been generally diffused. Their superiority over those usually cultivated by the natives has been conclusively established. The largest of Hindustan canes, ripe and trimmed ready for the mill, never exceeded five pounds, while it is by no means uncommon for an Otaheite cane under similar circumstances to weigh seven pounds. The extra weight arises proportionally from greater secretion of superior sap. The sugar is more abundant, granulates more readily, and has less scum. Its other superior qualities are that it ripens earlier, and is less injured by protracted dry weather.

Of the history of the sugarcane, the following popular tradition circulates amongst the natives :— In very ancient times, a vessel from their country happened to leave one of the crew, who was afflicted with a grievous malady, on a desert island at a great distance in the Eastern Seas, and, on returning after a time by the same route, they stopped at the island for the purpose of ascertaining the fate of their comrade, when, to their great astonishment, he presented himself in the flesh, perfectly restored to health, and even more than usually hearty. On eagerly enquiring for the means that effected this, they were conducted to some sugarcane plants, on which, he informed them, he had solely subsisted since their departure. Induced by this remarkable circumstance, occurring under their own observation, every care and attention was bestowed, we may well suppose, on the conveyance of such an invaluable acquisition to their own land, where the soil and climate have since contributed to its prosperity.

Soil.—The soil best suiting sugarcane is aluminous rather than otherwise, tenacious without being heavy, readily allowing excessive moisture to drain away, yet not light. A gentleman, one Mr. Ballard, has endeavoured to make the point clear by describing the most favorable soils about Ghazipore as "*light clays,*" called there *mootearee* or *doansa*, according to the presence of more or less sand in their composition.—*(Trans. Agri-Hort. Soc.*, I., 121.)

Mr. Peddington seems to think that calcareous matter, and iron in the state of peroxide, are essential in a soil for the production of the superior sugarcane. There can be no doubt that calcareous matter is necessary, but experience is opposed to his opinion with regard to the peroxide.

The soils preferred at Radnagore is there

distinguished as of "two qualities," being a mixture of rich clay and sand, and which Mr. Touchet believed to be known in England as a light brick-mould. About Rungpore, Dinajpore, and other low-lying places, the beds, where the cane is to be planted, are raised four or five feet above the level of the adjacent land.

The experience of Dr. Roxburgh agrees with the preceding statements. He says—" The soil that suits the cane best in this climate is a rich vegetable earth which, on exposure to the air, readily crumbles down into very fine mould. It is also necessary for it to be of such a level as allows of its being watered from the river by simply damming it up (which almost the whole of the land adjoining to this river, the Godavery, admits of), and yet so high as to be easily drained during heavy rains. Such a soil, and in such a situation, having been well meliorated by various crops of leguminous plants, or fallowing, for two or three years, is slightly manured, or has had for some time cattle pent upon it. A favorite manure for the cane with the Hindu farmer is the rotten straw of green and black pessalo *(phaseolus mungo max)*."

Many concurring opinions might be added to the preceding, but it is only necessary to observe further that "the sugarcane requires a soil sufficiently elevated to be entirely free from inundation, but not so high as to be deprived of moisture, or as to encourage the production of white-ants (*termes*)."

As the sugarcane plant withdraws exceptionally large portions of plant-constituents from the soil, and may thus be considered an exhausting crop, it is seldom cultivated by the ryot more frequently than once in three or four years on the same land. During the intermediate period, such plants are grown as are found to improve the soil, of which, says Dr. Tennant, the Indian farmer is a competent judge. He finds the leguminous tribe best suited for the purpose. But such long intervals of repose after a cane crop would not be requisite if a better system of manuring were adopted.

Mr. J. Prinsep has recorded the following analysis of three soils distinguished for producing sugar. They were all a soft, fine-grained alluvium, without pebbles. No. 1 was from a village called Mothe, on the Sarfee, about ten miles north of the Ganges, at Buxar; and the others from the south bank of the Ganges, near the same place. There is a substratum of *kunkur* throughout that part of the country, and to some mixture of this earth with the surface-soil the fertility of the latter is ascribed:—

Hygrometric Moisture on drying at 212°	2·5	2·1	3·6
Carbonaceous and Vegetable Matter on calcination	1·8	2·1	4·0
Carbonate of Lime No. 3 effervesced	1·6	0·6	3·9
Alkaline Salt, soluble	1·0	1·1	0·8
Silex and Alumina	94·1	94·1	88·2
Total	100·0	100·0	100·0

The earths unfortunately were not separated. Mr. Prinsep says the two first were chiefly of sand, and the third somewhat argillaceous. The former required irrigation, but the other was sufficiently retentive of moisture to render it unnecessary.—(*Jour. Asiat. Soc.*, II., 435.)

Manures.—The sugarcane being one of the most valuable crops of the ryot, he always devotes to it a portion of the fertilizing matters he can command, though invariably on too small a scale.

In the Rajahmundry district, previous to planting, the soil is slightly manured, either by folding cattle upon it, when their refuse spreads and saturates the ground, or by a light covering of the rotten straw of the green and black pessallo, which is here a favorite fertilizer. In some parts of Mysore, mud from tank-bottoms is employed, and this practice is more generally adopted in other places. Thus the fields were divided by deep ditches in Dinajpore, the mud of which, being enriched by the remains of animals and decayed aquatic plants, forms an excellent manure for the sugarcane. The ryot spreads this over the surface before ploughing is commenced, which when completed, the soil is further fertilized by a dressing of oil-cake and ashes.

Crushed bones would unquestionably be of the greatest benefit to sugarcane crops. For not only would their animal matter serve as plant-food, but their phosphate of lime, being one of the chief saline constituents of the sugarcane, would contribute in no inconsiderable degree towards the general result.

Salt is another valuable manure for this crop. Dr. Nugent, in a report to the Agricultural Society of Antigua, observes that salt has been found a most valuable auxiliary in cultivating sugarcane. Many trials of it, he says, have been made during successive seasons, applied generally to the extent of about nine or ten bushels to the acre. It destroys grub and other insects, and imparts to the canes increased vigour and ability to resist drought.

A remarkable incident was mentioned by the intelligent traveller, M. de Humboldt, while speaking of the practice adopted in the missions of the Orinoes. He states that when a cocoanut plantation is made, a certain quantity of salt is thrown into the hole that receives the nut ; and that, of all plants cultivated by man, there are only the sugarcane, the plantain, the mammee, and the Avocada pear which endure irrigation either with fresh or salt-water.

In the West Indies, when the cane-plants are affected by what is called there the *blast*, which is a withering and drying-up of the plants, the unfailing remedy is to water them with an infusion of dung in salt-water.

Preparation of Soil.—In the Rajahmundry district, during the months of April and May, the ground is frequently ploughed, until brought into a very fine tilth. About the end of May or beginning of June, the rains usually commence, and the canes are then planted. If the rains do not set in so early, the land is flooded artificially, and when converted into a soft mud, whether by the rain or by flooding, the canes are planted.

In Mysore the ground is watered for three days, dried for a like period, then ploughed, which is repeated five times during the following eight days. The clods during this operation are broken into small pieces by an instrument called *col-kudali*. The field is then ploughed a sixth time. After fifteen days it is ploughed again—twice in the course of one or two days. After an interval of eight days it is ploughed the ninth time. Altogether these operations occupy about forty-four days. For planting, which is completed in six days, an implement called *yella-kudali* is employed.

In Dinajpore, " the field, from about the middle of October until about the 10th January, receives ten or twelve double ploughings, and, after, each is smoothed with the *moyi*. During the last three months of this time it is manured with cow-dung and mud from ponds and ditches. On this account, the land fit for sugarcane is generally divided into fields by wide ditches, into which much mud is washed by the rain, and is again thrown on the fields when the country dries, and leaves it enriched by innumerable aquatic vegetables and animals that have died as the water left them. When the ploughing has been completed, the field is manured with ashes and oil-cake."

About Malda, " the land is first ploughed in the month of Kartick, length and breadth-ways, and harrowed in like manner ; four or five days after, it is again ploughed and harrowed, as before, twice. In the month of Aghun the whole land is covered with fresh earth, again twice ploughed, and harrowed in different directions, so that the clods of earth brought be well-mixed together with the land. This preparation continues until the 20th or 25th of the month of Paus."

In the vicinity of Dacca during " Kartick or Aghun (October, November), the ryots begin to prepare their ground. They first dig a trench round their fields, and raise a mound of about three feet in height. If the ground to be cultivated is waste, about nine inches of the surface are taken off, and thrown without the enclosure. The ground is ploughed to the depth of nine inches more. The clods are broken and the earth made fine. In Magh or Faghun (January, February) the sugarcane is planted ; a month afterwards, earth is raised about the plants, which is repeated after a month. The crop is cut in Paus and Magh (December, January). If the ground be not waste, but cultivated, the surface is not taken off. After cutting the crop, it is not usual again to grow sugarcane on the same ground for eighteen months, on account of the indifferent produce afforded by a more early planting."

In the Zillah North Moradabad, the land is broken up at the end of June. When the rains cease, it is manured, and receives eight or ten ploughings, which clears it of weeds. In February it is again manured and ploughed four or five times, and just before the sets are planted, some dung—four cart-loads to each *cutcha* beegah of low land, and five to high land—are added. The land is well rolled after the four last ploughings, and again after the cuttings are set.

About Benares and the neighbouring districts Mr. Haines says that, owing to the hot winds which prevail "from March until the setting in of the annual rains in June or July, the lands remain fallow till that period. In the meantime, those fields that are selected for sugarcane are partially manured by throwing upon them all manner of rubbish they can collect, and by herding their buffaloes and cattle upon them at night, though most of the manure from the latter source is again collected and dried for fuel. When the annual rains have fairly set in, and the Assaree crops sown (in some instances I have seen an Assaree crop taken from the lands intended for sugarcane), they commence ploughing the cane-lands and continue to do so four or five times monthly (as they consider the greater number of times the fields are turned up at this period of the season, the better the crop of cane will be), till the end of October, continuing to throw on the little manure they can collect.

"Towards the end of October and in November, their ploughs are much engaged in sowing their winter (or *rubbee*) crops of wheat, barley, grain, &c.; and at this period they make arrangements with the shepherds, who have large flocks of sheep, to fold them upon the fields at night, for which they pay so much per beegah in grain. During the latter part of November and early in December, the fields are again ploughed well, and all grass, weeds, &c., removed with the hoe, then the surface of the field is made as smooth as possible by putting the *hengah* (a piece of wood eight or ten feet in length, five to six inches in breadth, and three or four inches in thickness, drawn by two pairs of bullocks, and the man standing upon the wood to give it weight) over several times for three or four days in succession. This makes the surface of the field very even and somewhat hard, which prevents the sun and dry west wind from abstracting the moisture, which is of great importance at this period of the season, for, should there be no rain, there would not be sufficient moisture at the time of planting the cane to cause vegetation.

"In this state the land remains till the time of planting the cane cuttings, which is generally the 1st to the 15th of February; but should there have been a fall of rain in the meantime, or excess of moisture appear, the field is again ploughed and the *hengah* put over as before. A day or two previous to planting the cane, the field is ploughed and the *hengah* put over lightly."—*(Trans. Agri- Hort. Soc.*, VI., 45.)

Sets.—When the canes are cut at harvest time, twelve or eighteen inches of their tops are usually taken off and stored, to be employed for sets. These tops have several joints, from each of which a shoot rises, but seldom more than one or two arrive at a proper growth.

When cut from the stem, the tops intended for plants are tied in bundles of forty to fifty each, and are carefully kept moist. In a few days they put forth new leaves, are cleared of the old ones, and separately dipped in a mixture of cow- dung, pressed mustard-seed, and water. A dry spot is then prepared, and **loose rich** mould, and a small quantity of pressed mustard-seed, strewn over it; the plants are then placed separately therein, strewed between with a small quantity of earth, and covered with leaves and grass to preserve them from excessive heat. Ten or twelve days after- wards they are transplanted into the fields.

In Burdwan, the tops are cut into pieces four

to six inches long, thus having not more than four knots in each. Two or three of these plant-tops are put together in the ground, a beegah requiring from 7,500 to 10,240 plants. In Rungpore and Dinajpore about 9,000 plants, each a foot long, are required for a beegah; while in Beerbhoom 3,000 plants are said to be requisite for a beegah, each cane-top being about fifteen inches long. In the neighbourhood of Calcutta from 3,000 to 8,000 plants are required for a beegah, according to quality of soil, worst soils needing most plants. In Mysore an acre contains 2,420 stools, and yields about 11,000 ripe canes. Near Rajahmundry about 400 cuttings are planted on a *cutcha* beegah (one-eighth of an acre). In the Zillah North Moradabad, 4,200 sets, each eight inches long, are inserted upon *cutcha* beegah of low land and 5,250 upon high land.

In the district of Gollagore, the ryots cut a ripe cane into several pieces, with two or three joints to each, and put them into a small bed composed of rich mould, dung, and mustard-seed expressed of oil. At Radnagore, when cutting time arrives, the cane-tops are taken off, and placed perpendicularly in a bed of mud for thirty or forty days, being covered with leaves or straw, after which they are stripped of any leaves, and cut into pieces, having not less than two nor more than four joints each. These sets are kept for ten or fifteen days in a bed prepared for them, whence they are taken out and planted in rows, two or three together, eighteen inches or two feet intervening between each stool.

Planting.—The time and mode of planting vary. In the Rajahmundry Circar, Dr. Roxburgh says that "during the months of April and May the land is repeatedly ploughed with the common Hindu plough, which soon brings the loose, rich soil"—speaking of the Delta of the Godavery—"into very excellent order. About the end of May and beginning of June, the rains generally set in in frequent heavy showers. Now is the time to plant the cane ; but should the rains hold back, the prepared field is watered or flooded from the river, and while perfectly wet, like soft mud, the cane is planted. The method is most simple. Laborers with baskets of the cuttings, of one or two joints each, arrange themselves along one side of the field. They walk side by side, in as straight a line as their eye and judgment enable them, dropping the sets at the distance of about eighteen inches asunder in rows, and about four feet from row to row. Other laborers follow, and, with the foot, press the set about two inches into the soft, mud-like soil, which, with a sweep or two with the sole of the foot, they most easily and readily cover."—*(Roxburgh on the Culture of Sugar.)*

About Malda, in the month of Magh (January, February), the land is twice ploughed, and harrowed repeatedly, length and breadth-ways ; after which it is furrowed, the furrows half a cubit apart, in which the plants are set at about four inches from each other, when the furrows are filled up with the earth forming their ridges, and, the plants being thus set, the land is harrowed twice in different directions, fifteen or twenty days afterwards the cane sprouts, when the weeds that appear with it are eliminated. Ten or twelve days after this, the weeds re-appear, when they are again grubbed up, and the earth at the roots of the canes being removed, all the plants that have grown will appear.

At Ghazipore the rains generally set in at the beginning of March, when planting commences. Near Calcutta this process is inaugurated in May and June, while in Dinajpore and Rungpore the planting-time is February. About Commercolly it is performed in January. The field is divided into beds six cubits broad, separated by intervening small trenches fourteen inches wide and eight deep. In every alternate trench are small wells, about two feet deep. The irrigating water flowing along the trenches fills these wells, and is taken thence by hand and applied to the canes.

Each bed has five rows of canes. The sets are planted in holes about six inches in diameter and three deep ; two sets, each with three joints, are laid horizontally in every hole, covered slightly with earth, and over this a little dung.

When the canes are planted in the spring, the trenches must be filled with water, and some poured into every hole. At the other season of planting the trenches are full, it being rainy weather; but even then the sets must be watered for the first month. Mr. Haines says that in Mirzapore and the neighbouring districts, " in planting the cane they commence a furrow round the field, in which they drop the cuttings. The second furrow is left empty; cuttings again in the third; so they continue dropping cuttings in every second furrow till the whole field is completed, finishing in the centre of the field. The field remains in this state till the second or third day, when for two or three days in succession it is made even and hard upon the surface with the *hengah* as before stated."—*(Trans. Agri-Hort. Soc.,* VI., 5.)

Mr. Vaupell, in describing the most successful mode of cultivating the Mauritius sugarcane in Bombay, says that " after the ground is levelled, with the small plough called *paur*, in the manner of the cultivators, pits of two feet in diameter and two feet in depth should be dug throughout the field at the distance of five feet apart, and filled with manure and soil to about three inches of the surface. Set in these pits your canes, cut in pieces about a foot and a half long, laying them down in a triangular form, thus $\wedge$. Keep as much of the eyes or shoots of the cane uppermost as you can, then cover them with manure and soil; beds should next be formed to retain water, having four pits in each bed, leaving passages for watering them. The cutting should be watered every third day during hot weather, and the field should always be kept in a moist state."—*(Trans. Agri-Hort. Soc.,* VIII., 43.)

Near Benares, the sets require, after planting, from four to six waterings until the rains commence, and as many hoeings to loosen the surface, which becomes caked after every watering. In Bengal the moister nature of the soil renders these operations generally unnecessary.

After Culture.—In Mysore, the surface of the earth, in the hollows of which the sets are planted, is stirred with a stick as soon as the shoots appear, and a little dung is added. The following month the daily watering is continued, and then the entire field is hoed, a cavity being made round each stool, and a little dung added. In the third month water is given every second day: at its close, if the canes are luxuriant, the ground is again dug; but if poorly, the watering is continued during the fourth month, before digging. At this time the earth is drawn up about the plant, so as to leave the hollows between the rows at right-angles with the trenches. No more water is supplied, but the trenches between the beds are kept full for three days. It is then cut off for a week, after which, if it rains, no further water is requisite; if not, water is admitted once a week during the following month. The digging is then repeated, and the earth levelled with the hand about the stools.

The stems of each stool are about a dozen in number, but are reduced to five or six by the weakliest being now removed. The healthy canes are bound with one of their own leaves, two or three together, to check spreading; and this is repeated as required by their increased growth. In the absence of rain, the trenches are filled with water once a fortnight.

Whenever the *Puttaputti* is kept for a second crop, the dry leaves cut off in the crop season are burnt upon the field, which is dug over, and the trenches filled with water; and during six weeks the plants are watered every sixth or eighth day (unless of course rain falls), and the digging is repeated three times, dung being added each time. The after-culture is the same as for the first crop.

In the Upper Provinces, Dr. Tennant says, if moderate showers fall after planting, nothing more is done until the young shoots have attained a height of two or three inches, when the soil in their immediate vicinity is loosened with a small weeding iron, something like a chisel; but should the season be dry, the field is occasionally watered, the weeding being also continued, and the soil from time to time loosened about the plants. In August, small trenches are cut through the field, with little intervening spaces for the purpose of draining off the water if the season be too wet. This is very requisite, for if the canes are at this period of growth supplied with too much moisture, the juice is rendered watery and valueless. If the season, on the contrary, happens to be dry, the same dikes serve to conduct the irrigating water through the field, and to carry off the surplus that does not soak into the earth in a few hours. Stagnant water the natives consider very injurious to the cane, and on the proper contrivance of the drains depends in a great measure the ultimate result.

Immediately after trenching, the canes are propped, which are now about three feet high, each set having produced from three to six canes. The lower leaves are first carefully wrapped round the plant, covering it completely in every part; a strong bamboo, eight or ten feet long, is then inserted firmly in the centre of each stool, and the canes tied to it. This secures them in an upright position, and facilitates the circulation of the air.

Hoeing cannot be repeated too often. This is demonstrated by the practice of the most successful cultivators. In the Zillah North Moradabad, in April, about six weeks after planting, the earth on each side of the cane-rows is loosened by a sharp-pointed hoe, something in the shape of a bricklayer's trowel. This is repeated six times before the field is laid out in beds and channels for irrigation.— There, likewise, if the season is unusually dry, the fields in the low ground are watered in May and June. This supposes the existence of either nullahs or old *pucka* wells, otherwise the canes are allowed to take their chance, for the cost of sinking a well up-country is from ten to twenty rupees— an expense too heavy for an individual cultivator, while none would join in the expense, as perpetual disagreements and quarrels for the water would be the consequence.

In the vicinity of Benares, as the canes advance in growth, the leaves are wrapped, as they begin to wither, round the lengthening stem, which is bound to the bamboo higher up. Should the weather be wet, the trenches are carefully kept open; but if dry, water is occasionally supplied. Hoeing is also performed every five or six weeks. Wrapping the leaves around the cane protects them from being cracked by the heat of the sun, and prevent their throwing out lateral branches. In January and February the cane is ready for cutting. Its average height is about nine feet, foliage included, and the cane itself from one to one-and-a-quarter inch in diameter.

Near Maduna, the hand-watering is facilitated by cutting a small trench down the centre of each bed.

The beds are there a cubit wide, with only four rows of canes planted in each.

It is deserving of notice that the eastern and north-eastern parts of Bengal are more subject to rain at all seasons of the year, but especially in the hot months, than the western; which accounts for the land being prepared and the plants set so much earlier in Rungpore than in Beerbhoom. This latter place has also a drier soil generally; which is another reason why such stress is laid in the report on the necessity of watering there. Land about Benares is also drier than Bengal, and requires more watering in consequence.

At Malda, ten or fifteen days after the earth is removed from round the roots, and the plants appear, the land is slightly manured, well cleared of weeds, and the removed earth again laid about the canes. Ten or fifteen days after, it is well weeded, and again twenty or twenty-five days after that. It is necessary to follow this mode of cultivation until the month of Joyst. The land is ploughed and manured between the rows of canes in the month of Assar; fifteen or twenty days after which, the canes are bound, two or three together, with the leaves, the earth about the stems well cleaned, and that which was ploughed up, laid about the roots of the canes, a little raised. In the month of Saubun, twenty or twenty-five days after the preceding operation, the canes are tied as before, and again ten or fifteen days afterwards; which done, nine or ten clumps are tied together.

In the Rajahmundry Circar, on the Delta of the Godavery, Dr. Roxburgh states that "nothing more is done after the cane is planted, if the weather be moderately showery, till the young shoots are some two or three inches high; the earth is then loosened for a few inches round them with the weeding iron. Should the season prove dry, the field is occasionally watered from the river, continuing to weed and to keep the ground loose round the stools. In August, two or three months from the time of planting, small trenches are cut through the field at short distances, and so contrived as to serve to drain off the water, should the season prove too wet for the canes, which is often the case, and would render their juices weak and unprofitable. The farmer, therefore, never fails to have his field plentifully and judiciously intersected with drains while the cane is small, and before the usual time for the violent rains. Immediately after the field is trenched, the canes are all propped up; this is an operation which seems peculiar to these parts."

In Dinajpore, in about a month after planting, "the young plants are two or three inches high; the earth is then raised from the cutting by means of a spade, and the dry leaves by which they are surrounded are removed. For a day or two they remain exposed to the air, and are then manured with ashes and oil-cake, and covered with earth. Weeds must be removed as they spring up; and when the plants are about a cubit high, the field must be ploughed. When they have grown a cubit higher, which is between the 13th June and the 14th July, they are tied together in bundles of three or four, by wrapping them round with their own leaves. This is done partly to prevent them being laid down by the wind, and partly to prevent them from being eaten by jackals. During the next month, three or four of these bunches are tied together; and about the end of September, when the canes grow rank, they are supported by bamboo stakes driven in the ground. They are cut between the middle of December and the end of March."

If the canes grow too vigorously, developing a superabundance of leaves, it is a good practice to remove the decayed ones, usually low down, that the stems may be fully exposed to the sun. In the West Indies this is called *trashing* the canes. It requires discretion; for in dry soils or seasons, or if the leaves are removed before quite dead, more injury than benefit will be occasioned.

Harvesting.—The seasons when the canes become ripe in various districts has already been noticed when treating on their cultivation. Supplementary thereto I may state that, in the Rajahmundry Circar, about the mouth of the Godavery, Dr. Roxburgh adds that "in January and February the canes begin to be ready to cut, which is about nine months from the time of planting. As this operation is the same as in other sugar countries, I need not describe it. Their height, when standing on the field, will be from eight to ten feet (foliage included), and the naked cane from an inch to an inch-and-a-quarter in diameter."

In Malda the canes are cut in January and February. In North Moradabad, upon the low lands the canes are ripe in October, and upon the high lands a month later. The fitness of the cane for cutting may be ascertained by making an incision across the cane, and observing the internal grain. If soft and moist, like a turnip, it is not yet ripe; but if the face of the cut is dry and white particles appear, it is fit for harvesting.—(*Fitzmaurice on the Culture of the Sugarcane.*)

Injuries.—1. *A wet season*, either during the very early or in the concluding period of the cane's vegetation, is one of the worst causes of injury; for the absence of the usual intensity of light and heat causes the sap to be very materially deficient in saccharine matter. But, on the other hand,

2. *A very dry season*, immediately after the sets are planted, though partly compensated for by artificial means, causes the produce to be but indifferent. These inconveniences are of a general nature, and irremediable.

3. *Animals.*—In India, not only the incursions of domesticated animals, but in some districts of the wild elephant, buffalo, hog, and porcupine, are frequent sources of injury. Almost every plantation is liable also to the attack of the jackal, and rats are especially destructive.

4. *White-ants.*—The sets of the sugarcane must be carefully watched to preserve them from the white-ant (*termes fatalis*), to attacks from which they are subject until they have begun to shoot. To prevent this, the following mixture has been recommended :—

Assafœtida (*Hing*) ....8 chittacks.
Mustard-seed Cake (*Sarsum ki Khalli*)...8 seers.
Putrid Fish ....4 ,,
Bruised Butchroot, or Muddur ....2 ,,

Mix them together in a large vessel, with water sufficient to make them into the thickness of curds ; then steep each tip of cane in it for half an hour before planting ; and lastly, water the lines three times, previous to setting the cane, by irrigating the water-course with water mixed with bruised butchroot or, if not procurable, muddur.

A very effectual mode of destroying the white-ant is by mixing a small quantity of arsenic with a few ounces of burned bread, pulverized flour, or oatmeal, moistened with molasses, and placing pieces of the dough thus made, each about the size of a turkey's egg, on a flat board, covered with a wooden bowl, in several parts of the plantation. The ants soon take possession of these, and perish, while the poison is transmitted to their successors who feed upon them. They are said to be driven from a soil by frequent hoeing. They are found to prevail most upon newly broken-up lands.

In Central India, the penetration of white-ants into the interior of the sets, and their consequent deterioration, is prevented by dipping each end into buttermilk, assafœtida, and powdered mustard-seed, mixed into a thick compound.

5. *Storms.*—Unless very violent, Dr. Roxburgh observes, "they do no great harm, because the canes are propped. However, if they are once laid down, which sometimes happens, they become branchy and thin, yielding a poor watery juice."

6. *The Worm* "is another evil which generally visits them [the cane-plants] every few years. A beetle deposits its eggs in the young canes; the caterpillars of these remain in the cane, living on its medullary parts till they are ready to be metamorphosed into the chrysalis state. Sometimes this evil is so great as to injure a sixth or an eighth part of the field; but, what is worse, the disease is commonly general when it happens—few fields escaping."

With regard to manures for sugarcane, the village compost, containing an admixture of night-soil and village-sweeping, will be about the best and cheapest manure available to the Indian ryot. The following give the results obtained by manuring with different composts for sugarcane :—

BOMBAY, *March* 1874.

From

The HON'BLE F. S. CHAPMAN,

Chief Secretary to the Government of Bombay.

For the information of the Government of India. Results obtained from experiments with various manures made by the Superintendent, Government Botanical Gardens, at this Presidency :—

EXPERIMENT WITH MANURES, NATURAL AND ARTIFICIAL.

The field on which the experiments were made was the deep black soil that is common in the Deccan. The ground had been slightly manured the year previous; in 1873 the ground was prepared by ploughing several times, and laying up in ridges, as is the custom for planting sugarcane in this country; plots were marked off 10 yards wide, and the manures applied to every alternate plot, the alternating plots being left without manure. Artificial manures and guano were applied at the rate of 4 cwts. per acre—estimate cost per acre, Rs. 28; night-soil, 10 tons per acre—estimate cost, Rs. 20; village sweepings, 20 tons per acre—estimate cost, Rs. 20. The results are as under :—

Name of Manure.	Weight of Produce of Sugarcane per acre.		Remarks.
	Tons.	Cwts.	These results need not be taken as depreciating the value of artificial manures. They are made for particular soils and particular conditions of exhaustion of these soils, and we have first to learn what the soil is in want of, before we can apply the artificial manure that will be useful.
Hop Manure	29	0	
Peruvian Guano	37	6	
Dissolved Bones	21	12	
Superphosphate	27	2	
Nitro-phosphate	26	10	
Urate	20	12	
Nitrate of Soda	21	11	
No manure	19	0	
Wrack of Village Sweepings	41	5	Contains ashes of cattle droppings, goat droppings, &c.
Crude Nightsoil	48	2	
Deodorised Nightsoil	45	3	The value of sugarcane in this district is about Rs. 6 per ton when plentiful.
Nightsoil supplied in Irrigation Water	49	6	

In the case in which the largest yield was obtained, *viz.*, 49 tons 6 cwts. per acre, the means of applying the nightsoil were as follows :—A pit was dug in the line of the water-channel filled with nightsoil, and water made to pass through it, a few thorny branches being placed to prevent solid matter from passing. The water, in passing, absorbed and dissolved so much of the properties of the manure, that in a very short time the matter in the pit had lost its disagreeable smell, while the soil purified the water so quickly that not the slightest nuisance was created; the native workmen used the water for watering quite freely. I found that, if the pit could be covered, and an arrangement made whereby the insoluble matter which accumulates could be removed without being handled, native prejudice would be defeated entirely. I have procured two iron tanks, which I believe will answer the purpose, and I intend to arrange them for use during the ensuing season.

CHAPTER IV.

COTTON.

Cotton, the staple clothing of India.—Cotton in the East, and cotton in the West.—The superiority of American cotton, due to what causes.—Difference between "New Orleans" and "Fair Dhollera."—Causes of the inferiority of Indian cotton.—The ryot and the middleman.—The cotton industry of England in its relation to America and India.—The attempts of the Indian Government to introduce the American variety.—The deterioration of acclimatized exotic cotton in India.—Deterioration of cotton in America.—Extract from the Report of the Agricultural Department, Washington.—Improvement of the indigenous staple *versus* the acclimatization of an exotic staple.—Cotton cultivation in the Berars, and the influence of railways and roads.

The rational culture of the cotton plant in India.—Soils adaptable for cotton.—Preparation of the soil.—The tap-roots of the species "Gossypium."—Deep-ploughing.—Mr. Rivett-Carnac on deep-ploughing of cotton-fields, and results obtained on the Berar model-farms.—Levelling and ridging.—Mr. Login on "Ridging" in India.—Selection of seed.—The time for sowing.—Soaking the seed and sowing.—Thinning the plants and weeding.—Topping.—The time and mode of gathering.—The drying of cotton.—Noxious influence of sun and dew.—Mr. Login's experiments.—Cost and results of the Egyptian method of cotton cultivation.—The object of cotton-culture.—Improvement of the soil should affect the parts of fructification.—Analysis of cotton-wool and cotton-seed.—The proportion of phosphoric acid in "Orleans" and "Surats."—Cotton manures.—Return of plant and seed to the soil.—Professor Hilyard on the withdrawal of soil-ingredients by cotton-wool and cotton-seed.—Experiment of manuring cotton with super-phosphate of lime, and results.

IN the present civilized state of mankind, material for clothing must be regarded as almost equally important as material for food ; and while rice and wheat demand our chief consideration as the staple food, cotton claims equally prominent notice as the staple clothing, of India.

Cotton, then, is the filamentous substance which envelops the seeds, and fills up the cavities in the seed-vessels, of plants belonging to the species "Gossypium." Cotton has been spun and woven into garments for the use of mankind from remote ages, and is the chief raw material which clothes India's millions of inhabitants.

A small portion of the cotton goods used in India is manufactured in this country, but by far the larger portion is imported from England, chiefly spun from American cotton.

There appears to be two chief varieties of the cotton-plant—the one the native of India, of the East ; the other the native of America, of the West. Though cotton has undoubtedly been cultivated from earlier times in India than in America, and has been spun into the most beautiful fabrics even long before America was discovered, the American variety, when cultivated, succeeded in a short time in driving the

Indian cotton, and the fabrics spun therefrom, out of the European markets.

Whether we have to attribute the rapid development of American cotton-culture entirely to the superiority of the staple, or to the advantages of a soil recovered fresh from nature's hands, or in a greater degree to the energy of European enterprize, is difficult to say, but I am of opinion that, if India's soil had been cultivated by Europeans for the same period as American soil has been, the quality of its cotton would have now surpassed the American staple in the same ratio as it is the reverse.

The filaments of the East Indian cotton, as grown at present and known in the markets of the world as "Dhollera" and "Surats," are considerably shorter than those of the American variety, and as, therefore, only the coarser descriptions of yarn and cloths can be spun from them, they realize comparatively poor prices. East Indian cotton, however, is valued for its color and noted for its strength; but its chief defects, as reported upon in England, are—the dirty state of the staple, the admixture of impurities, and the wilful adulterations that are practised.

The causes of these defects we must attribute to the ignorance and poverty, as also to the apathy and indifference, of the Indian ryot. For, as he is obliged to sell his crop, very often before it is ripe, in order to pay the land-tax and defray the expenses of cultivation, he has no interest in picking his crop as it ripens and the pods open ; he has no interest in keeping the first and best picking separate from the inferior cotton picked afterwards ; he has no inducement to trouble himself in keeping aside the rubbish collected from the ground. For, however careful and circumspect he may be, he receives not a farthing more for his pains from the money-lender who has bought his crop. Hence it is that the cotton is not picked from time to time as it ripens, but is allowed to remain till the whole field is ready for picking, by which time a great portion of the crop is deteriorated by dews, by the pods falling off, and by dry leaves and other foreign substances getting mixed up with it.

Dirty and impure as the cotton is when it passes out of the hands of the ryot, it becomes worse when passing through the hands of the middleman, whose interest it is to increase the weight by all sorts of contrivances and all kinds of admixtures, and has not the slightest hesitation in spoiling a good quality of cotton by mixing with it an old, inferior, or altogether unsaleable quality. In fact, it appears to be more profitable, to the ryot as well as to the middleman, to produce inferior and dirty cotton in preference to a selected and good article.

But some improvement in the cleanliness of the staple has been effected of late years by the mercantile houses of Bombay sending agents into the cotton-growing districts, and thus coming into closer communication with the cultivator. This system will doubtless, in course of time, obviate the intervention of the obnoxious middleman, while effecting a permanent improvement in the staple.

The cotton industry of England has, during the present century, assumed enormous proportions, and millions of sterling are paid annually to America for the raw material consumed in Manchester. It is therefore simply a matter of State policy and self-interest for England and its Indian Dependency to make all possible exertions and suffer any outlay to enable the produce of India not only to compete with, but to supplant, American cotton in the European markets. The sudden but continuous fall of silver, the depreciation of the rupee, and the heavy loss in exchange that India suffers by the drawings of the Secretary of State, afford to the Government of India more powerful reasons than ever to develop the culture of this most important staple.

On account of the greater length of fibre and the general superiority of the American cotton, it was but natural that the Indian Government should have concentrated its attention in the attempt to introduce and acclimatize in India the American variety of the cotton-plant. These attempts—dating from the year 1788, when the Court of Directors called the attention of the

Indian Government to the cultivation of cotton in India, " with a view to affording every encouragement to its growth and improvement"—have entailed considerable expense, while it cannot be acknowledged that Government has succeeded in the task it set itself.

True, the exotic variety is now grown to a certain extent in Guzerat and other parts of Western India with apparent success, the returns per acre being larger, and the produce cleaner ; but we have unmistakeable evidence to show that the best crops are obtained only from freshly-imported seeds, and that the exotic variety grown from acclimatized seed is rapidly degenerating.

Even in America a deterioration of the staple is going on, as would appear from the following extract :—

(DEPARTMENT OF AGRICULTURE, WASHINGTON.)

"The production, sale, and consumption of cotton are subjects of so much interest, that everything pertaining thereto should be well understood. Planters, as well as merchants and manufacturers, may profit by lessons elicited by a comparison of the experiences and observations of those engaged in its cultivation, marketing, and manufacture. The correspondence of this Department with intelligent planters of the South, made the impression that the quality of cotton offered in our markets had greatly deteriorated within the last twelve years, and thus induced me to prepare the following circular, requesting cotton-growers of the South, and manufacturers of the East, to furnish the results of their observations on the subject :—

"'To——————————

"'Questions of some importance to the country have arisen, which it is desirable should be solved by the opinions of manufacturers as well as planters.—1. Has the staple of American cotton deteriorated in quality within the last twelve years? If so, (2) to what cause is it attributable?

"'It has been suggested that deterioration is traceable to certain phases of the cotton market, which induce planters **to study** quantity rather than quality; that dealers do not judiciously discriminate between qualities in fixing the price. To aid this Department in the investigation of the **subject** for the benefit of manufacturers and planters, **I will** be obliged to you for your opinions, predicated upon your experience and observation of the subject.—I am, most respectfully, your obedient servant,

FREDK. WATTS,
Commissioner of Agriculture.'

"This circular was directed to fifty manufacturers of the Eastern States, and to as many planters of the Southern States; and from very many of both classes answers were received, satisfactorily showing that, while the quality of cotton now brought to market is *quite inferior* in condition to what was **produced** twelve years ago, that condition is attributable **to** causes which do not necessarily enter into the production or sale of the commodity. It seems **to be very** clear that the present production is, in **a large** measure, in the hands, and under the direction, of a less intelligent class of planters, who do **not** appreciate the importance of a judicious selection of seed, proper cultivation, and especially a careful preparation for the market. Now, while there are other planters who are intelligently guided in these requisites, the productions of both classes meet in the same market, and should command a discrimination as to quality and price, which, it is complained, they do not get. On the contrary, the conclusion is that dirty cotton is most profitable, because it brings more money per acre than that which is sold by the careful planter.

"This seems to be an evil which time and circumstances must cure; and it is therefore an injudicious conclusion that it would be better to adopt the example of the planter who sells dirty cotton. It cannot be that the merchant or the manufacturer will long fail to discriminate between the good and the bad, when they are marked by such distinctive qualities as clean and dirty. This, then, may be looked upon as a temporary evil. And we may hope that its cure will necessarily work a corresponding change in the careless class of planters to which we have alluded; for if they have to pay for hauling dirt, for which they get no price, and which decreases the value and price of their cotton, their losses will teach them to separate the former from the latter. It is assuming too much to suppose that both the merchant and the manufacturer will continue insensible to the advantages which arise from a choice between good and bad. The evil complained of may last for a time, but detection and change are certain.

"We cannot doubt for a moment that the spirit of improvement in agriculture actuates the planter of the South as well as the farmers of the North; and that the fact that better seed will produce better products, is greatly appreciated and acted upon everywhere. But if the merchant and manufacturer fail to appreciate the value of a good article of produce as compared with an inferior one, it will go very far to discourage the effort to excel."

A correspondent of the *Times of India*, writing from Berar, says on the subject of cotton improvement :—

"You get plenty of information about the cotton of this cotton-growing land; but I have never seen any allusion to the *main* cause of its being of different qualities and of some of it being dirty and some clean. Much has been written about the respective qualities of different kinds of seed, and much trouble has been taken, and much expense incurred, to produce and to distribute among the cultivators what are considered to be the best varieties; but I believe that all who have sojourned much among the real cultivators will agree with me in saying that difference in the quality of seed has comparatively little to do with the difference in the quality of the crops. Railways and roads make nine-tenths of the difference. Other things being equal, the best seed will of course produce the best cotton; but the difference in other things is so great, that difference of seed is scarcely worth taking into account in calculating the results.

"In the vicinity of the railway, and of made roads leading to the cotton depôts, that is to say, where sufficiently potent influence has been brought to bear upon cultivators to induce them to deviate from their ordinary modes of procedure, the fields are well ploughed, and the ground thoroughly prepared. The seed is very carefully drill-sown. The plants are thinned where necessary, and the fields carefully weeded—kept, indeed, as clean as a well-tended garden, which they require to be. The picking is begun as soon as a quantity of the capsules have opened, and before any of the cotton has fallen to the ground. Three *well-timed* pickings suffice to secure the whole crop without any of it being allowed to fall to the ground. It is thus got in clean and in the best condition.

" To see the reverse of this, we have only to go twenty miles—often much less—from the railway on the one or two made roads, and the further we recede from them the greater is the contrast. The ploughing becomes less thorough; the clods are not pulverized; the seed is carelessly sown; the plants are not thinned when thinning is required; the weed and grass are not eradicated, but allowed to grow up, depriving the cotton-plants of their nourishment, and stunting their growth. In places far removed from the made-roads, it sometimes requires close inspection to discover the cotton-plants amidst the more luxuriant weeds and grass.

" But the worst is still to come. The value of the cotton in the remoter districts is not sufficient to induce the cultivator with his household to undertake the troublesome work of picking it from the pods. It is allowed to fall to the ground, and is then gathered up at one gathering, with whatever soil may adhere to it. Should rain fall in the interval, as happened last season, it is of course battered into the black soil which is converted into mud; and it is thus lost, for all the purposes of commerce except adulteration, though still available in some measure for the cultivator's own use.

" I need scarcely tell you that the latter phase of cotton-culture is the original and normal one, in this part of India at least, and that the extraordinarily different mode recorded in the preceding paragraph, has been brought about by roads and railroads, the only way by which the 'schoolmaster' has hitherto operated with much effect on the genuine agriculturist, the real holder of the plough.

"It is not, however, cotton cultivation only that the roads and railways **have affected thus** powerfully. The effect on wheat and jowari (staples of these provinces) is equally striking. Away from roads and railways, care and industry are conspicuously awanting. Although drill-sowing was practised in this country a thousand years before it was heard of in England, so little care is taken in ploughing and cleaning the fields and pulverizing the soil, that the wheat has the appearance of having been sown broadcast, mixed with an equal proportion of weeds and grass. Like the cotton in similar circumstances, it is stunted in its growth, and the produce very inferior. In striking contrast with this, we see near the roads and railways in the cold season, fields of wheat rivalling in appearance those of England. Mile upon mile is to be seen drill-sown, perfectly regular, and without a weed. Before it ripens, the vast expanse of bright green brings vividly before the Englishman his own fertile land.

"Nothing will move the cultivator to work in any other way than according to his normal lazy, procrastinating mode, except a stirring appeal to his self-interest. Where, from difficulty and expense of conveyance, his market is confined to the villages in the vicinity of his fields, he has no inducement to cultivate much land, or to take any particular trouble with what he does cultivate. The demand is small, and little care or labour is required to produce enough to satisfy it. Toil beyond this would be unremunerative. But when, by means of roads and railways, the market is extended, there is of course a proportional rise in price which, operating on the strongest propensity in man, savage or civilized, produces results such as I have described."

It is my firm conviction that if the labour, time, and money devoted to the acclimatization of the American cotton in India, had been spent on the improvement of the indigenous staple, Government would long before this have enabled the ryot to send a quality of cotton into the markets fully able to compete and hold its own against the best " New Orleans."

I would exceed the limits of this work were I to give even an outline of the various experiments made by Government for the purpose of acclimatizing the American variety, and to note the majority of failures and the inadequate success attained—inadequate considering the labour, time, and money spent on them; but a careful perusal of all the official reports on this subject cannot fail to leave an impression upon the mind, that, as asserted before, if such labour, time, and expense had been devoted to the improvement of the indigenous cotton, magnificent results would have been obtained.

The culture of the cotton-plant has been brought to greatest perfection in America, and we need do little else, here in India, than adopt the mode of cultivation followed there, with such alterations as the peculiarities of districts and soils may demand.

Soil.—The deep, black cotton soil of the Deccan

and Guzerat, the red soil of the Berars—in fact, all loamy and even sandy soils—will be found suitable for the cultivation of cotton. Too rich soils are apt to make crops run into stalks and leaves, and should therefore be avoided, as well as stiff, clayey, and damp soils.

The land should have a deep trench, so as to drain off all stagnant water, which has been found to vitally injure the plant.

Preparation of the Soil.—The species "Gossypium" belongs to those kinds of plants which, in addition to their lateral rootlets, have top-roots that penetrate, according to the nature of the soil, more or less deeply into the subsoil. It is essential, therefore, to prepare the soil with due regard to this peculiarity.

Deep-ploughing, more or less advantageous for all crops, is eminently so for the cultivation of cotton, favouring, as it does, the development of the top-roots. In one of the very first reports Mr. Rivett-Carnac submitted on the model-farms in the Berars, we are told that the combined effect of deep-ploughing and careful selection of seed was in one case an outturn of 255 lbs. of clean cotton to the acre. He proceeds to say—" The case was, it is true, an exceptional one, as the soil of the field in which the crop was sown was superior to the ordinary run of the cotton-growing tracts. But, from ordinary fields in the farm, during this, an unfavorable season, as much as 176 lbs. of cleaned cotton was picked from the acre. The results are therefore encouraging."

In another part of the report, he says with reference to the Bolundshuhur model-farm :— "So far as can at present be judged, it would appear that deep-ploughing is of great benefit to the plant. Those parts of the seed farms which have been thus treated, show very favorably by the side of the fields cultivated according to the ordinary native method. The plants on the well-ploughed fields were much stronger and healthier than their neighbours, and, as already noticed, 180 lbs. of clean cotton per acre was picked from these fields. This season, an ordinary native field hardly yielded 50 lbs. to the acre."

Deep-ploughing will not only enable the plant to obtain an extra amount of nourishment from a hitherto untouched source, but the deep penetration of the roots into the soil will enable the plant to withstand droughts and sudden changes of climate much better than it does at present. It is preferable that the ploughing should be done with the hoe, and extend as deep as possible, the land being afterwards levelled, and all clods carefully broken.

The soil is then thrown up into ridges, sufficiently apart to enable the plants to extend laterally as much as possible, but still close enough for the plants to shade the soil and prevent it becoming too rapidly dried up by the direct rays of the sun. In America the ridges are five to **seven feet** apart and ten inches high, but **for the** Indian cotton-plant a distance of three feet is sufficient.

Mr. Login, to whom we are deeply indebted for his trouble in introducing the Egyptian method of cotton cultivation into India, describes **the** process of ridging as follows :—

" To many this may appear a difficult process, though in fact it is most simple, once the men get into the way of working the *jindrah*, which is a shovel made from a one-inch plank about two feet long and nine inches deep, the **lower** edge of the plank being chamfered off a little, like the edge of a chisel, so as to give a slightly cutting edge. At right-angles to the length of the boards, and at the back of it, is attached a pole some eight feet long, so that this shovel has something the appearance of **the** letter T inverted, the arms being the **board**.

" A rope is attached to the two arms like a punka rope, which a man pulls, while another holds the pole or handle and directs the shovel; so that at each complete motion, one-half of a ridge two feet in length is thrown up, **and** it is completed in a similar manner when the men pass down the other side of the ridge. The work is both simple and expeditious, which most cultivators in this neighbourhood perfectly understand ; for whenever there is irrigation from wells, **they** throw up similar ridges to divide their field **into** small squares called *kearaha*, some two hundred square feet in area, so as to prevent the waste of water."

Selection of Seed.—The cotton seeds intended for sowing should be subjected to the most rigid selection. The best-bearing and healthiest plants in the field should be selected for the purpose, and only the largest and best-developed of the pods picked from each tree. There is every reason to believe that this system of selection, carried on scrupulously for several years, will result in a most marked improvement of the staple.

Sowing.—The best time for sowing cotton in Western India appears to be after the first heavy rains of the S.W. monsoon—not before, the young plants being very easily injured by heavy floods. But it will be well to be guided by the custom of the native cultivator, whom the experience of hundreds of years has taught the right time of sowing.

The seeds should be soaked either in a mixture of cow-dung and water, or in a diluted solution of saltpetre, and exposed for about an hour to the sun to dry. Four or five of them are then dropped into holes made on the top of the ridges about three inches deep and **two** feet apart, and covered lightly with a little earth.

Thinning.—When the plants **sprout** and begin to develop the third leaf, each cluster of them should be thinned, leaving only the two most vigorous plants. The ridges, which the heavy rains will have partly washed down, must be repaired by shovelling up the earth, taking care, however, that none of the young plants get buried in the soil during the process.

At this time also, all grasses and weeds that may have appeared in the meantime should be thoroughly eradicated, by the hoe preferable. In a week or ten days the plants will be sufficiently matured to suffer further thinning, only the strongest plant of each cluster being now left.

Weeding must be closely attended to, all interlopers being carefully destroyed, and the soil washed down from the ridges should occasionally be drawn up round the plant as before.

Topping.—When the plant evinces a disposition to produce wood and leaves at the expense of flowers and seeds, the tops should be nipped off when the podding commences; this will generally have a most material effect in increasing the outturn by encouraging the growth of the lateral branches.

Gathering.—The cotton should be gathered when the pods burst, as exposure to sun and dew deteriorates the staple to a considerable extent. The picker should be provided with a couple of bags, for the purpose of keeping the best and cleanest sort separate from cotton gathered from inferior pods. Special care should be taken that none of the leafy enclosures of the pods gets mixed with the cotton; and a premium should be given to the gatherers for the largest percentage of clean cotton.

Drying.—When drying, cotton should **never be** exposed to the dew, but dried in the shade, which will improve the staple greatly both in glossiness and general appearance.

The above described method of cultivation is in principle the same as that so admirably advocated by Mr. Login as the Egyptian method of cotton cultivation. Soils **cultivated by** this method have yielded on an average 267 lbs. of clean cotton per acre, while the average yield by native culture is 50 to 60 lbs. per acre, inferior in quality as in quantity.

The following represents the cost and the results of the Egyptian method of cultivation as given by Mr. Login :—

Abstract showing the proportional cost of working the Egyptian and Native systems of Cotton Cultivation.

	Egyptian.			Native.		
	Rs.	a.	p.	Rs.	a.	p.
Ploughing	3	3	2	3	3	2
Ridging	2	15	9	0	0	0
Sowing	0	7	0	0	1	1
Watering	1	10	3	1	10	3
Drainage	0	5	2	0	5	2
Weeding	8	5	4	8	5	4
Thinning	0	2	8	0	0	0
Topping	0	1	0	0	0	0
Clearing	0	4	1	0	4	1
Total outlay on labour ...Rs.	17	6	5	13	13	1

The above return is obtained from the expenditure on experiments at Chundee; yet, though showing the comparative expenditure of the two modes of culture—that is, that the ridge system exceeds the broadcast by one-quarter—the sums Rs. 17-6-5 and Rs. 13-13-1 must far exceed the outlay of a native cultivator; for at the Chundee farm the work was not started till the last week in May, and highly-paid labour had to be employed.

With the native cultivator, on the other hand, *time* would be of no consequence, and he would never think of carrying on farming by daily-paid labour and hired bullocks; and, in addition to this, weeding—which in this case is the largest item—costs the zemindar comparatively little, as the grass obtained by weeding is utilized as fodder for cattle.

For the above reasons, almost one-third might be fairly deducted from the above amounts, but even if we reduce them only by one-fourth, we have Rs. 13-0-10 and Rs. 10-6-0 for the two systems; so, if to this Rs. 13 an acre we add Rs. 7 for land-rent and manure, the whole outlay in cultivating by the Egyptian system, *where irrigation is available*, can hardly exceed Rs. 25 an acre, while Rs. 20 will be sufficient to cover all expenses where there is not, against Rs. 17-5-2 by the broadcast or native system.

281

ABSTRACT showing the results of Mr. Login's Cotton Experiments during 1872.

Locality.	Nature of Soil.	Crop of last Season.	Average No. of times Ploughed.	Ditto Irrigated.	Ditto Weeded.	Date of Sowing.	Area in Acres.	Yield in Maunds of "Kapas" per Acre.	Value of Kapas at Rs. 5 per maund per Acre.	Yield of Clean Cotton per Acre.	Remarks.
								Md. sr. ch.	Rs. a. p.	lbs.	
Shahabad	⅔ Maisah ⅓ Rousiah	Wheat and Grass	4½	0	3½	From 24th to 30th June	7·689	13 25 3	68 2 5	363½	The eight fields at Shahabad which were partially manured but not irrigated.
Kurnool	Maisah	Cherrie	4	7	5	27th May	0·208	20 2 5	100 5 7	535	
Ditto	Do.	Do.	4	5	4	23rd June	0·199	14 17 8	72 3 0	387	
70 miles north of Delhi	⅔ Maisah ⅓ Rousiah	Wheat	2	2½	4	27th June	2·111	9 29 2	48 10 5	259	
,, 50 ,, ,,	Fair	Wheat chiefly	1	0	2	About 25th June	1·458	3 9 5	16 2 11	86	This result was from seven small fields that were sown the day after ploughing.
,, 22 ,, ,,	Maisah	Second crop of Cotton	0	6	6	10th May 1871	0·756	5 18 8	27 5 0	144	Second crop injured by insects.
,, 22 ,, ,,	Do.	Grass	7	5	5	24th May 1872	0·323	9 8 8	46 1 0	246	
,, 15 ,, ,,	Do.	Do.	4	2	2	15th June	0·400	10 5 0	50 10 0	270	
Chundee Govt. Farm 30 miles north of Umballa	Fair	Wheat	2	3½	4	From 13th June to 18th July	44·000	4 16 4	22 0 6	117½	The small result was owing to the lateness of the season.

The above return shows the result of a set of private experiments along the Grand Trunk Road between Umballa and Delhi, from which some idea can be formed of the probable profits under careful cultivation.

Mr. Login says—"From this abstract, it will be seen that, in the case of the experiments at Shahabad, where there was *no irrigation*, with Kapas selling at **Rs. 5** a maund, the value of the yield was no less than Rs. 68-2-5 per acre on an outlay of Rs. 20, or Rs. 48-2-5 profit ; so that, allowing for picking as well as ordinary and extraordinary charges, the zemindars who cultivated these $7\frac{2}{3}$ acres at Shahabad must have cleared over two hundred per cent. net profit on these particular fields."

This is the result where excessive care was *not* taken ; but where a small patch of ground at Kurnoul was sown a month earlier than at Shahabad, and was both watered and manured, the value of the outturn per acre was above Rs. 100, the late Mr. Deacon having obtained not less than 535 lbs. of clean cotton per acre, while the average at the Chundee farm, owing to the lateness of the season, was only $117\frac{1}{2}$ lbs. per acre, or less than one-fourth of his.

Manures.—The object of cotton-culture being to obtain a large yield of the filamentous substances enveloping the seed of the plant, with wool of good color, fair length and strength, and free from dirt and other foreign matter, we must consider how to improve the soil so as to yield a large outturn and a good quality of the staple, and what substances and conditions would favor the development of the *parts of fructification* and also study the influence of their component parts. Dr. Royle gives the results of an analysis of cotton-wool and cotton-seed made in New Orleans in December 1843:—

"*1st Analysis—Cotton-Wool.*

One hundred parts of cotton-wool, on being heated in a platinum crucible, lost 85·89 parts. The residuum, on being ignited under a muffle till the whole of the carbon was consumed, lost 12·735, and left a white ash which weighed nearly 1 per cent., or 0·937; of this ash, nearly 44 per cent. was soluble in water. Its constituents were as follow:—

Carbonate of Potash (with a trace of Soda)	44·29
Phosphate of Lime (trace of Magnesia)	25·34
Carbonate of Lime	8·97
,, Magnesia	6·75
Silica	4·12
Sulphate of Potash	2·90
Alumina	1·40
Chloride of Potassium ⎫ ,, Magnesium ⎪ Sulphate of Lime ⎬ and loss Phosphate of Potash ⎪ Oxide of Iron (a trace) ⎭	6·23
	100·00

Supposing the carbonic acid in the abovementioned salts to have been derived during the incineration of the cotton, the following will more accurately express the important mineral ingredients abstracted by the cotton from the soil, for every 100 parts of its ash:—

Potash	31·05
Lime	17·09
Magnesia	3·24
Phosphoric Acid	12·32
Sulphuric Acid	1·20

So that, for every 10,000 lbs. of cotton-wool about **60 lbs.** of the abovementioned ingredients are abstracted from the soil, in the proportion indicated by the following figures, omitting the fractions :—

Potash	31 lbs.
Lime	12 ,,
Magnesia	3 ,,
Phosphoric Acid	12 ,,
Sulphuric Acid	1 ,,

"*2nd Analysis—Cotton-Seed.*

One hundred parts, heated as before, lost 77·387, and the residuum, after being burned under a muffle, left 3·936 parts of a perfectly white ash, the composition of which was as follows :—

Phosphate of Lime (with traces of Magnesia)	61·34
,, Potash (traces of Soda)	31·73
Sulphate of Potash	2·65
Silica	1·68
Carbonate of Lime	0·47
,, Magnesia	0·27
Chloride of Potassium	0·25
Carbonate of Potash, Sulphate of Lime, ,, Magnesia, Alumina, and Oxides of Iron and Manganese, and loss	1·61
	100·00

A comparison of the above **table** with that afforded by the cotton-wool, will show **a great** dissimilarity between the two. The ash of **the** cotton-seed is fourfold that of the fibre, while the former has also three times as much phosphoric acid as the latter, **as will** appear on presenting the analysis in a form corresponding with the second table under cotton-wool :—

Phosphoric Acid	45·35
Lime	29·79
Potash	19·40
Sulphuric Acid	1·16
	95·70 "

M. Crace-Calvert determined the percentage of phosphoric acid in different samples of cotton-wool, and he found that—

New Orleans contained 0·079 per cent., while Surat contained only 0·027 per cent.

Can it be that the inferiority of Indian cotton is due to deficiency of Phosphoric Acid in the soil?

From these analyses we find that wood-ashes and bone-dust, the latter preferably as superphosphate of lime, are the principal manurial substances likely to have a direct influence on the development of cotton-wool and cotton-seeds.

All nitrogenous manures—guano, nightsoil, &c.—should be avoided, as they assist any tendency of the plant to produce wood and leaves at the expense of flowers and fruits.

The plant remaining after the cotton has been gathered should be burnt and ploughed into the field, and on no account disposed of otherwise unless an adequate return of its ashes is made. The seed may be deprived of its oil, and the remaining oil-cake returned to the soil, either direct, or through the medium of cattle, for which it will prove a most valuable food-stuff.

Professor **Hilyard**, of Mississippi, makes the suggestive statement that when the lint only of the cotton-crop is removed from the land, it takes no more than four pounds of soil ingredients for each bale of cotton, but when both lint and seed are permanently removed, the land loses on an average forty-two pounds of soil ingredients for every bale. In the former case, the cotton is one of the least exhaustive of known crops; in the latter, one of the most exhaustive.

Mr. **J. W. Roberts**, of Osyka, Mississippi, reports to the Agricultural Department, Washington, the results of an experiment in fertilizing about $1\frac{1}{2}$ acre of poor upland soil, not capable of producing without manure more than 500 lbs. of seed-cotton. The ground was ploughed to a good depth, and otherwise well prepared; was manured with 370 lbs. of Pierce's superphosphate of lime, and planted with "Dickson" seed; with the following result :—The crop of seed-cotton amounted to 1,300 lbs., making 433 lbs. of baled cotton, which, after defraying all expenses, yielded a net profit of 49 dollars 52 cents. According to this exhibit, the fertilizer should be credited with an increase of at least 800 lbs. of seed-cotton on the area named.

FINIS.

www.ingramcontent.com/pod-product-compliance
Lightning Source LLC
Chambersburg PA
CBHW022055230426
43672CB00008B/1179